In the Shadow of Prison

In the Shadow of Prison
Families, imprisonment and criminal justice

Helen Codd

WILLAN
PUBLISHING

Published by

Willan Publishing
Culmcott House
Mill Street, Uffculme
Cullompton, Devon
EX15 3AT, UK
Tel: +44(0)1884 840337
Fax: +44(0)1884 840251
e-mail: info@willanpublishing.co.uk
website: www.willanpublishing.co.uk

Published simultaneously in the USA and Canada by

Willan Publishing
c/o ISBS, 920 NE 58th Ave, Suite 300,
Portland, Oregon 97213-3786, USA
Tel: +001(0)503 287 3093
Fax: +001(0)503 280 8832
e-mail: info@isbs.com
website: www.isbs.com

First published 2008

ISBN   978-1-84392-245-2 paperback
       978-1-84392-246-9 hardback

British Library Cataloguing-in-Publication Data

A catalogue record for this book is available from the British Library

Typeset by GCS, Leighton Buzzard, Bedfordshire
Printed and bound by TJ International Ltd, Padstow, Cornwall

Contents

In loving memory of Sheila Beedle,
a good friend who died while this
book was being written.

Acknowledgements

Much of this book is about women, and without the friendship, support and encouragement of some of the most fantastic female friends anyone could wish for, this book would probably never have been started, let alone finished. Barbara Hudson has been an inspirational and supportive colleague and mentor and has taught me that it is possible to combine being a brilliant and productive scholar with a love of good food, gin and tonic and luxury department stores. Elaine and Lin Jenkinson-Bennett have been generous and loving friends throughout and deserve many, many thanks. My only hope is that, when I give them a copy of this book, their Labrador Reuben will not eat it. Alice Mills has shown me that co-authoring can be enjoyable and rewarding, and, again, deserves many thanks. Rachel Hartland has been a caring and encouraging presence in my life for a very long time and deserves huge amounts of appreciation for her patience, prayers and wise advice. Eilidh Grant has given me praise, encouragement and late-night text messages, and been there when my confidence in this project has wavered. Julia Turner, too, has been a wonderful companion in motherhood, books and coffee. On a more academic note, Belinda Crothers at the Institute of Advanced Legal Studies has been constantly encouraging and interested in my work, and I am grateful to the IALS for granting me an Associate Research Fellowship which allowed me access to unparalleled library facilities and gave me an alternative location in which to write and think.

It is important, however, not to leave out the men who have been supportive. David Scott has been an endless source of encouragement, good humour and confidence in my abilities. Fr. Damian Feeney has provided spiritual guidance, wonderful coffee and huge amounts of enthusiasm for this book. Brian Willan has been inordinately patient in waiting for this manuscript. My greatest thanks and appreciation go also to a man – my husband Nicholas Palmer. He has somehow always been with me throughout my adult life, first as a friend and then later as a partner. By the time this book is published he will have been around for over twenty years, and for this he deserves much praise, many thanks and probably a medal.

Heartfelt thanks are due to my parents, Alan and Jane Codd, especially for their willingness to take my daughter on a 'little holiday' so as to enable me to attend the Law and Society Assocation Conference in Berlin in July 2007. Finally, I'd like to send thanks and cuddles to my beautiful daughter Alexandra. The proposal for this book was written during her afternoon nap-time when she was a few months old and the final manuscript was submitted as she was close to her fourth birthday. Being her mummy has taught me that it *is* possible to write while exhausted (but that usually it's better just to sleep) and has also made me realise just how horrendous it must be to experience separation from a child as many mothers in prison have to. I'm grateful to her for her joy, laughter, love and boundless wonder.

The papers were heavy, and when she had to wait at the level-crossing while a train went by, she rested the parcel on the top of the gate. And idly she looked at the printing on the paper that the parcel was wrapped in.

Suddenly she clutched the parcel tighter and bent her head over it. It seemed like some horrible dream. She read on – the bottom of the column was torn off – she could read no farther.

She never remembered how she got home. But she went on tiptoe to her room and locked the door. Then she undid the parcel and read that printed column again, sitting on the edge of her bed, her hands and feet icy cold and her face burning. When she had read all there was, she drew a long, uneven breath.

'So now I know,' she said.

From *The Railway Children* (1906) by E. Nesbit.

Chapter 1

The landscape of punishment: family ties and penal policy

Introduction: about this book

Most prisoners do not exist in a vacuum. They may stand alone in the dock in court and serve a prison sentence alone, but most prisoners are members of family, kin and friendship networks (Paylor and Smith 1994). While prisoners experience the primary effects of detention and deprivation of liberty, their families live their lives in the shadow of prison. This shadow is cast not only over individuals but also over entire communities. The partners and children of prisoners experience the effects of imprisonment most acutely during the sentence but also often have to cope with the manifold challenges posed by prisoner release and community re-entry. Even when an individual has been released from prison their future job and housing prospects, relationships and social status can be affected by their previous incarceration, and the circumstances and lives of their family members will often have undergone major change.

There has been an expansion of interest in prisoners' families in the last five years, which in the UK has been prompted by the publication of the influential Social Exclusion Unit Report (2002), which identified the positive role played by prisoners' families in relation to resettlement. In an era of the decline of social work, this offered a new strategy for dealing with offenders leaving prison, stressing the responsibilities not only of prisoners but also their family members. In the US, the decimation (or worse) of the population of some urban areas as a consequence of mandatory minimum sentencing policies and a shift towards longer prison sentences has led to an explosion of research on urban inequalities and the mass imprisonment epidemic, this research including consideration of the experiences of prisoners' families. There is, as a consequence, a deluge of published literature.

This book offers an introduction to the situation of prisoners' families, primarily in the UK but also in a range of other jurisdictions, particularly those such as the US and Australia which, like the UK, are experiencing a dramatic increase in the prison population and a shift towards punitive policies in sentencing. The book offers an introduction to this diverse field and encourages further research, debate and discussion. It does not claim to identify all possible relevant issues nor does it claim to have answers to every dilemma or controversy. The book draws on empirical research conducted by the author and others in the past and more recently, and although based in the UK incorporates extensive references to current research emerging from other jurisdictions, particularly the US.

The book begins with a discussion of the social and penal backdrop to a discussion of prisoners' families, and Chapter 2 offers a range of explanations and justifications for supporting and researching prisoners' family members. Chapter 3 provides an extensive summary of the many and diverse impacts of imprisonment for prisoners' partners and children. Unusually for books such as this, this book then includes a chapter on law. After all, it is mechanisms of the law and legal process which render families subject to the effects of imprisonment. The prison itself operates as an arm of the state and is created, regulated and managed within a framework of legislation and case law. While it is possible to consider prisoners' families from a sociological or social work-based perspective, their position is so intertwined with law, especially in relation to human rights, that it is essential in my opinion to include a consideration of legal responses to such families.

Following on from the law chapter is a chapter in which family relationships are considered. The family relationships of female prisoners have, with the exception of women's relationships with their children, hardly been researched. To discuss these issues is timely due to policy shifts over the last decade which have led to a dramatic increase in the female prison population in a number of jurisdictions, with many associated consequences particularly for children. The penultimate chapter offers examples of current and/or recent programmes in relation to prisoners' families and provides potential evidence of good practice in service provision. The book concludes with a critical commentary and suggestions as to responses to the current situation of prisoners' families both in the short and long term. This book offers the reader an introduction to the current issues, with the caveat that the literature is already extensive and being frequently augmented, and thus this book offers an introduction. If the reader wishes to know more then the reader is urged to listen to the voices of prisoners' partners and children themselves as they speak through the research data.

The impetus for this book came from several strands of ongoing research in criminology and criminal justice and has been particularly influenced by feminist perspectives and research into gender, sentencing and punishment. For over thirty years feminist writers have questioned the relationship between women, crime, criminology and criminal justice, documenting and challenging the injustices faced by women in prison; the poor conditions; the unsupportive and oppressive regimes; and the specific needs of imprisoned mothers, pregnant women and women with complex mental health and substance abuse needs. These feminist perspectives have also been visible in work on prisoners' partners originating from outside the UK, such as the work of Ann Aungles (1994), Lori Girshick (1996) and Laura T. Fishman (1990). It is often said that regardless of the gender of the inmate it is women who bear the burdens of caring. To be blunt, if a man is imprisoned then he can probably rely on his male friends to have a party or take him to the pub and buy him drinks when he is released, but it will be his mother, partner, sisters and female friends who will visit, provide extra clothes, books and hobby materials, pay for phone calls and write letters. Thus, although it is almost universal that there are far more men than women in prison, regardless of the jurisdiction, women are not immune from the consequences of imprisonment; they experience these impacts in a variety of forms and contexts beyond the immediate experience of loss of liberty and freedom.

As writers such as Pat Carlen (1983, 1990) and others have shown, women's prisons and women's experiences of imprisonment are different from those of men. An extension of a feminist discussion of female imprisonment is to question how women are affected by male imprisonment. In her discussion of the possibilities for the development of a 'women-wise' penology Pat Carlen (1990) proposed this as involving two elements. First, that the penal regulation of female law-breakers does not increase their oppression *as women* still further, and second, that the penal regulation of law-breaking men does not brutalise them and make them even more violently and ideologically oppressive towards women in the future. It is a matter of constant awe to me that families cope with often objectively almost impossible circumstances and still manage to keep the relationships together. I have seen women – for it is more often women – see their lives turned upside down and found themselves living through a period of immense turmoil and struggle, but have seen women find inner strength, power and determination. Equally, I have seen women cowed, depressed and ill as a consequence of the extreme stresses and anxieties that imprisonment can bring to a family. From a feminist point of view, the evidence is indisputable that women are often profoundly affected by the imprisonment of men. It is thus an integral element of feminist approaches to imprisonment to not only consider women as prisoners but also their role as partners of men. Very little, however, is known of who visits women prisoners, or indeed of who, if anyone, provides the kind of emotional and practical support which is often provided to male prisoners by female relatives and family members.

The shadow of prison?

> Right now, the shadow of prison squats at the corners of, and often at the center of nearly every black family's life in this nation (Dixon 2005).

The image of living in the shadow of the prison resonates throughout research into prisoners' families and their communities, not only in relation to black people as referred to in the above quotation but in relation to families generally (see Combessie 2002; Roberts and Gabor 2004; Comfort 2007). The idea of the shadow as a metaphor in this context has many aspects and implications. For a shadow to exist there must be a source of light and an obstruction. That is, in criminal justice terms there are policies and penal establishments which may have implications for the lives and circumstances of people who are not themselves living in the prison. A shadow can be bigger than the object creating it, and distorted so it is not the same shape. In terms of prisoners' families, the impacts of imprisonment may affect many more people than are actually incarcerated and these impacts may be diverse and broadly spread. Shadows fall differently depending on the time of day; the impacts of imprisonment vary with changes in the social and penal climate. It is often cold in the shadows, as I experienced in downtown San Francisco when I walked around the bottom of the well-known landmark, the Transamerica Pyramid.[1] The height of the surrounding skyscrapers means that little sunlight

4

makes it through to street level, so at the base of the pyramid there is not only less light but it also feels colder than in more open areas of the city. This uncomfortable coldness can reflect the social coldness sometimes experienced by prisoners' families.

People standing in the shadows may not be able to see clearly due to the lack of light. A shadow is impossible to pin down; it shifts. It is possible to draw around the edges but then it moves again, as does penal policy. One cannot pick up and contain a shadow; similarly it may be impossible to identify and quantify all the impacts of imprisonment and all the families and individuals affected. Unless viewed in the context of shadow-puppetry or silhouette portraits, the shadow is not the main focus or aim; rather it is a consequence of light hitting an object. In policy and research terms the focus usually falls on prisoners, and not their families. Sometimes people seek out shadows, for example when standing in the sun feels too hot and the sun is too bright; the shadow may provide respite from the heat and glare, rather as Comfort's work has talked about prison as a source of relief and support (Comfort 2007). To find shadow on a hot day can be essential for survival or comfort and well-being. The bigger the object the bigger the shadow; so the more people in prison the more aspects of family and community life affected. Although, as for some plants, shade can be a health-promoting environment, the absence of sunlight can have a negative impact on health; for example, Vitamin D is obtained by the body from food and is also produced as a result of the skin's exposure to the UV rays in sunlight. Vitamin D deficiency, such as that due to insufficient sunlight exposure, can lead to serious illness. With this brief consideration in mind, it is clear that the idea of 'the shadow of prison' has many implications and connotations for understanding the impact of imprisonment on families.

Families: a note on terms

The situation of prisoners' partners arises as a consequence of their relationship with someone else. The term 'prisoner's family' itself places the prisoner in the possessive position. In my view, however, defining the prisoner as the subject and defining the family in relation to the prisoner does not give sufficient attention to family members in their own right and there is (arguably) a need to reconceptualise the debate even down to the terminology. This is difficult if we are to avoid clumsiness. I would be far happier reconceptualising the debate as involving 'families in which one or more family members are in prison' in that this terminology prioritises and foregrounds the family and not the prisoner. It places the emphasis on the ongoing familial circumstances and stresses that the family exists even if one or more members are in prison. This viewpoint would make sense in the context of the research, such as that by Megan Comfort (2002), which has documented the lengths to which family members go to play out family lives, rituals and decision-making in the environment of the visits room. Her phrase 'the prison as a domestic and social satellite' stresses the idea of the family having to live out its family life in multiple locations, one of which is a prison. However, although this appellation is ideologically desirable in my view, it makes for clumsy writing. Thus, reluctantly I have chosen to continue to refer to 'prisoners' families', but with an express statement from the outset that a family- rather than prisoner-based perspective is a desirable goal to be worked towards in future research and writing.

The penal context

The experiences of prisoners' families are not simply the product of individual responses to imprisonment but reflect broader shifts in penal practices, criminal justice and societal attitudes to crime and criminals. Most of the research referred to in this book has emanated from the UK and the US, both nations having recently experienced sharp rises in their prison populations and a swing towards more punitive sentencing policies and practices (Pratt *et al.* 2005). To fully understand and appreciate the impacts of imprisonment, it is necessary to look beyond the individualistic focus on the offender and instead recognise that imprisonment affects family members and, as has been considered in recent research from the US, communities. Other research has documented the impacts of other non-custodial penalties, such as fines and curfews, and the possible impacts on other family members (Aungles and Cook 1994). It is imprisonment, however, which has the greatest impact on families. Of course, sometimes it is the best possible outcome for a family which has suffered; on other occasions it creates a range of difficulties and challenges

The US – mass imprisonment and its collateral consequences

A number of countries including the UK have experienced a dramatic growth in their prison populations during the last decade, some of the most drastic changes being seen in the prison population in the US. For some young men from socially excluded communities, especially members of urban minority ethnic groups, imprisonment has become as commonplace as the 'gap year' for middle-class white young men, with associated discourses of freedom, responsibility, self-discovery and new life experiences.

Indeed, the growth and consequences of the prison population has led to writers such as David Garland (2001) referring to 'mass imprisonment', which has emerged in the US during the last twenty-five years and which has two defining features. The first is 'sheer numbers', that is, a rate of imprisonment and a prison population which is markedly above the norm for similar societies. Second is 'the social concentration of imprisonment's effects', as he explains:

> Imprisonment becomes *mass imprisonment* when it ceases to be the incarceration of individual offenders and becomes the systematic imprisonment of whole groups of the population (Garland 2001: 6).

Writing in 2001, Garland argued that we have scarcely begun to address the question of the extent of the impact of 'mass imprisonment', pointing out that

> we have libraries of criminological research about the impact of imprisonment upon the individual offender, but scarcely anything on its *social* impact on communities and neighbourhoods. (2001: 6).

Since 2001, academic and policy-orientated research publications have begun to assess these broader implications of the mass imprisonment epidemic, some of these addressing the precise question of the impact on communities (Travis and Waul 2003a; Braman 2004; Mauer and Chesney-Lind 2002). This recent research on the unintended and associated consequences of imprisonment has focused not only on the impact of incarceration on inmates themselves, their families and their children, but also on their communities and on society as a whole, building on the research into the impact of imprisonment on families which has been published in the US since the 1960s (Brodsky 1975; Swan 1981; Fishman 1990; Girshick 1996; Gabel and Johnston 1995). Echoing the language of the military, some writers have labelled these unintended impacts the 'collateral consequences of imprisonment'. These 'invisible punishments' have, in the words of Marc Mauer and

Meda Chesney-Lind 'transformed family and community dynamics, exacerbated racial divisions and posed fundamental questions of citizenship in a democratic society' (2002: 1). The steady stream of research on these 'collateral consequences' of imprisonment in the US shows that, for many prisoners and their families, there is a range of associated negative consequences. Some relate to the offenders themselves; others, more subtly, to their family members. In the UK-based literature, there has been a tendency to draw a distinction between prisoners and 'prisoners' families'. The recent US-based research has adopted a more holistic approach and has linked the impacts of penal sanctions on offenders themselves with other impacts on communities. For offenders themselves, imprisonment may result in a number of additional civil consequences, some relating directly to citizenship and opportunities. A task force report by the American Bar Association (2002) found that these consequences include dis-enfranchisement, deportation, loss of professional licences, felon registration and ineligibility for many welfare benefits. Additional consequences can include prevention from serving on a jury, running for public office, collecting military benefits, parental rights, possessing firearms and receiving public assistance (Wheelock 2005). The consequences of imprisonment in the US are extensive, but are not simply limited to incarcerated individuals and ex-prisoners. Far more than in the UK, the consequences of a felony conviction alone can be substantial, and there are at least an estimated nine million ex-felons in the US at the moment (Wheelock 2005). The controversial US Presidential election in 2000 made the question of felony disenfranchisement more visible both inside and outside the US, and prompted debates around the operation of disenfranchisement legislation which, for a number of reasons, has had a significantly racialised impact (Uggen *et al.* 2003b). A majority of states have laws restricting the voting rights not only of imprisoned felons but those on probation or parole; some states also include ex-felons (see Manza and Uggen 2004). Four states bar convicted felons from voting for life. An estimated 1.4 million African American males, 13 per cent of the adult African American population, have lost the right to vote under this legislation (Mauer and Chesney-Lind 2002).

The challenges of obtaining employment have been augmented by challenges in relation to education, following recent changes to the eligibility of ex-prisoners for student financial aid (known as Pell Grants) (Page 2004); Wheelock states that 92,841 students have been denied funding due to a drug offence and that the estimated number of disqualified students is growing (Wheelock 2005; Levi and Appel

2003). Of particular concern in relation to families are the restrictions on public assistance for ex-felons. Individuals in violation of a condition of their parole or probation can be barred from receiving federal welfare benefits (Temporary Assistance to Needy Families [TANF]); food stamps, Supplemental Security Income and access to public housing (Rubinstein and Mukamal 2002). Individuals convicted of a drug felony can be permanently barred from receiving TANF or food stamps (Travis and Waul 2003a). When set in the context of offending patterns, these provisions can have a profound impact on African American families and families of female offenders. Families of colour are most affected by welfare bans; Allard (2002) reported that 92,000 women face collateral welfare restrictions, and of these women, 35,000 (38 per cent) are black. This, of course, affects families: there are an estimated 135,000 children whose mothers are disqualified from public assistance as described. Similarly, in relation to public housing, a high proportion of those relying on public housing are black women with children (Wheelock, 2005).

The civil consequences of imprisonment are underpinned by legislative foundations. Questions of family life, rights to intimate relationships and parent–child interaction have occupied the US legal system in relation to both legislation and recent case law. One aspect of imprisonment which can have a direct impact on prisoners' family relationships is that of 'permanency planning' for prisoners' children. Under the Federal Adoption and Safe Families Act 1997, where a child 'has been in foster care under the responsibility of the State for fifteen of the most recent twenty-two months' then the State is required to file a petition to terminate the parents' rights. The average length of sentences served by both men and women means that termination proceedings will be legally mandatory in the majority of situations involving incarcerated parents whose children are cared for by State agencies (Gentry 1998).

One of the most significant contributions to the debate has been the development of awareness of the impact of mass imprisonment not only on individuals and their families, but also on communities, including children (Hairston 2003; Wacquant 2001). As Donald Braman writes in the context of policy debates, both liberals and conservatives 'forget that offenders not only offend against, but come from, communities' (Braman 2004: 4). More than two million children are estimated to have parents in prison (Mazza 2002) and many more experience the incarceration of a parent at some time during their childhood (Seymour 1998). Other writers (see Travis and Waul 2003a) have assessed the impact on offenders 'home' communities. One of the most immediate social shifts is the change in 'the ratio'; that is, the gender ratio of males to females (Braman 2002). Combined with the impact of HIV/AIDS and drug use, the levels of imprisonment of males, specifically African American males, means that many children are growing up in matriarchal communities. This has effects on the behaviour of both men and women, with exaggerated perceptions of the 'male shortage' meaning a decline in men's accountability and responsibility within relationships and the community. Linked to this is the rising number of children raised by grandparents, one of the consequences of shifts in drug policies which have contributed to the drastic rise in the women's prison population (Minkler and Roe 1993; Dressel and Barnhill 1994; Cox 1999).

When this situation is assessed in the context of research on the links between parental imprisonment and subsequent offending, the future impact of these policies may well lead to more crime, rather than less. The situation is complex however, and recognised by Donald Braman (2004) in his book based on ethnographic research in Washington DC. It is the same communities that experience high levels of imprisonment which also experience high levels of criminal victimisation, and so sometimes there are high levels of community support for the imprisonment of offenders. The omnipresent prison means that children can grow up accepting imprisonment as an ordinary aspect of life, and Wacquant (2001) has analysed perceptively how through a variety of strategies and policies the ghetto is becoming more like the prison and the prison more like the ghetto. There is no similar research into the impact on communities of imprisonment in the UK, however.

Prisoners' families in the UK – 'now you see them, now you don't'

For some categories of offender, tracing the evolution and implementation of penal policies is fairly straightforward. For example, for young offenders broad policies can be traced through research documents, proposed and actual legislation, official reports and official speeches (Morgan and Newburn 2007). Trying to identify penal policy in relation to prisoners' families is a frustrating exercise, made more difficult by a lack of co-ordination between all the organisational elements which may contribute to that which could be called 'policy'. In contrast with other areas of criminal justice, where there has been a number of influential reports followed by statutory developments, to understand current policies in relation to prisoners' families necessitates an awareness not only of criminal justice but also of multiple aspects of law, social security, employment, education and childcare, and involves knowledge of the activities of a number of different agencies and public bodies.[2] There have been policy initiatives and research into prisoners' families, but this research has tended to be narrowly focused on one aspect of families' experiences and needs, such as visiting; mother and baby provision; education and prisoners' children, and resettlement. There is no joined-up thinking, and although it is attractive to argue that the newly-constituted Ministry of Justice might offer a co-ordinated response this is not immediately in prospect. There have been initiatives focusing on particular topics, such as the work of the Department for Work and Pensions (DWP) in relation to employment of ex-prisoners, and work by other government departments on families in relation to resettlement, but there has been no real co-ordinated policy focus on prisoners' families.

In her recent book *Criminal and Social Justice* (2006) Dee Cook advances the image of an 'upside down duck' as a means of explaining social policy interventions under New Labour:

> [If] we were to see society as a pond, we could envisage the policy process (policy-makers and implementers) operating like ducks, smoothly moving through sometimes troubled waters, their calm vision and direction steering social policies, which are implemented through the firm direction of the paddling webbed-feet, working rhythmically and powerfully below the surface, translating policy into action and direction (2006: 120).

She then goes on to argue that, staying with this analogy, the duck's channel through social waters has not been smooth, and the duck has in fact been 'turned upside down by a plethora of government papers, policies and initiatives which have literally swamped those agencies ... charged with their implementation'. The duck's rapidly-paddling feet 'flay energetically in mid-air without firm strategic direction' but at the same time little is actually happening underwater. Before long, of course, as Cook points out, the duck is likely to drown (Cook 2006: 120–121).

If we adopt this image of the duck as a way of visualising policies in relation to prisoners' families, then the duck may not necessarily be upside-down as there has not been the same deluge of reports, documents and initiatives raining down on its head. Rather, the prisoners'-families policy-duck is an intermittently-appearing duck, which spends some time invisible. Unlike Cook's duck, this duck has very weak feet and is scared of paddling too vigorously for fear of upsetting the other occupants of the pond. Indeed, it may appear to be more concerned with appearing to paddle than actual paddling. It quacks enthusiastically on occasions, but then lapses back into silence then gradually disappears. Reflecting the intermittent input into prisoners' family policy, it is always underfed and hungry as it is neglected by those people on the river bank who could feed it bread, who instead ignore it no matter how loud it quacks unless it can serve a useful purpose to them. This neglected and weak duck, ignored unless it can be useful, offers a symbolic representation of current UK prisoners' family policy.

One of the key contentions of this book is that prisoners' families are always marginalised. They are socially marginalised as the stigmatised families of prisoners, marginalised as only secondary actors in the criminal justice process, and marginalised in almost any academic discipline in which they are mentioned. They do not 'belong'; they are always added on or left out completely. In schools, the needs of prisoners' children may not be understood, and whilst there is a high level of public awareness of the impact on children of divorce, for example, there is little similar awareness of the experiences of the children of prisoners. Some of this reflects public attitudes; it is particularly difficult to engender public support for prisoners' families in the UK where families often experience the 'familial taint' of offending even though they are not themselves offenders. Prisoners' families not only live their lives in the shadow of prison, but often live metaphorically shadowy lives, never really belonging to a discipline or discrete area of professional practice but instead existing and moving somewhere near the edges.

Members of prisoners' families experience a form of 'selective visibility' which varies depending on the context. For example, from a prison management perspective family contacts necessitate provision for visits; raise security questions; and are linked to prisoner well-being. In the actual prison context the day-to-day realities of visits involve officers and prisoners alike in rules, regulations, procedures and routines which make these visits possible. In this context, families are always either present or imminently present. From a policy point of view, however, they are an additional optional consideration. For example, it may be a matter of custom and practice to take family considerations into account in sentencing, and indeed some recent cases have considered the impact of a prison sentence on the offender's children, but this approach is not universal (Piper 2007). Although, as in many other aspects of criminal justice and penal policy, prisoners' families have not been immune from a governmental tendency to promote 'sound-bite policies' such as the proposed 'targeting and tracking' of prisoners' children (Woolf 2004), the potential impact of policy developments on families is not routinely discussed. Prisoners' families are not always ignored but are not always visible in policy terms. For example, electronic tagging has been argued to lead to an increase in crime in the home, but this emerged as a consequence of the evaluation process and the question of the impact on families was not raised *ab initio*. Similarly, in discussions of changes in sentencing practice family considerations are peripheral, in contrast to discussions of resettlement where families have become the 'flavour of the decade'. They are thus selectively visible, considered when policy-makers want to utilise them but always less important than other groups. For example, increased attention has been paid to questions of justice for victims and the role of victims in the courts and it is largely accepted that the 'traditional' court process has left them feeling excluded. Prisoners' families often feel the same exclusions, but in the UK have less legitimacy as actors.

The inexorable rise in the prison population in England and Wales, along with the emergent research into the links between strong family ties, social capital and the successful community re-entry of ex-prisoners, has meant increasing interest by policy-makers in prisoners' families. However, such interest has often owed more to rhetoric and the desire for electorally attractive sound-bites than actual funded policy initiatives (Clarke 2005). In considering penal policy and prisoners' families however, there is more to it than simply considering specific, actual targeted initiatives for families. Put simplistically, the higher the prison population then, intuitively, the more families affected. Families experience the waves made by penal policy changes, for good or bad. For example, if a jurisdiction were to drastically cut the rate of imprisonment then it is possible that a family might continue to suffer the problems of a criminal member bringing criminal activity and a criminal lifestyle into the home. As changes in mental health provision have meant that sometimes crises have resulted due to individuals being released without accessing appropriate support, so, it could be argued, a sudden downturn in the use of imprisonment may create problems for families.

Comfort (2007) argues that in era of welfare cuts in the US the prison is the one consistent state institution which can provide help: thus although families suffer many negative consequences of imprisonment, there are so few community resources available that imprisonment may offer some positive benefits. The converse is also true and the effects of this upward shift in the use of imprisonment can be seen not only in the UK but, more acutely, in the US. In textbooks on imprisonment it is customary to include a chapter on the aims of imprisonment and these aims can have an associated impact on families. For example, a shift towards retributive justice may lead to longer (or possibly shorter) prison terms, or rehabilitative policies may change the nature of the establishment in which a prisoner is detained or the regimes governing prisoners' daily lives. The period of the sentence given and served may be the same in both cases, but the nature of the prison may change, and thus so may the nature of the visiting facilities; the tenor of visits; the experiences of visitors and so on.

The social atmosphere around sentencing, imprisonment and criminal justice may also have a profound impact on families. Some offences are more unpopular than others and sometimes elicit public sympathy and sometimes condemnation. These public attitudes may change over time. That said, from reading the extensive literature which has emerged since the 1960s (Morris 1965) the constant, continuous theme tends to be one of unpleasantness, struggle and hardship. The precise nature of these hardships has in some ways changed and in some ways stayed the same. For example, prisoners now may find it easier to keep in touch by means of telephone calls, which were not available routinely in the time of Morris's research. However, many prisoners' families still experience financial hardships, difficulties visiting, lack of information and housing changes. Although a number of support groups have grown since Morris was writing (and some, such as Aftermath, have come and gone), the voices of prisoners' family members still resonate with those of forty years ago. What to tell the children, how to deal with the stigma and shame, how some communities support and some do not: all these things would be familiar to the prisoners' partner from today travelling through time and and ending up in 1965, or conversely, for one of Morris's interviewees travelling forwards from 1965 to the present.

It is tempting to argue that despite ostensibly important reports such as the Woolf Report (1991), and its talk of community prisons and 'the permeable wall', or legislation such as the succession of criminal justice acts over the same period and the expansion in available forms of community penalties, for many families little has changed. It could be argued that imprisonment is now so common that it bears no stigma: this may be true in some communities where it is simply part of daily life, but so much depends on the offence type, on the individuals concerned and their previous place and role in the community, and whether members of the community or the community environment itself were victimised. Donald Braman (2004), in his insightful and perceptive ethnographic work on Washington DC, points out that high levels of support for imprisonment exist even in the communities where imprisonment has taken away the most people, and he points out that the communities which have the highest levels of prisoner residence may also have the highest levels of criminal victimisation. Clearly there have been some profoundly important new initiatives, and individual establishments have worked, especially in relation to prisoners' children, to develop extended visits schemes and programmes such as 'Storybook Dad', but to some extent it is tempting to argue that little has changed. Indeed, it could be argued to be worse because more and more people are being imprisoned and therefore more families affected and, perhaps most significantly, a higher proportion of these individuals who are now imprisoned, who may not have been for similar crimes fifteen or twenty years ago, are women.

Although there have been legal changes in visit entitlements since the research of Morris (1965) other policies and shifts in attitudes have worked together to make things harder for families. The shift towards more punitive penal policies and increased use of imprisonment has meant that, as well as more families being affected, the attitudes of policy-makers have made the maintenance of prisoners' family relationships more challenging. Prisoners' families suffer from the intersection of social and criminal justice policy, as they are, even if not at the beginning, usually suffering financial hardship. Cuts in services, lack of public and/or affordable housing, stigmatisation at the hands of the media, shifts in benefits entitlements and a general move away from probation as a support agency towards probation staff as criminal justice enforcement and surveillance personnel, have all had a negative impact on prisoners' families. They are always an afterthought, or figure solely in policy discussions of other people or single-issue aspects of their lives.[3] Policy-making in relation to prisoners' families becomes fraught with electoral dangers for governments, who do not want to be viewed as soft on crime and viciously attacked for this by the media. At a time when some aspects of crime continue to fill many column inches, the question of 'what about their family' is almost never asked in a sensitive way. They may be mentioned, or blamed, are assumed to have known, but there is still little appreciation of the impacts of imprisonment for families. They are, quite literally, the forgotten casualties of 'tough on crime' policies, which, bluntly, have translated into being 'tough on families' and 'tough on children'.

The social context and the persistence of family-blaming

In the UK and the US there is still a persistent tendency to blame prisoners' families for their own situation and as Condry (2007) found in her research with families of serious offenders, this stigmatisation has a gendered aspect, especially for mothers. It is of course correct that sometimes prisoners' partners acquiesce or are complicit in their partner's offending, but in public and media discussions of the issues prisoners' families often receive little public support. This blaming of the family has a long history and in some jurisdictions in the past was explicitly endorsed. For example, during the Nazi era in Germany the Third Reich brought in *Sippenhaft*, a system whereby the family members of political offenders were punished as well, justified by reference to criminal bloodlines and genetics.[4] The punishment of family members is a 'stock-in-trade' of dictators, although it is fair to say that the motivation may have more to do with deterrence of others than punishment of those assumed to be complicit. However, what is important is the commonplace nature of this dragging of family members into a web of punishment even in the absence of evidence that they have committed any infractions themselves. Agozino (2005) makes the point that in Africa it is common for the wives, mothers, sisters or girlfriends of army officers who are suspected of plotting unsuccessful coups to be harassed, maimed, killed or detained even without being suspected of any crime themselves. Although this policy clearly does not operate explicitly in the UK, there are resonances of this idea of the 'familial stain', 'kin contamination' and family blaming (Condry 2007). For example, in the wake of the terror attacks on New York in 2001 the British government proposed new anti-terrorist legislation which would have allowed for the detention of a person who 'has links with a person who is a member of, or belongs to an international terrorist group'. These links were not defined in the Bill and could potentially have allowed for the detention of family members of suspected international terrorists, although this clause was never approved and never made it into the statute book.

Echoes of this interpretation of the transmission of criminality, either biologically or socially, are seen in the debates around prisoners' access to artificial insemination facilities in attempts to conceive children, as discussed later in this book. Although prisoners' children are more easily perceived as 'innocent' they may also be defined as a 'chip off the old block' and rendered potentially criminally suspect or labelled as a potential problem at an early age. The negative reactions of the press to Maxine Carr, who gave a false alibi to her partner Ian Huntley, who in December 2003 was convicted of murdering two young girls, is a good example of the readiness of the UK press and public to condemn prisoners' family members and partners. Her subsequent imprisonment and hounding after her release has failed to portray her as a woman who testified in court that she was scared of her partner and wanted to protect him from the negative mental effects of what he had told her was a false allegation; rather than being portrayed as a woman who, although having made a mistake, sought to support her partner, she has been portrayed as the natural successor to Myra Hindley who, in contrast, took an active role in the abduction and murder of a number of children (Jewkes 2005). Families, and especially women, become easy targets for the media. It is hard to identify an example of a male partner of a serious female offender for whom the same argument of 'he must have known' is used by the tabloids; partly this reflects that women's offending is more minor, but women are often made responsible for male behaviour, either as mothers or partners. Women who are the mothers of criminals may be made to feel that the offending behaviour was the consequence of poor parenting or bad mothering; similarly, the wives of male offenders may find themselves accused of being somehow responsible, and assumed to have always known what was going on.

The best analysis of this concept of familial blame is that developed by Rachel Condry (2007) in her vivid ethnographic account of the impact of conviction and sentence on the families of serious offenders. Her discussion of the 'web of shame' and kin culpability consider, in particular, the dominance of psy-discourses and mother- and partner-blaming and she explores how familial blame can attach itself to omission, commission and continuation. The continuation of a relationship with an offender can lead to further stigmatisation, but to end their connection with the offender could not challenge the other forms of blame and stigma consequent upon the offending behaviour. Sometimes family members are not happy to even be associated with the offenders, but regardless of this continue to be societally deemed as legitimate targets for public disapproval and hostility (Condry 2007). Even where family members sever ties with offenders, this 'family-blaming' may persist. For example, a recent case in Lancashire illustrates this vividly. A young man who lived with his parents was convicted of sending obscene, harassing text messages to many women linked to the charity where he worked. Although after the story appeared in the local newspaper (Lancashire Evening Post 2006a) his parents asked him to leave their home and disowned him, their home was later the target of abusive graffiti. Family-blaming is a persistent and powerful undercurrent in relation to the experiences of prisoners' families.

The research context

Depending on your viewpoint, there has either been a significant development of relevant research into issues relating to prisoners' families over the last five years or, alternatively, there has been little relevant research and much of it has been small-scale. This difference in perspective reflects different approaches to methodology. From a quantitative point of view, it is fair to say, as does Joseph Murray (2005) that there has been little detailed research into prisoners' families. If, however, we recognise the different strengths of qualitative work then we have seen insightful and detailed studies being published based on, for example, the committed ethnographic work of Megan Comfort who 'hung around' the 'Tube' (i.e. the visitor's entrance) at San Quentin State Prison in the US so she could write about the women visitors (Comfort 2002), or Rachel Condry's immersion into the world of a self-help group for the families of serious offenders (Condry 2007). Rose Smith and Roger Grimshaw's team have published a detailed, vivid and harrowing account of poverty and financial disadvantage amongst prisoners' families, which goes beyond pure financial questions and documents a range of other economic and social difficulties (Smith *et al.* 2007). Although the studies referred to may each have been conducted on a small scale, the commonalities of experiences and needs lead to the deduction that the small-scale findings may be representative of the situation on a larger scale. Whilst writers such as Murray have indeed provided important data such as that on whether or not prisoners' children are more likely to become offenders, others, often women, have worked with and amongst prisoners' partners and children and thus have been able to provide thought-provoking interview data.

In my view, the commonality of experiences and the vividness of these accounts as garnered by researchers offer far more value to someone with a genuine interest in the issues than pure numbers. It is, after all, an altogether different matter to read that a high proportion of women prisoners are mothers compared to reading accounts of the sheer desolation experienced by an imprisoned woman separated from her children. Similarly, a statistic that a high proportion of prisoners' partners suffer financially is one thing, but to hear the voice of a woman explaining how she has gone without even basic items herself so as to support her partner is another. The voices of children too are there, albeit they are not as audible as for practical and ethical reasons they are often regarded as too young to be interviewed. The children of prisoners express themselves in different ways, however, not only verbally, and their experiences and emotions are there to be seen if they are appropriately approached. In contrast with quantitative work such as that of Joseph Murray and David Farrington (2005, see also Murray *et al.* 2007) this book recognises the value of qualitative data in providing vivid and detailed information on the lives of prisoners' families which perhaps could not be elicited using purely quantitative research methods. Thus, at risk of sounding like an unthinking disciple of qualitative research methodology in this regard, whilst quantitative data may be of use in determining basic statistical linkages, the textured nature of qualitative enquiry provides the foundation stones for this book.

Conclusion

It could be argued that this book is flawed in that it focuses almost exclusively on the female partners of male prisoners and upholds the dominant stereotype of the heterosexual family which has dominated the literature, despite criticism. The literature, however, still very much focuses on this. There is almost no published research on the male partners of female prisoners and as men in this position do not tend to involve themselves in support groups, they constitute an almost invisible population. In addition, when men are imprisoned their children are highly likely to stay with their mothers but when women are imprisoned they tend not to go to their fathers but to other female relatives. The literature says a little about the mothers of prisoners, who often continue to visit prisoners serving very long sentences after other relationships have broken down, and who may, for example, continue to visit those who have committed shocking offences with which other family members such as partners cannot cope, as in the case of some sex offenders (Condry 2007). The lives of gay partners of prisoners of either gender are almost invisible. It is beyond the scope of this book to try and document the experiences of these invisible and marginalised groups, as there is a need for detailed empirical research, but it is important to critically identify this. I am thus aware, in writing this, of the difficulties of criticising a position which I may appear to be propagating; that is, the continued dominance of a model of 'the prisoners' family' which is that of a male inmate, young female partner and young children. This image takes no account of the experiences of other groups, such as the families of older prisoners or the older partners of prisoners (but see Codd 2000). We know little, for example, of the impact on adults of the imprisonment of a parent. Although there has been a recent expansion in research into prisoners' families, there are still many questions yet to be addressed and a substantial need for further, detailed research in the future.

Notes

1   Many thanks are due to Graham Steventon for his expertise and enthusiasm in showing me the architecture of San Francisco, including the Pyramid.
2   For example, at the time of writing the Department for Education and Science (DfES) has been conducting a study into improving outcomes for prisoners' children.
3   Rather as in a multi-user fantasy-based computer game developed in the 1980s, one user, when logged in as herself, was unable to see a fulsome description of a beautiful character based on her, although this was visible to everyone else playing the game, sometimes policy-makers seem unable to see things which are not only visible but dominate the lives of others.
4   For a discussion of how this took place after the executions of Sophie and Hans Scholl and other members of the 'White Rose' group involved in peaceful resistance, see Dumbach, A. and Newborn, J. (2006) *Sophie Scholl and the White Rose*, Oxford: Oneworld, especially pp. 167–169 or, in German in relation to the Scholl family, Scholl, I. (1993) *Sippenhaft: Nachrichten und Botschaften der Familie in der Gestapo-Haft nach der Hinrichtung von Hans und Sophie Scholl*, Büchergilde Gutenberg: Frankfurt am Main. Four days

after Hans and Sophie Scholl were executed their flat was raided and a number of family members were placed in detention. For a discussion especially of how it linked to fear, see Loeffel, R. (2007) 'Sippenhaft, Terror and Fear in Nazi Germany: Examining One Facet of Terror in the Aftermath of the Plot of 20 July 1944', *Contemporary European History* 16: 51–69.

Chapter 2

Why care? Family ties and other justifications

Introduction

One of the underlying themes of this book is that families living with imprisonment merit far more attention from policy-makers and academics than they currently receive. This chapter offers some justifications for increased awareness of and support for prisoners' families. It is a disturbing reflection of public attitudes to crime and punishment in the UK that research into and support for prisoners' families needs to be justified at all: rather than recognising prisoners' families as often fragile families in need of help, prisoners' families often attract the same stigma and social disapproval as offenders themselves (Codd 1998; Peelo *et al.* 1991). Families of prisoners are categorised as 'undeserving' and, in an atmosphere of negativity, support for prisoners' families and attempts to encourage closer relationships between prisoners and their children are often vilified in the press.

There are, however, a number of reasons why relationship ties between prisoners and their families are important and also pragmatic, philosophical and humanitarian arguments as to why these relationships merit more attention and support than is currently the case (Hairston 1991). Family ties may benefit not only prisoners but also society as a whole, in the present, the near future and also the long term.

Family ties during the sentence

For many families, relationship bonds, including the bonds of marriage, intimacy and the bonds between parents and children, mean that imprisonment poses a challenge to their relationship but does not end it. Many families continue to care for prisoners because despite the locks, bars and bolts an imprisoned family member is still a family member. The continued existence of family ties is not to be taken for granted, however. Imprisonment, by its very nature, challenges relationships between prisoners, family and kin, friends and other members of their communities. Although much of the literature views this as a by-product of incarceration, some writers have seen this as a core aspect of the punitive element of imprisonment and as one of the unstated aims of the sentence (No More Prison 2006). Some families sever contact with an inmate, and some inmates sever contact with their families, but that does not change the fact that a family member is imprisoned. Even if a prisoner's wife, for example, decides to end the relationship, she cannot return to her previous status of never having been married to a prisoner (Codd 2000, 2002).

Family ties may offer benefits both to prisoners and 'outside' family members at various points during the sentence and, for men, also play a fundamental role in preventing recidivism (Ditchfield 1994). As will be discussed later in this book, however, the same linkage between family ties and the prevention of reoffending cannot be presumed to exist for women leaving prison. The research evidence shows that male prisoners benefit from supportive family relationships during and after the sentence, although a corresponding benefit for partners cannot be assumed.

Research on prisoners' family ties tends to focus on the importance of family contact for prisoners; the importance of family contact for the maintenance of the family unit, especially in relation to parent–child relationships; the role of supportive family ties in promoting the successful community re-entry of prisoners and subsequent decreased likelihood of recidivism and most recently the contribution of family relationships to the offender's process of desistance. It is commonplace to consider the importance of family ties for prisoners, but, with the possible exception of the impact on prisoners' children, relatively little attention has been paid to the question of the importance for families of maintaining ties with prisoners. By deduction, through interviews and from reading postings on the Prison Chat UK website, it is clear that keeping in touch with prisoners, by visiting, writing letters, sending tapes and so on, is a key activity of prisoners' outside partners and one of concern and anxiety should anything go wrong or should there be any problems. Qualitative data from interviews conducted with prisoners' partners emphasise the importance placed by many partners and children on keeping in touch (Codd 2002). The consequences of keeping in touch, and of supportive ties, have been well documented for prisoners, especially for the post-release period, but not for families. Difficulties visiting and communicating create anxiety and stress for family members, but, for example, it is not easy in the absence of research to argue that the maintenance of these ties benefit partners in the long term in the same way as imprisoned men benefit both during and after the sentence.

Family ties and prisoner well-being

Supportive family ties can be extremely important for the well-being of prisoners but the strength and operation of these bonds are challenged by imprisonment. Laing (2003) refers to Brodsky (1975) and argues that strong family relationships tend to get better and bad family relationships tend to get worse, continuing in the pattern which existed prior to imprisonment (Swan 1981), the greatest deterioration in relationships being with female friends, then spouses, the least affected being those with parents (Brodsky 1975). This echoes anecdotal evidence that where long-term sentences are being served it is, by the end, only mothers who visit and support inmates. Loneliness, isolation and lack of contact with family and friends are often identified as the most disturbing and distressing aspects of imprisonment and have been argued to constitute a key aspect of the punitive elements of the loss of liberty (Flanagan 1980; Richards 1978; Murray 2005). In Mills' study (2005), for the majority of prisoners interviewed the hardest aspect of being in prison was being separated from family and friends, often feeling powerless and frustrated when they could not do anything if their families were experiencing problems, as well as coping with communication difficulties and uncertainty as to their partners' feelings. For women inmates estrangement from children is a primary concern for the majority (Dodge and Pogrebin 2001). Alice Mills suggests that active family support can help ameliorate the 'pains of imprisonment' (Sykes 1958) and potentially reduce the risks of suicide and self-harm, as loss of or limited contact with families has been linked to an increased likelihood of attempted suicide, with family relationships and visits issues often acting to trigger acts of suicide/self-harm (Mills 2005;

Liebling and Krarup 1993; Liebling 1992, 1999). Loss of contact with family and friends, or separation, can lead to feelings of isolation, loneliness, guilt, anger and despair and Adams (1992) found that prisoners' loss of connection with family members, especially children, was linked to depression. In contrast, family support can enhance what Dodge and Pogrebin (2001) call 'emotional survival' providing love and lifting self-esteem. The prison suicide/self-harm prevention implications of supportive family ties should not be underestimated, and initiatives aimed at promoting family contact can also potentially reduce the risks (Mills 2005, citing McCarthy 2004).

The maintenance of family ties for prisoners has been linked to a lower level of 'institutionalisation' into the prison subculture. As well as contributing to psychological difficulties such as depression, paranoia, anxiety and suicidal tendencies, the isolation, it has been argued, pushes prisoners to adapt to the prisoner subculture (Gordon 1999). Identification with the prison subculture can lead to lower compliance with institutional rules and norms and, after release, can make community entry more problematic (Wolff and Draine 2004; Gordon 1999).

Family ties and family well-being

As has already been described, there has been limited discussion of the impact on non-imprisoned family members of policies which encourage the maintenance of family ties (Codd 2007a). While the well-being and mental health of prisoners is clearly helped by family contact, there is little published literature on the mental health needs of prisoners' partners, with the exception of Lowenstein's (1984) work which indicated that the female partners of male prisoners experience high levels of stress and anxiety. It cannot be assumed that contact between a prisoner and his or her family is automatically of benefit to the family. Similarly, where an initiative apparently benefits inmates by allowing contact, it cannot be assumed that it is welcomed or experienced as beneficial by partners. For example, since 1986 prisoners have been allowed access to telephones, following a limited experimental introduction of access which was later extended to cover the rest of the prison estate. This has been welcomed as providing opportunities for prisoners to maintain contact with their families, but has been experienced by some prisoners' partners as a form of control by their imprisoned men, who use the telephone as a method of remote surveillance, expecting women to be at home when they call and then quizzing them as to their activities if they are not available. Similarly, as will be discussed later in the book, telephones may enable prisoners to keep in contact with their families even if they are a long way from home but the pressure to fund phone calls, at rates which are set at levels much higher than usual for calls outside prisons, may lead to extreme anxiety and self-deprivation in outside partners. Sometimes telephones can be used for threats and intimidation, continuing a pre-existing abusive relationship pattern.

Visits are recognised as highly important but Mills (2005) argues that there has been little research into prisoners' experiences of visits and little research into men's experience of visiting, either as male partners of female prisoners or as same-sex partners of male inmates. Children often find visits stressful, especially closed visits (Richards and McWilliams 1996). For many female partners of male prisoners visits are a source of anticipation, joy, stress and sadness (Fishman 1990; Girshick 1996; Christian 2005). Many women report the combination of excitement and stress experienced, as preparing for a 'date', the visit often necessitating a whole day off work or a day away from home and often involving travelling long distances. The visit itself can be short and intense with high levels of anxiety in case of an argument, or women feeling they have to present a rose-tinted version of how they are coping so as not to upset the man. This presentation of one's ability to cope may not be restricted to visitors: Grounds and Jamieson (2003) found that the Republican ex-prisoners whom they studied reported hiding their worries and difficulties from their visitors and reassuring them that everything was alright. The security processes and lack of privacy may also take their toll: the graphic accounts of sexual activities reported in some US prison visits rooms (Fishman 1990) do not seem to be mirrored in the UK and family members may feel they do not have enough opportunity to show affection. For example, HMP Styal has banned visitors from kissing the female prisoners on security grounds in order to prevent the bringing in of drugs (Bunyan 2006).

While the evidence is clear that supportive family ties are of benefit to prisoners during the sentence, there is a scarcity of research into the well-being of families and it cannot therefore be assumed that family contact is as beneficial to 'outside' family members as prisoners. Of course, for those outside the benefit accrued may take the form of pride at 'standing by their man' or 'not giving up' on a son or daughter, but the evidence is not clear from the limited amount of published research.

Family ties after the sentence: re-entry and resettlement

> Family is important to understanding the reintegration of former prisoners, yet we know little about its precise impacts (Visher and Travis 2003: 98).

There has been a substantial recent expansion in interest in the role of prisoners' family ties in resettlement and in reducing reoffending by ex-prisoners and this has been recognised in several official reports and research studies (Social Exclusion Unit 2002; Home Office 2004, 2006; HMIP 2001). Much of the recent interest in prisoners' families in the UK has been prompted by the research finding that prisoners without active family support during their imprisonment are between two and six times more likely to offend in the first year after release than those who demonstrate or receive active family interest (Ditchfield 1994). A number of different research studies have confirmed the relationship between strong family ties during imprisonment and better outcomes after release (Ohlin 1954; Holt and Miller 1972; Visher and Travis 2003), but much of this research is dated and the strength of the relationship seems modest (Hairston 1991). Strong family ties can assist in prisoners' successful community re-entry and recent research into desistance has foregrounded families (Mills 2005; Maruna and Immarigeon 2004; Maruna 2001; Social Exclusion Unit 2002). Family support, which is not necessarily the same as the maintenance of family ties, can make a fundamental contribution to preventing reoffending after release and also, such as where family contacts provide post-release accommodation or employment opportunities, can assist in the community re-entry of offenders. Families may offer practical and emotional support immediately after release, such as by providing housing. Family acceptance and encouragement were found in one study to relate to the greatest chance of post-release drug abstinence, employment and optimistic attitudes (Nelson *et al.* 1999). The precise nature of this relationship and how it operates, however, has not really been ascertained.

American research has shown that incarcerated fathers who maintain family ties and who rejoin family life after imprisonment are less likely to be rearrested (Petersilia 2003) and in the UK, *A Five Year Strategy for Protecting the Public and Reducing Re-Offending* (Home Office 2006) recognises that supporting offenders' social and family links is key in successful resettlement and proposes that 'social and family links are at the heart of offender management' (Home Office 2006: 29). Re-establishing a commitment to family roles can be critical to developing a non-criminal identity (Visher and Travis 2003). That is not to say that this applies to all prisoners, in that many prisoners may not step back into a familial role immediately on their release, but the importance of a familial role as one aspect of identity transformation is significant (Visher and Travis 2003: Uggen *et al.* 2003a). Family ties may give ex-prisoners a reason to cease offending and to refuse criminal opportunities (Sampson and Laub 1993; Garland 2001 cited in Mills 2005). The recognition of the link between family ties and successful re-entry is not new; Ohlin (1954) found that 75 per cent of those he studied whom he categorised as maintaining active family interest were successful on parole, compared to 34 per cent of those categorised as loners. Follow-up studies in the subsequent twenty years gave similar results (Glaser 1964). More recent studies have supplemented this evidence and it is clear that prisoners' family relationships and ties to those family members during the sentence improve the chances of successful community re-entry on release (Hairston 1991, 1998; Laub *et al.* 1998; Sampson and Laub 1993). Most of the studies, however, define success in terms of non-recidivism, and it can be argued that there are many other aspects of reintegration which should be considered. From the perspective of policy-makers reoffending rates are clearly a valuable measure of one aspect of a person's successful reintegration, but there are other issues which are often viewed by prisoners themselves as more important signs that they are 'making it in the free world' such as obtaining secure accommodation and establishing relationships with children (O'Brien 2001; Visher and Travis 2003). This research can also be criticised for its focus on male released inmates and has been criticised for not sufficiently assessing issues such as the strength of the effects of different family relationships and how the quality of family ties should be assessed (Visher and Travis 2003).

As Mills and Codd (2008) argue, while there has been considerable research on the question of 'what works' in reducing reoffending, much less attention has been directed towards *why* and *how* processes of reintegration and resettlement work (Farrall and Maruna 2004). Little is known about the nature of any causal links between family ties and reduced recidivism and there have been few attempts to explore 'the impact of family influences in an individual's transition from prison to the community' (Visher and Travis 2003: 99). Some theorists, such as Farrall (2004), Sampson and Laub (1993) and Wolff and Draine (2004), have drawn on the concept of 'social capital' to provide key insights into the significance of prisoners' family ties and Mills and Codd (2008) discuss potential ways in which offender managers could mobilise this social capital by helping to support family relationships and involving families in reintegration.

It is important, however, to exercise caution in basing justifications for supporting prisoners' families on the grounds of their potential positive role in resettlement and in preventing reoffending. Although it is attractive to argue that families are beneficial support systems for offenders, families are not homogeneous and it is important not to romanticise the concept of 'family'. In encouraging families to play a role in re-entry planning, programmes must recognise that not all families offer positive environments. The government's recognition of the value of family ties, as, for example, propounded by the former Home Secretary Charles Clarke in his address to the Prison Reform Trust (Clarke 2005), relies on the assumption that family ties are in themselves a good thing. Although a growing body of research considers the links between family ties, community re-entry and also desistance, the concept of the family, and its role, has not really been interrogated. However, despite the government's willingness to endorse the importance of maintaining prisoners' family ties, a number of concomitant problems arise. First, there is the key problem of the 'criminal family': criminal behaviour has for a long time been linked to family attributes and family functioning (Klein *et al.* 2002). Families can themselves be criminogenic, providing a crime-friendly environment and, sometimes, assistance for offending which can jeopardise successful re-entry (Wolff and Draine 2004). Sometimes the social environment of a family may be linked to future offending. It thus becomes problematic to adopt an idealised view of the family as a valuable agent in preventing reoffending if that is not the case. Indeed, the same family and friendship bonds which could aid in prisoner resettlement may allow the prisoner to slip easily back into relationships with old accomplices in familiar environments.

Other prisoners may have limited family ties as a consequence of cutting off from abusive families, or through growing up in local authority care. For foreign national prisoners, family relationships may exist but be of little de facto help in enabling them to cope. Indeed, the existence of the relationship between a foreign national prisoner and his or her family may generate far more stress than support, with, for example, mothers worrying about who is caring for their children and, in some countries, children being in real danger of experiencing abuse or homelessness. The vision of the loving supportive family committed to helping an offender 'go straight' is an enticing one, in the same way as the vision of the supportive family and community group is in relation to family group conferencing and restorative justice, but in reality families can be unpleasant, abusive, manipulative and sometimes criminal, and it is thus highly naïve to unquestioningly argue that family ties are to be promoted. In addition, the government's enthusiasm for this romanticised notion of 'family' sits uneasily with the rhetoric of anti-social behaviour, the eviction of 'neighbours from hell', parenting orders and an emphasis on control and policing of these 'problem' families. In fact, the families whose children are the subjects of applications for anti-social behaviour orders may well be the families of prisoners, bearing in mind the statistical evidence and the socio-economic background of offenders. Thus the concept of 'the prisoner's family' is more complex than recognised in much government policy and may indeed not play the offender management role as envisaged in policy documents. This does not mean that prisoners' families should not be involved in decision-making, nor that family ties should not be supported, but a naïve endorsement of a 'happy families' model is simplistic and ignores the reality of many prisoners' family members, and the impacts of other government policies on families.

Societal and philosophical justifications

Pragmatic justifications for supporting prisoners can be subject to criticism. For example, justifying family support on the grounds that strong family ties can reduce the risk of reoffending and assist in resettlement is a dominant theme in penal policy but, as will be discussed in more detail later in this chapter, shifts a gendered burden to women (Codd 2007a). Such schemes are also of little value where prisoners are serving life sentences, where their release may never take place, or they are old, ill and likely to die in jail. Obviously for some life sentence prisoners release may be a realistic possibility, but for others, such as those with a whole-life tariff, it will not be a possibility. In such situations family contact needs to be justified in other terms, including but not limited to the benefit to the other members of the family. These justifications can be broadened out to include societal and philosophical questions.

Financial justifications

Put simply, if family ties can contribute to an increased likelihood of desistance, then supporting family ties could save the State, and therefore taxpayers, money. There are sound financial reasons for supporting prisoners' family ties in relation to desistance, as explored in a report for New Philanthropy Capital (NPC) (Brookes 2005). NPC is a charity that advises donors and funding sources on how to give more effectively, aiming to increase the quantity and quality of resources available to the charitable sector, and their recent research has explored the role played by charitable organisations in relation to prisoners and their families. The report focuses specifically on the costs and benefits of supporting prison visitors' centres in the context of research linking family ties to a decreased risk of reoffending and suggests that increased funding of visitors' centres would be 'an incredible bargain' in terms of the return generated by the initial investment. Brookes (2005) gives an example. If the cost of funding a visitors' centre was around £40,000 per annum (Loucks 2002) then if this were doubled then the cost of the centre would be £80,000. Brookes argues that the cost to the public purse of the average reoffender if they reoffend again after release is at least £111,300. Thus, he argues, if only one prisoner were to be assisted in their desistance by strong family ties which have been facilitated by a visitors' centre, this is still an excellent investment. He then extrapolates from this for the average prison and the number of prisoners likely to benefit from increased investment in a visitors' centre, pointing out that the costing of running a visitors' centre is about the same as the direct cost of imprisoning one inmate for a year. This research is valuable in that it attempts to quantify the financial consequences of a rising prison population with a correspondingly high reoffending rate, and offers financial reasons for supporting prisoners' family ties which take the debate beyond humanitarian justifications which may not be universally supported or accepted.

Interestingly, the report makes clear throughout its calculations that other factors could push up the savings; thus the figures quoted would seem to be conservative. The financial calculations presented in this report clearly identify that investing in visitors' centres could prove a sound investment. Of course, a better-funded visitors' centre is not a magic wand and investing in visitors' centres does little to challenge the basic costs of a high rate of imprisonment to begin with. Nor does such investment deal with the substantial negative financial consequences of imprisonment for families as identified by Smith *et al.* (2007). The financial argument presented by NPC may, however, be more persuasive to pro-imprisonment conservatively-minded policy-makers as a means by which visitors' centres can be funded, and families supported, without policy-makers appearing to be soft on crime. There are issues, however, of assuming that the entire financial burden should fall on third sector bodies, in that it suggests government creates the chaos and voluntary bodies go around sweeping up the mess, but it is promising. There is a need for caution, however, in accepting the linkage made by NPC between visitors' centres, family ties and decreased likelihood of reoffending, and more research is needed into whether good visitors' centres play such a central role in promoting family ties as NPC believes. It may be intuitively attractive to argue that family ties can be improved and reinforced by providing well-staffed visitors' centres, but there could be other initiatives which might be equally important. The other critical question is a financial one, and involves asking whether it is not more cost-efficient to argue simply for a significant reduction in the use of imprisonment, and whether building visitors' centres is simply a cosmetic improvement which ultimately supports the current system without challenging it. After all, the most straightforward method of ensuring that a prisoner's existing supportive family ties remain supportive is to minimise absolutely the number of people imprisoned, recognising the calls of penal abolitionists.

There are other financial arguments for minimising the negative effects of imprisonment on families. Until recently the best which could be achieved in terms of quantifying the total costs of imprisonment for families and State agencies was based on an informed guess. However, the research into poverty and disadvantage amongst prisoners' families funded by the Joseph Rowntree Foundation (Smith et al. 2007) estimated the actual costs of imprisonment by analysing the cases of five families who had participated in the study. Although the research was not designed to gather information about such costs, the interviews yielded valuable information concerning household finances and service use.[1] The case studies include the mother of a prisoner; a grandparent; a resident partner with one child; a resident partner and a non-resident partner with children. After imprisonment the weekly incomes of the five families fell and, for nearly all the five families, their only source of income was income support and housing benefit. The study estimated the costs of their use of NHS and social services resources: for example, in one of their cases two children received foster care, at a cost of £350 per week; in another case the child had social worker supervised weekly visits, at a cost of £104 per child per week. This estimation of the financial costs recognises the financial consequences of imprisonment not simply for families but for society as a whole. The total cost to agencies over a six-month period averaged £4,810 per family. After taking into account costs of providing items, travel and, the most significant impact, that of taking responsibility for children, the full cost per family averaged £5,860, including the cost to families and the cost of support provided by families and relatives. The average personal costs to the family and relatives over six months was £1,050, with the average loss of earnings being £6,204 over six months. If these costs are added to the usual figure of the cost of imprisonment, such as that of £37,500 per year given by the Social Exclusion Unit in 2002, then the additional costs to families and the public purse takes the total to £49,220.

The sample studied was small, and the cost of keeping one prisoner for a year will have risen since 2002, but what is clear from this study is that not only does imprisonment directly cost society the obvious incarceration costs, and entail families undertaking clearly visible costs such as travel and provision of goods, but also hidden social costs arise in relation to healthcare and social services. If we consider children, then additional costs can arise in terms of school exclusion and individual tutoring or alternative provision; psychological and behavioural services for children; counselling and related responses to the emotional and behavioural effects of imprisonment. For caregivers, there may be additional healthcare costs linked to stress, anxiety and mental distress, but for older carers there may also be physical consequences such as back and muscle pain from carrying toddlers, for example, or simple physical exhaustion from the demands of caring for young children. Thus the financial arguments based on preventing reoffending rehearsed earlier are persuasive, but on a more basic and obvious level imprisonment is extremely costly, not only in terms of the costs of incarceration but in relation to other associated expenses linked to the effects on families and the consequent need for the provision of support services. While some of these effects can be ameliorated by improved provision, such as visitors' centres, the effects based on trauma of separation and anxiety are less easily dealt with but clearly often involve costs linked to social work and healthcare.

The Smith et al. (2007) study offers an innovative and timely perspective on the issues, and in a world in which resource considerations are omnipresent the cost arguments may provide a valuable tool in the armoury of those who seek to improve the situation for members of prisoners' families. For example, government policy-makers may not be persuaded by philosophical or humanitarian arguments to limit drastically the use of imprisonment, when there is a risk that right-of-centre media commentators will immediately accuse them of being 'soft on crime', but fiscal arguments may be more persuasive, particularly as there does not seem to be any suggestion that the ever-rising prison population will not be accompanied by a rise in these 'collateral costs'.

Social inclusion

Considering the impact of imprisonment on families, and seeking to challenge the negative elements, can be viewed as a social justice project of fundamental importance. This approach can perhaps best be seen in Renny Golden's inspirational book, *War on the Family* (Golden 2005). Prisoners' families are in many ways the embodiment of multiple deprivations and socio-economic challenges, prisoners' children being one group of children at high risk of living in poverty (Walker and McCarthy 2005).

For many members of prisoners' families, who are already socially marginalised due to existing social and economic circumstances, imprisonment adds or exacerbates elements which ensure that they remain, to develop Jock Young's terminology (Young 1999) 'outside the track', allowed to spectate but not participate. As the research indicates, their children may also experience the same exclusion later in their own lives. Whilst prisoners' family members may have some difficulties in common with other people who are not experiencing a family member's imprisonment, it is the precise combination, combined with the institutional elements, which is significant. Whilst the individual components of the common impacts of imprisonment on families may not be specific purely to that experience (for example, just because a family is living in poverty it does not mean that they have an imprisoned family member), it is the conjunction of all these aspects which make the specific experiences of prisoners' families particular. Poverty, housing problems, loneliness, social stigma and practical problems of separation all combine to produce a particular set of challenges and difficulties which are experienced by many members of prisoners' families. Members of prisoners' families are the subjects of decisions over which they have no control and in relation to which they have no real *locus standi* as they are not the person on whom the sentence of imprisonment has been passed. Mirroring their exclusion in societal terms, prisoners' families exist on the margins of different disciplines and practice areas and indeed, live in the shadows, both overshadowed by the power of the prison but also 'out of the sunlight', almost in the dark, not focused on but out on the edges.

There are a number of justifications for just, lawful and proportionate punishment of offenders but the secondary punishment of non-imprisoned family members is more problematic. To be interested in prisoners' families one merely has to be interested in justice: the whole question of justice for victims and offenders includes family members. A great deal of attention is paid to homeless people; individuals with substance dependencies; and unemployment. The effects on children of divorce and other forms of family breakdown are well-publicised and matters of public concern. The large group of people affected by imprisonment receive less attention. This is because prisoners' families are often reacted to as responsible for their own fate, or as being themselves criminal. Whilst it is possible to attempt to raise funds openly for Victim Support, it is more problematic to campaign openly for the families of convicted murderers and rapists (Condry 2007). Yet, from a child's point of view, for example, suffering, hardship and loneliness are still suffering, hardship and loneliness, no matter what the cause. Thus, to be concerned about prisoners' families is to be profoundly concerned about social justice, about empowerment and inclusion.[2] It is about seeking not to punish people for crimes of which they have not been convicted in a court of law by due process. It is about challenging binary thinking which entails thinking about supporting victims *or* offenders as if the two are mutually exclusive. It is about recognising that, as crime harms many people, so does imprisonment. Our legal system, in its adversarial foundations, is based on this binary thinking. Families have little place in sentencing in an age of risk management and punishment. Whilst victim impact statements are fashionably discussed in relation to their viability at the sentencing stage, except in terms of the pre-sentence reports members of offenders' families do not have the same visibility or legitimacy. To be concerned about prisoners' families is interpreted by the media as involving being soft on crime and pro-criminal, whereas this is certainly not the case. From a social justice perspective prisoners' family members are often invisible, stigmatised and alone. Even prisoners' children receive only a limited amount of specific recognition of their needs. Schools vary in knowledge, understanding and attitudes and government policies for children do not focus on them specifically. The stigmatisation of prisoners' families in our culture can make it especially hard for children to seek help. Recent research by Janet Walker has illustrated how prisoners' children benefit from the support of their own peer group and how friendships can amount to almost surrogate family relationships for them and commonality of experiences can be particularly important (Walker 2006a).

Hudson (2006) considers how we could, and indeed should, do justice to those who are at the borders of our communities, or beyond, the central question being 'how can we provide justice for those with whom we feel no sympathy, and whose actions we cannot understand?' In her insightful discussion she employs the categories of 'aliens' and 'monsters'. 'Monsters' are offenders whose actions we cannot understand, whose actions and attitudes are beyond the boundaries of our understanding. Hudson describes 'monsters' as 'people who do not share our moral universe' (2006: 238), people with whom we feel no common humanity. These 'monsters' can include perpetrators of horrific, violent and shocking offences, but also in more routine categories such as young people who deliberately steal from the elderly. A monster can cease to be a monster when its humanity becomes visible, and Hudson argues that criminal justice processes should be active in this re-humanisation process. Hudson then follows up by discussing the alien, who is 'a figure we have not yet judged'. We do not know, as Hudson argues, whether the alien will be a monster or will have qualities we would recognise as human. These conceptions of the person at, or outside, our various communities, be they geographical, political, moral or cognitive, have great relevance to an understanding of societal responses to prisoners' families. Monsters, after all, may not spring fully formed from nowhere, as if some kind of golem created for their creator's own ends, as in Frankenstein's monster, but, if human, begin as babies with, if not actually present for their upbringing, at least a biological mother and father.

The way in which the media and society responds to prisoners' families reflects the dominance of the image of the monster as coming from a family of monsters, or from a family with a tendency to transmit monsterhood. In some contexts, offenders are situated by the media as coming from a predominantly criminal background, or as having criminal parents, and the whole milieu is described as predisposing the individual involved to 'monsterhood'. Sometimes the apparent normality of an offender's family is juxtaposed with the actions of the offender, but it is a rare family which escapes the mechanisms of family-blaming. Some try, through allegations that they have tried to stop the offending, or were too scared to intervene, but if a family appears to be essentially law-abiding and respectable then the tendency is for the media and social reaction to treat the family as rather like some science-fiction or horror film characters who can make themselves appear human but are monsters underneath. This implies sometimes some kind of calculation to deceive, or an inbuilt corruptness which the family may have failed to notice. Thus mothers of offenders become mothers of monsters, blamed as a consequence of nature or also nurture. Either way, the mother bears some responsibility for the production of the monster. Hudson makes the point that 'we need strong ideals of justice to counteract the ever-present spectre of the monster, and to counter the tendency to strengthen the borders of community and to treat aliens as monsters' (2006: 244).

In the criminal context, the offender-as-alien is a less likely figure than the offender-as-monster, but this relates more to arrested and unconvicted offenders such as those on remand, or those who have been acquitted of offences prompting a public outcry. In these situations, their culpability is an unknown quantity but the temptation is to treat them as monsters anyway. Hudson's point about the fear and hostility shown by adults to the alien, E.T., in the film of the same name, in contrast with the curiosity and lack of preconceptions of the children, is relevant here. Where, for example, someone is a suspected child sex offender, then this curiosity by children may be seen as a further mark of their cleverness, as a mark of their skills in relating to and manipulating children. Aliens may represent an entire race of aliens which might want to come and live on our planet to co-exist contentedly, or, as in *Independence Day*, to wipe us out entirely. The fear of the alien is also the fear of the unknown; fear of the terrorist suspect, for example; fear of the not-yet-caught murderer or rapist. They may turn out, for example, to be profoundly mentally disordered and in need of help, or to be wrongly suspected, but the tendency is for an easy slippage from categorising the person as alien to categorising the person as monster. Condry's work (2007), although it does not use these conceptual frameworks, demonstrates exactly how the families of serious offenders are indeed categorised as monsters by reason of their biological or familial proximity to the monster. Sometimes the media become obsessed with whether monsterhood is contagious, or whether two monsters together, as in Myra Hindley and Ian Brady, can create the acts of some kind of über-monster, capable of greater acts of cruelty and non-morality than one alone. What we see also then is the assessment of the monster's family, and more often than not either clear blame apportioned or, at very least, an argument based on their apparent normality which misrepresents their tendencies to monsterhood underneath. Condry pays particular attention to the stigmatisation of women linked to offenders, such as wives and mothers, and it could be argued that 'monsterhood' is in some ways viewed as matrilineal, as being

37

transmitted via a 'bad' mother. There are, after all, many shocking offenders in both real-life and fictional popular culture whose offending is claimed or interpreted as being linked to their abusive, neglectful or inadequate mothers, from Norman Bates in Psycho to some real-life serial killers.[3] In responding to these 'other' beings the concept of common humanity becomes essential here, as is argued by Coyle (2001) and others:

> Why should we be concerned about the human rights of prisoners, of men and women who are criminals or who are accused of being criminals? The answer to that question goes straight to the root of our civilisation. It is relatively easy for human beings to show respect and humanity to those who deserve that respect or who themselves show it to others. But what sets us apart as human beings is our ability to differentiate between who a person is and what he or she does and in so doing to recognise the need to show respect and humanity even to those who, by our estimation, do not deserve it (Coyle 2001: 8).

This argument is often used in relation to prisoners, but is also relevant to their families as supporting prisoners' families as families in need reflects a society which cares about its weakest members and which recognises the inherent dignity of all, simply by reason of being human. As the European Court of Human Rights pointed out in *Wainwright v. UK*, a case relating to the strip-searching of a prisoner's mother and half-brother visiting a prison, the family members had done nothing wrong and were unconvicted. Although it often seems that in England and Wales we have not yet totally abandoned the desire to see offenders suffer, as was the case when corporal and capital punishments were carried out under the public gaze, it could be argued that prisoners' families should be treated with greater respect and dignity. That is not to say that I am arguing that prisoners' families do not deserve to be treated well; rather an argument that even if one believes that prisoners' families deserve to suffer with their family member, a humanitarian and forward-thinking approach would be to treat them better than one feels they deserve. In my view, prisoners' partners and children are not to be reacted to as criminals themselves, but even if one thinks that family members deserve to suffer, an application of Coyle's statement indicates that we should, as a 'civilised' country, treat people not as they deserve but as they should be treated.

Feminist justifications and women-wise penology

The development of feminist perspectives in law, criminology and criminal justice has highlighted the gendered nature of imprisonment. On the whole, it is mostly men who populate the prisons. On a world level women usually make up no more than 10 per cent of the prison population in any jurisdiction and in many countries the proportion is substantially lower than this (Carlen and Worrall 2004). The explanations for this are linked to women's role expectations and the nature of female offending. It is, however, long-established that the experience of being imprisoned differs for men and women, and male and female prisons may differ in their environments, regimes and operation.[4] Women's imprisonment has become a key focus of feminist research and campaigning in criminal justice. In the UK, however, little research on prisoners' families has been feminist in its origins and methods, and the gendered nature of the prisoner's partner role has, with a few exceptions been mostly invisible (Codd 2002, 2007a; Condry 2007). In the US, in contrast, the day-to-day lives of prisoners' partners have been analysed 'through a gendered lens'. Research has shown that, regardless of the gender of the inmate, it is women who bear the burdens of caring. The term 'prisoner's family' usually implies children, and usually women caring for them. Megan Comfort's insightful ethnographic research with women visiting San Quentin is a good example: the gendered impact of the experience is integral to her work. Both Girshick (1996) and Fishman (1990) offer gendered insights into the women's lives and their relationships with male prisoners.

Pat Carlen's 'women-wise penology' can be interpreted and expanded to include the women who are left outside. The study of imprisonment from a feminist perspective needs to take account of all who are sucked into its field of impact, not just prisoners. This broader perspective includes those who are left to live on the outside, including those who for whatever reason choose not to support or continue relationships with someone in prison but whose lives have been affected by the incarceration decision and process. The multigenerational impact also needs clarifying and developing. Wacquant (2001) has, in his 'deadly symbiosis' piece, argued that in the US the ghetto is becoming more like the prison and the prison more like the ghetto, considering how children become acclimatised to a prison-type setting in their everyday lives. This process could of course be said to be gendered: while boys are learning about crime and imprisonment, girls are more likely to be learning about 'riding the bus' (Christian 2005), learning how to visit and how to create a home-like domestic atmosphere in the prison visitors' room, and how to conduct a relationship under the constant eyes of the guards. Thus, if we are to really care about criminal justice and women, we should consider the impact of the system not only on offenders and victims, but also on families who are affected by criminal justice measures.

Current initiatives which link family ties with desistance appear to recognise family ties merely as a means to an end; that is, the prevention of reoffending. Thus women become co-opted into the process of prisoner resettlement: women become responsible for helping ex-offenders 'go straight' and they are supported because of their instrumental value, not because of any commitment to maintaining families for their own sake (Codd 2004b, 2007a). This reinforces women's roles as law-abiding carers, and, as the term 'prisoner's family' suggests, foregrounds and prioritises the prisoner and not the family. In women's prisons, motherhood itself justifies prisons developing new, family-friendly initiatives such as all-day visits: for male inmates, family-friendly projects are justified not purely by reference to parenthood but to research into reoffending. This again reinforces gendered ideologies of women's care. The emphasis on desistance and reintegration of prisoners puts the focus squarely on the inmate, rather than on the family: families are supported because they can play a key role in resettlement, not because of their need for support as a family in their own right.

Critical perspectives: prisoners' families and penal policy

It is commonplace in discussions of prisoners' families to refer to families as 'the other victims of crime' or as 'forgotten victims' (Codd 1998; Light and Campbell 2006). This approach has been criticised, however (No More Prison 2006) because it can obscure the question of *why* prisoners' families are experiencing difficulties. It leads to an extension of the offender's responsibility and, by blaming the prisoner, can fail to question the systematic institutional and policy failure to respect prisoners' families. Renny Golden and others have discussed the so-called 'war on drugs' in the US in relation to prisoners, and prisoners' families can be seen as the 'walking wounded' of a system which only pays lip-service to the notion of family. Critical criminologists (Barton *et al.* 2006) have argued for 'expanding the criminological imagination', that is, encouraging and enhancing 'a kind of criminological imagination that is able and willing to break free of old constraints and look at the problems of crime and punishment with fresh eyes' (Currie 2002 quoted in Barton *et al.* 2006).

Prisoners' families could be argued to be the innocent victims of current penological policies; they are the casualties of the move towards mass imprisonment and the dominance of imprisonment as the paradigmatic criminal sanction. A critique of penology and the use of imprisonment, therefore, entails a recognition and understanding that families are suffering along with inmates. Thus, to care about prisoners' families is a logical extension of a concern with punishment and its uses, and an integral element of an awareness of critical issues in punishment and prisons. Thus, if we are to adopt critical perspectives which challenge power differentials then caring about prisoners' families is entirely merited and indeed necessary. It is rather like saying not only look what imprisonment does to offenders but look what imprisonment does to lots of other people as well. Thus, to care for prisoners' families is to care for the victims of current penal policies and negative social attitudes which build on discourses of risk and fear to stigmatise not only the criminal but anyone associated with them.

In contrast with this kind of critical perspective, some commentators have expressed views similar to those of Phil Gallie, the Conservative Member of the Scottish Parliament cited by Laing and McCarthy (2005) as saying:

> I recognise the soul-destroying effect that a parent's imprisonment must have on a youngster, but there should be no off-loading of responsibilities for who caused this anguish. The responsibility lies firmly with the individual who landed in prison as a result of their decision to break the law. The offender must take full responsibility (Gallie 2002).

This is a brilliant example of the kind of 'sound-bite' approach to crime and justice policies exposed and criticised by Michael Welch (2005). It, however, begs the question of how this responsibility is to be borne and exercised by prisoners. Even if the offender regrets their offending, while they are in prison there is little they can do to help their family. As Gallie was responding to suggestions that it should be made easier for prisoners to receive visits from their families, is he arguing that families should continue to experience often-unsatisfactory visits, and that this would be acceptable as, after all, it is the prisoners' responsibility? It is a kind of criminological 'but for' test, to borrow a term from the criminal law of causation: 'but for' the offender's actions the family would not be in this position at all. Clearly this is unarguably the case, and one only has to talk to prisoners and those with whom they work, especially counsellors and staff such as chaplains, to see that many prisoners emphatically do recognise their responsibility. This is why some choose to 'do hard time' and not see their families, so as to save their families the stress and unpleasantness of visiting. Many do experience remorse, guilt and anxiety and want to do more to help their families. Gallie does not, however, explain how they can do this. Prisoners' wages are not 'real' wages for the work they do; family contact is limited; and bluntly there are aspects of families' experiences which are made worse by the prison establishment and which are not an automatic corollary of the prison sentence. For views such as Gallie's to be tenable, the situation of the prisoner's child needs to be understood. It makes little difference to the experience of suffering and loneliness, or stigma, of a prisoner's child if the prisoner is at fault or the prison system: after all, the child is still suffering. Surely, the question is 'what is to be done?' The 'who is to blame' question is a linked one, but blaming the parent alone does nothing to help the child.

Conclusion

This chapter has explored the question of why we should care about prisoners' families and the justifications for paying increased attention to families are persuasive. Families matter not only for today's prisoners but also for family life and for children in the future: one does not have to condone or forgive what an offender has done in order to believe that their partner or child should not suffer as a result. The phrase 'if you can't do the time, don't do the crime' becomes completely irrelevant in the context of prisoners' families: a prisoners' partner or child may suffer a range of negative outcomes and experience an overflow of the punishment meted out to the offender. The impact of punishment flows around like a liquid, and is not restricted to one individual. It changes its nature and shape, shifts from one person to another and affects more people than those to whom it is initially directed. It is clear, however, that a number of tenable justifications exist in support of arguments that academics, practitioners and policy-makers should pay more, and better-focused, attention to members of prisoners' families.

Notes

1   Note that the study focused on the families of prisoners who were living in poverty, i.e. living with a household income of 60 per cent or less of the median household income in 2005. The families selected were chosen on the basis of variation in terms of age, ethnicity, family structure before and after imprisonment, service use, employment history and status. Their imprisoned relatives were serving sentences of between six months and eight years. Three families were white British; two were of Afro-Caribbean heritage. More detail as to the cases is given in the report (Smith *et al.* 2007: 41–42).

2   For some, faith and spirituality can provide justifications. Faith and spirituality are often entwined with prisons, sometimes controversially, and caring for prisoners and their family members can be seen as a spiritual activity. For example, for Christians the Bible mentions prisoners not infrequently and many Biblical figures were at one time or another imprisoned. Indeed, it is often forgotten in Christian discussion that, as Mark Lewis Taylor (2001) points out, the nature of the Crucifixion is inherently the operation of the state-sanctioned execution of a prisoner. Effectively in the light of the procedural and evidential irregularities, it is an execution as a consequence of a miscarriage of justice involving prisoner brutality, corruption and torture. For Roman Catholics in February 2007 Pope Benedict XVI called upon Catholics to visit prisoners and to give them spiritual care. The so-called 'Golden Rule', common across many world faiths and also called the 'ethic of reciprocity', would cover prisoners and their families without a problem, recognising the obligation to take care of families who are suffering.

3   There is also the possibility that if one comes from a family of monsters then law-enforcement agencies may define all children of that family as potential monsters too.

4   The needs and experiences of women prisoners will be discussed in Chapter 5.

Chapter 3

Who cares? The effects of imprisonment on families

Introduction: who are prisoners' families?

Prisoners' families are not a homogeneous group although despite this much of the literature is still predicated on the heterosexual family unit, usually involving an imprisoned father and a non-imprisoned young mother caring for young children (Morris 1965; McDermott and King 1992; Shaw 1992; Boswell and Wedge 2001; Paylor and Smith 1994). This image of the stereotypical 'prisoner's family' assumes the imprisonment of the man: male non-imprisoned partners of female prisoners are notably absent in the literature, as are same-sex partners. As anyone who has ever worked for, volunteered with or researched a self-help or support group for prisoners' families will know, such groups are often almost entirely populated by women. This reflects the simple demographics of imprisonment in the UK, where there are many more men in prison than women, and also may reflect gendered attitudes to help and support. The expectations of hegemonic masculinity may mean that men feel the need to be seen to be coping, and therefore to participate in a support group is akin to an admission of weakness and failure. For example, several years ago when I was teaching an access course a student stayed behind after the class to talk about his wife who was imprisoned for benefit fraud. He described with great enthusiasm how he and some of the other 'dads' he met whilst visiting the prison all met up for a cup of tea beforehand, telephoned each other if they had problems and had taken all the children on a outing to Blackpool Zoo. I commented that it sounded like a support group, but he responded that none of the men needed one of those (!).

Diversity and difference

There is still a tendency in the UK for discussions of prisoners' families to be 'race-blind' but in the US questions of race and ethnicity are so embedded in any discussion of imprisonment that these issues are more visible. Although the UK has seen a gradual expansion in academic interest in older prisoners (Wahidin 2004; Crawley and Sparks 2005) the move into considering older prisoners' families has been only briefly undertaken (Codd 2000) and the 'greying' of the prison population has not yet led to published research on the adult children of elderly prisoners. Little is known of prisoners' mothers, and even less about siblings. Paylor and Smith (1994) demonstrated that the family and kinship ties of prisoners are more diverse and varied than suggested by the published literature at their time of writing, and include not only actual but 'fictive' kin. Friends, unless they are treated as kin, tend to be omitted from specific consideration although prisoners' children can benefit greatly from supportive friendship groups in coping with the experience of parental imprisonment (Walker 2006b). Thus, the term 'prisoner's family' may imply greater diversity, and more fluid and dynamic relationships rather than simply blood- or marital-kin ties.

Grandparent caregivers

A particular current concern is the role of prisoners' parents, who may find themselves raising their grandchildren as a consequence of parental imprisonment, usually of mothers. The needs, experiences and struggles of grandparents came to public attention in the US during the 1990s, when the 'war on drugs' combined with the AIDS epidemic led to demographic shifts in communities and more and more children being brought up by grandparents (Minkler and Roe 1993; Dressel and Barnhill 1994; Cox 1999). In the UK Islington Council has recognised the needs of this increasingly significant group, and has published their *Guide for Grandparents Caring for the Children of Prisoners*. That is not to say that all grandparent caregivers are old. In Minkler and Roe's (1993) American study some of the grandparent caregivers were in their thirties. However, many grandparent caregivers are at least middle-aged themselves and very often more elderly.

Whilst grandparents may experience the same problems as partners in terms of visits and information, their difficulties may be compounded if they are elderly, in poor health, are having difficulties claiming benefits and having to deal with social service agencies and so on.

There are also theoretical dilemmas about allowing and encouraging grandparents to care for prisoners' children: if, as some writers suggest, family background and childrearing practices can predispose individuals to criminal behaviour, then it may be unwise to leave the next generation in the same environment which contributed to their parents' offending. Grandparents can act as bridges within families where there are conflicts between the prisoner and other adults, ameliorating the worst effects of separation for children by enabling children to retain some contact with an incarcerated relative. In the case of relationship breakdown, grandparents can act as relationship facilitators, in that even if a prisoner is no longer in a relationship with a child's other parent a grandparent may enable parent–child contact by taking the child to visit. Grandparents often also play a key role in helping families to cope, through providing financial, practical and emotional support. For example, in an earlier study an interviewee's father added the interviewee to his car insurance policy so that she had access to a car after financial difficulties meant that she had had to sell her own (Codd 2002).

Caring as a gendered activity

In stressing diversity, however, there is one key fact which underpins not only this chapter but also this book. It makes no difference to the burden of caring responsibilities whether the prisoner is male or female. Age is also insignificant here. The key fact is that regardless of the gender of the inmate, it is *women* who bear the burdens of caring from the outside. Although statistically men are more likely to be imprisoned, the burdens of caring are taken up by women. That is not to say that all women, to use a hackneyed phrase, 'stand by their man', but that where men receive visits, financial support, correspondence and gifts from outside, it is likely to have been given by women. Thus it follows that where prison regimes provide limited facilities or provisions, where telephone costs are high, or visitors' centres have expensive facilities, or, as is usual in the UK, prison wages are so low that prisoners need outside financial support, on the whole it is women who are providing these things, sometimes at great cost to themselves. The gendered nature of the responsibility for caring for prisoners 'on the outside' has been documented in research from the US (Girshick 1996; Fishman 1990), the UK (McDermott and King 1992; Devlin 2002; Condry 2004; Codd 2002) and Australia (Aungles 1993). When coupled with inequalities linked to socio-economic factors, such as pre-imprisonment social exclusion, when discussing the consequences of imprisonment for prisoners' partners, on the whole it is women who experience these hardships. There is, however, no detailed research into whether the impact on children is gendered although there is some evidence in the psychological literature that boys and girls, especially adolescents, display different behavioural reactions to the imprisonment of a parent.

The effects of imprisonment on families

Incarceration reaches more deeply into the substance of family and community life than standard accounts of criminal sanctions suggest. Forcefully transforming the material and social lives of families, incarceration creates a set of concurrent problems, which, in combination, strain relationships and break apart fragile families. The accounts of families attempting to cope with incarceration, typically missing from criminal justice and child development literatures, illustrate a broad array of consequences for families as a whole and for children in particular (Braman and Wood 2003: 159).

The impact of imprisonment goes beyond the prisoner; rather like ripples on a pond, a range of consequences commonly results. Some of these consequences may have positive benefits. For example, the imprisonment of a drug-using parent may lead to a better experience of parenting for their children where children experience stability and good substitute care (Eddy and Reid 2003). Similarly, if a parent is imprisoned for offending within the family, then the quality of life of the family could be substantially enriched by their absence. Removal of a dangerous persistent offender from a community may promote public safety. In the absence of other public services and in the context of profound deprivation and social exclusion, imprisonment of male partners may offer women some control over their lives (Comfort 2007). However, many of the other consequences at best pose challenges for families, and at worst lead families to experience profound difficulties and stresses and sometimes family relationship damage or disintegration.

Imprisonment, marriage and relationships

There is little accurate data as to the precise impact of imprisonment on relationship stability, but Action for Prisoners' Families suggests that 45 per cent of offenders lose contact with their families while serving a sentence, and 22 per cent of married prisoners divorce or separate as a result of their imprisonment (Salmon 2007).

More recent American research (Lopoo and Western 2005) has begun to unravel the complex relationship between incarceration and marriage, unpacking findings that while incarceration is highly disruptive and reduces the likelihood that a man will marry while imprisoned, and dramatically elevating the risk of divorce in first marriages, these effects do not seem to be persistent, and other research has confirmed that a strong and long-lasting emotional attachment, which need not necessarily be marriage, helps to divert men from crime (Laub *et al.* 1998; Uggen and Wakefield 2005; Warr 1998). Notably, the same correlation does not appear to exist for women prisoners in relation to men (Leverentz 2006). The relationship between prison and marriage runs both ways. It is commonplace to discuss the impact of family relationships on crime, and to link stable marriages to desistance and a lower chance of reoffending after release. It is difficult, however, to ascertain the precise impact of incarceration on marital and partnership relationships, and to assess whether imprisonment leads to divorce and separation, in that it is difficult to separate out the effects of imprisonment from the effects, for example, of involvement in a criminal lifestyle. Imprisonment has not only an impact on the particular marriages of particular inmates but may affect marriage rates generally, which is significant because marriage rates have been linked to societal stability (Lopoo and Western 2005; Western 2006).[1] The impact of incarceration on the incidence of marriage in the context of the rising imprisonment rate has been assessed in the context of the declining rate of marriage in the US during the last forty years which is particularly visible amongst African Americans with low educational attainment. The published research has developed the arguments of Wilson and Neckerman (1986), who linked low marriage rates amongst poor urban African Americans with a shortage of 'marriageable men' as a consequence of low rates of employment and high rates of imprisonment. Lopoo and Western expand Wilson and Neckerman's thesis by suggesting that ex-prisoners may remain undesirable marriage partners after release, and convicted husbands may have high risks of divorce because of the time they spent in prison. They consider how 'the incapacitative effect of incarceration is likely to prevent marriage among those who are single and increase the risk of separation among married couples' (2005: 723). The role of marriage is important because, as they identify, there is evidence that declining marriage rates amongst disadvantaged couples increase the likelihood of non-marital childbearing and risk of resultant poverty, and also because strong stable marriages can provide a route out of crime (Uggen and Wakefield 2005; Laub *et al.* 1998). They conclude that although incarceration is highly disruptive for an individual's chances of marriage, the effect of incarceration on the national prevalence of marriage is very small. They also argue that the likelihood that a marriage will fail in a year when a man is incarcerated is about three times higher than that for a man who is not incarcerated. This is specifically linked to an increase in divorce in first marriages. They conclude, however, that we still know little about the effects of incarceration on marital relationships.

One of the things which we do know from the research is that imprisonment places marital relationships under stress, sometimes as a consequence of the nature and circumstances of the offending and sometimes as a result of the stresses of separation and other difficulties during the sentence (Codd 2002; Lowenstein 1984). Prisoners in the UK have a high divorce rate and the Social Exclusion Unit (2002) found that over half of male prisoners and one-third of female prisoners were living with a partner or spouse before imprisonment, but that approximately one in five prisoners who are married when they enter prison divorce or separate during their sentence.[2] Separation by imprisonment can exacerbate pre-existing relationship difficulties (Klein *et al.* 2002; Fishman 1990) and may be the last straw in a marriage characterised by what Fishman (1990) calls the husband's 'fast living'; that is, a criminal lifestyle (Christian 2005). Indeed, incarceration may provide spouses with the opportunity to take the first step in severing ties with an offender after a history of marital problems (Struckhoff 1977). In contrast, for some couples imprisonment can allow for social distance which can improve existing relationships by removing strains which had existed prior to the sentence (Wolff and Draine 2004). There is a romantic view that imprisonment can bring a couple closer together emotionally: as one wife of an incarcerated man said to me during an interview, 'you've never had a love letter until you've had a letter from a prisoner'. Some relationships benefit from the separation in that the enforced separation can promote 'renewed courtship' (Fishman 1988b) and new romance, especially through letters, and joint daydreaming or planning about hopes and dreams for the future. For some couples, imprisonment offers a break from the day-to-day realities of their lives together, and allows for reaffirmation of the relationship itself and new expressions of love and commitment (Kotarba 1979; Fishman 1988b).

However, hardship and emotional difficulties are more prevalent than this romanticised view would suggest. It is not purely intimate relationships which are affected as imprisonment can also disrupt relationships within the families coping with imprisonment from the outside. For example, families may disagree and differ in their attitudes to the offending, or to the trial process, or the sentence. They may apportion blame or responsibility – 'why didn't you stop him robbing the bank?'; 'it's his upbringing which has made him a rapist'; 'he hit you because you deserved it' – they may display denial, through either a genuinely-held belief in the relative's innocence, or a public display of this belief. Sometimes family relationships are damaged by the crime or its nature, such as where the victim is someone within the family, as in the case of domestic violence or sexual abuse. The responsibility and agency of offenders is undeniable; however, it is clear from the research evidence that prison policies and programmes can affect the impact of the sentence itself on the ties of the inmate. Ties which exist when an inmate is sentenced can be profoundly damaged by the challenges of conducting a relationship from a distance and the unsympathetic visiting conditions in some institutions.

The financial impact

The financial consequences of imprisonment for families are well documented in the research literature (Davis 1992; Smith *et al.* 2007). It is clear, however, that poverty and imprisonment are strongly interwoven (Smith *et al.* 2007). Across jurisdictional boundaries, the experiences of prisoners' families, although varying in the intensity and causes of their financial impoverishment, are almost universally experiences of extreme financial difficulties. Most families experience financial losses and/or incur additional expenses (Hairston 2003). Parental incarceration results in major economic strain for children and families, but the dynamics of incarceration as a cause of economic strain have led to less attention than other forms of strain, such as unemployment and industrial restructuring (see Braman 2002; Braman and Wood 2003; Western *et al.* 2002). The destitution of families supporting prisoners 'on the outside' has been described as 'a shadow punishment [which] is marginalised and largely invisible to the public gaze' (Aungles 1993).

Families experience varying difficulties at different stages of the processing of the prisoner from arrest, possible remand, custodial sentence and release. At each of these stages prisoners' families experience a range of personal, financial and social consequences, and these reinforce each other: hence, to some extent, it is difficult to isolate and identify purely financial consequences (Davis 1992). For some families, imprisonment means the loss of a main family income, even if that income may have been illegally earned: as Morris said, 'although few [prisoners] had actually saved money from criminal earnings in order to provide for their families in case of imprisonment, some wives were certainly better housed and clothed and had more opportunity for going out and about as a result of such ill-gotten gains' (Morris 1965: 153). Morris documented the acute anxiety of family members about money, especially since at the time she was writing many women were unused to taking responsibility for the allocation of the total household income and became anxious when responsibility was forced upon them.[3] For the families of some recidivist prisoners, their financial situation improved (Morris 1965: 216), although there is little evidence of this improvement of financial circumstances in the more recent published empirical literature in the UK (Codd 1998; Davis 1992). However, in her discussion of prisoners' families in the US, Creasie Finney Hairston points out that since just over half of prisoners indicate that they were not employed before incarceration and most report a history of drug problems, and it is reasonable to assume that before imprisonment they were drains on the family income, not contributors, and that their imprisonment places their families in an improved financial position (Hairston 2003, citing Mumola 2000).

The financial impact of imprisonment is greatest where families try to maintain their relationship with the imprisoned person and still view the incarcerated family member as a family member, albeit living elsewhere; and where the imprisoned family member fulfilled a functional parenting role prior to their period of custody (Hairston 2003). This maintenance of the family unit despite imprisonment, that is, the concept of 'families living with one member in prison', entails greater associated subsequent financial burdens for the non-incarcerated family members. Conversely, where family members were not part of prisoners' lives before their incarceration then the financial impact is lessened, although there may still be subsequent financial losses such as the loss of child support payments from the non-resident parent (Hairston 2003). The prisoner's non-resident family status is not altered by their incarceration, but they become no longer able to provide the financial support that they may have done previously. These consequences are not restricted to immediate family members such as partners; where grandparents care for the children of prisoners, especially for the children of imprisoned women, they will certainly experience financial costs. In the US even if the mothers were in receipt of benefits prior to their incarceration, these benefits are not automatically transferred to caregiving grandparents (Hairston 2003) and grandparents caring for grandchildren have identified financial difficulties as one of their main problems. For these parent-surrogate caregivers, their costs rise if they encourage and facilitate contact with the imprisoned parent: telephone calls cost money and visits entail a range of expenses.

Davis (1992) found, in her small-scale study of eight prisoners' wives, that the initial process of arrest and remand was associated with both disruption of the family income and the wives' role in relation to it: they felt disorientated, and their energies were mostly focused on locating their partners and establishing contact. During this transition into what Davis refers to as 'a new world of loss and uncertainty' (1992: 77), financial issues assume low priority. During this stage, partners' difficulties are exacerbated by lack of advice and knowledge of where to go for support: women may not wish to discuss the matter with their imprisoned partner because that would add to the prisoner's worries. The feelings of shame experienced by many prisoners' partners may also make it hard to discuss the situation with family and friends, these feelings of shame being linked not only to the circumstances of the prisoner, but also to their own perceived inability to cope. There may be delays in accessing social security benefits, which again may be exacerbated by a lack of knowledge of entitlements and application procedures. The loss of an income is usually accompanied by the associated additional costs of maintaining relationships between the prisoner and the family. Different financial stresses occur at different points in the process, and impact on both families' income and also their expenditure. Supporting inmates in prison creates additional demands on families, although families may be more than willing to make sacrifices in order to provide for an inmate. Davis found women married to remand prisoners coping with conflicts about how to meet the needs of their partners and children as well as themselves, these competing demands usually meaning that women 'get by' simply by putting themselves and their own needs at the lowest level of their priorities (1992). At the later and subsequent sentencing stage, financial problems have mounted, and at this point women have to take charge of the finances. For some women, this is their first experience of financial independence and responsibility, and can for some women prove to be an empowering experience. That said, the benefits of being able to budget and plan operate in the context of an ongoing struggle to live within the limits of the income available, and of course the costs of providing for an absent partner are not provided for by an associated supplement to welfare benefit rates. The Assisted Prison Visit Unit funds visits for those on low incomes but the costs of visiting go beyond the simple transport costs. As Davis sums up the UK experience:

> Travelling long distances with children is not just tedious, it is expensive. It was not only a question of making sure that everyone looked well turned out; there were the costs of feeding children on journeys or using cafés in order to get hot water to heat babies' feeds at regular intervals. Where public transport connections were missed, taxis were the only available alternatives to the women and their children, desperate not to miss visiting times at remote prisons. The conditions in which the women and their children had to wait before being admitted to some prisons meant that clothes and other belongings were ruined by rain as families stood in the open (Davis 1992: 81).

The period leading up to the prisoner's release can create its own pressures, some women becoming apprehensive about 'losing control' over their finances once their husband has been released, others concerned that their partners would react badly if they had not coped well financially in their absence. Interestingly, in Davis' study none of the women reported a feeling of increased financial security following their partner's release.

Debt is gradually being recognised as another dimension of the financial consequences of imprisonment. In an Australian study of the links between imprisonment, debt and crime, Anne Stringer (2000) explored the cause, extent and effects of debt problems amongst prisoners and their families. The project found that debts are created unnecessarily by a prison sentence; that existing debts increase unnecessarily during imprisonment, and that family members impoverish themselves by unnecessarily paying prisoners' debts. Stringer argues that, during the term of imprisonment, families often suffer the most from prisoners' debts, since they may worry more; they may be harassed by debt collectors and they may lose their own income through repaying debts which they, themselves, did not incur (2000: 3). In addition, Stringer stresses the vulnerability of family members in the context of debt, many of whom are unaware of their rights and vulnerable to 'unprincipled and unlawful debt collection practices'. Family members may pay prisoners' debts for them, either as a consequence of pressure from the prisoner or debt collectors, because they believe they are legally responsible, or in order to preserve the asset, such as a car, for which the debt was incurred. These difficulties are exacerbated by lack of access to responsible financial advice. In the 1960s, Pauline Morris discussed the problems of hire purchase agreements and 'tallymen': these have now been replaced by credit cards, high-interest debt consolidation loans and other forms of marginal financial practice, including loans from so-called 'loan sharks'. Although the debt levels of prisoners' families has not been the focus of extensive specific published UK research, it would seem unusual for prisoners to be debt-free at the point of incarceration, unless at that point they are socio-economically so excluded that even 'second-tier' financial services are unavailable to them. Of course, such debts may be familial, informal or quasi-legal: families may become the targets for unpaid and angry drug dealers, or for the lenders of unpaid informal loans. Smith *et al.* (2007) found that prisoners' family members were particularly likely to get into debt through the use of store cards and loans from private loan companies, which require the payment of higher rates of interest than many other forms of debt. The issue of prisoner debt, and the debts of families, merits much further discussion. If, as argued by Manning (2000) in his searing analysis, credit is deliberately being marketed to the poor and socially-excluded, sometimes at exorbitantly high rates of interest or with punitive charges for 'delinquency' and default, such as exceeding a credit limit or missing a payment date, this may adversely affect prisoners' families. Many more families live with high-level debt than at the time Morris was writing, and, as identified by Manning in relation to the US, rates of personal bankruptcy are increasing. Although little of this is evidenced in the research literature, the role of credit in the lives of prisoners and their families is worthy of further consideration. Manning cites case studies of individuals receiving targeted marketing offers at specific times of economic and social vulnerability and transition: at the point of a partner's imprisonment, a credit card or other loan may offer an apparently temporary solution which, in contrast to the 'old' methods of credit, such as neighbourhood businesses offering goods 'on tick' or 'on the slate', credit cards and other loans permit family members to maintain the secrecy of their situation and sidestep the public shame they fear as a consequence of their disclosure of their partners' imprisonment and also as a consequence of their disclosure of their financial difficulties.

The expense of visiting inmates is a 'formidable' one (Comfort 2002), including not only travel costs but the costs of snacks, overnight lodging where necessary, incidental expenses and also lost income (see Davis 1992; Grinstead *et al.* 2001; Braman 2002; Marchetti 2002). Vending machines in visiting rooms in the US, from which snacks and drinks can be purchased, often charge high prices and, in the US, prison rules which stipulate that only, unopened, factory-sealed food can be brought in also increase costs (Comfort 2002). Comfort writes that several of her interviewees 'and numerous other low income women forfeit the quality or quantity of their own intake both inside *and* outside the prison – scrimping on their personal food budgets or skipping meals altogether – so as to be able to afford the appeasement of their mate's appetite' (Comfort 2002: 479). Under the governorship of Ronald Reagan in 1968, California introduced overnight visits. This involves extra expense for family members, although these visits are often highly valued (Comfort 2002; Bandele 1999).

In his discussion of the collateral consequences of imprisonment for families in the US, Braman (2002) explores the costs of incarceration for families. The costs of supporting inmates from the outside are exacerbated in the US by the high costs of reverse-charge telephone calls permitted by the correctional authorities, and the costs of purchasing goods for inmates via the prison commissary system: 'One of the more unpleasant surprises to many families is the high costs of phone calls from prison. Inmates can only call collect, and additional charges for monitoring and recording by the prison phone company add up quickly – indeed, many families have their phones disconnected within two months of an incarceration' (Braman 2002: 120). The rules on which goods, and how much money in the form of postal money orders, can be sent to inmates vary from state to state, but when combined with the costs of visits themselves it is easy to understand why a high proportion of the family income of prisoners' partners can be consumed by the demands of maintaining family relationships. Other less visible costs may include childcare (so that the outside parent can work), or, in countries such as the US, medical expenses, especially those linked to stress. Braman emphasises the fact that the costs of incarceration 'bear down disproportionately on families that are least able to absorb them' (Braman 2002: 122), arguing that many of these families are already struggling to make ends meet so any additional expenses or burdens have a greater impact. Consequently, any self-denial of the fulfilment of needs by family members in low-income families is likely to be significant and not simply involve a reduction in the provision of luxuries or a decrease in the amount of money spent on leisure. As Braman explains in the context of one of the families in his case study, one mother of a prisoner struggles to buy groceries, keeps her lights off and does not use the air conditioner in the summer. As he observes, 'given her limited income, any additional sacrifice is a significant one'. For example, in her detailed and vivid exposition of how partners try to integrate family life into the prison setting, creating prison as a 'domestic satellite', Megan Comfort describes how the women she observed and interviewed visiting at San Quentin went to great lengths to provide food, especially for special occasions and extended family visits (Comfort 2002). Hairston referred to the provision of money and other items for inmates as 'a by-product of maintaining family contact' (Hairston 2003: 265).

In the UK, as in other jurisdictions, family members supply funds for telephone calls, clothes, magazines, books, educational and hobby materials, and toiletries (Codd 2000, 2002). This provision of food and other items is not simply of practical significance. Food and gifts signify expressions of love and caring, and provide women with a way of maintaining their role as a caring partner, wife or mother despite the absence from the home environment of one or more family members. Food has both practical and symbolic significance, both in terms of its provision and preparation and also in terms of eating together as a family. Some prisons recognise this as an inhererent part of visiting, as demonstrated by the visiting rooms at Tegel Prison in Berlin where facililities for cooking and eating together are recognised as facilitating a key aspect of family life, especially for the families of Turkish inmates. Many families of prisoners continue to provide food, gifts and even contraband in order to assist their family members. Where prisoners are substance-dependent, family members may interpret smuggling drugs into a visit as a helpful act: similarly, smuggling drugs into an inmate, or throwing a drug-filled tennis ball or a mobile phone over the wall into the exercise yard can be viewed as a means of helping the inmate 'do his time' and making prison more bearable.

Stigma

The feelings of shame and stigmatisation experienced by the families of prisoners is a recurrent theme in the research literature. Although stigmatisation of the family of an inmate is usually identified as one of the consequences of imprisonment, the extent, impact and nature of this is a matter for discussion. Fishman suggests that it 'is usually discussed in vague and general terms' (1990: 284). In one of the most influential articles on the topic, Davies argues that 'shame' and 'stigma' are not sufficiently differentiated: shame is subjective, whereas stigmatisation refers to actual hostility and/or lack of respect based on the individual's status as a prisoner's wife (Davies 1980). Stigmatisation may be a minor concern in the context of the other problems families face. There is also a distinction to be made between shame and stigmatisation as a consequence of conviction, and shame and stigmatisation as a consequence of imprisonment.

The classic formulation of the concept of stigmatisation in a range of situations is that of Erving Goffman (1963). The stigmatised person is defined and treated as somehow 'different' or 'other', this stigma being so powerful that families may not be able to avoid it (Fishman 1988a). Stigmatisation, which can arise in a range of contexts, implies a perception of difference, which is then linked to undesirable traits (Smith 1992). It is clear that the process of arrest, trial, conviction and imprisonment is a legal manifestation of the social stigmatisation of an individual, the consequences of this stigma following the prisoner throughout the sentence and afterwards. The families of prisoners take on what Goffman (1963) terms a 'courtesy stigma': the family share the 'spoiled identity' of the inmate.

Although stigmatisation is omnipresent in the literature, it is not as simple to describe and analyse as first supposed. Whilst in the eyes of the popular press and news media there may be undertones – or even open discussion – of the complicity of the family (as evidenced in the use of phrases such as 'she must have known'), or the perceived benefits experienced by the family as a consequence of the offending, families may also experience friendship, sympathy and support from friends and neighbours. Families may be presumed to be 'guilty by association' (Codd 1998), but the precise manifestations of this are more complicated. A key component of this is secrecy: while family members may conceal their partner's whereabouts or fabricate a reason for their absence, if the truth is concealed then this may limit the prisoner's social contact. The fear of the 'courtesy stigma' (Goffman 1963), which arises through affiliation with the stigmatised, can cause family members further stress through the pressures of maintaining secrecy.

There is an important distinction between subjective feelings of shame and actual hostility. These feelings of shame may also be experienced by the prisoners themselves (Bates et al. 2003). Morris

(1965) reported that feelings of shame were experienced by the wives of first-time prisoners and were found to fade quite quickly, so the wives of recidivists claimed that they were not ashamed. In contrast, in a recent study of ex-prisoners, adult children and caregivers, the caregivers describe the experience as embarrassing and shaming (Bates *et al.* 2003). These feelings of shame and 'alienation from mainstream society' prevented families in one recent US study from seeking social services (Bates *et al.* 2003). These feelings, however, vary socially, ecologically and historically. For example, Morris (1965) identified the absence of a man from a woman's household as a source of shame; however, there are strong arguments for suggesting that changes in family composition and changes in social attitudes mean that the absence of a man is no longer likely to result in social stigmatisation, since many households are headed by one member. Clearly, there are some families that suffer assaults, criminal damage, and threats (Codd 1998). However, for many other families the level of fear experienced is greater than the experience of actual hostility. However, as has been shown in the fear of crime literature, living with a constant high level of fear creates its own problems. This fear is greatest for the families of offenders convicted of shocking or 'taboo' offences, especially sexual offences, or where the case has led to particular local anger. In these situations, the fear of retaliation may lead to family members changing their names, moving house, or living in fear of going out in public because of gossip or worse.

The question of whether families experience stigmatisation and consequent hostility from their communities has varied answers. For some families, especially in this era of mass imprisonment (see Wacqaunt 2001), imprisonment is simply a fact of life: the family is experiencing the absence of one member and living out their family life in and between the home and the prison (Comfort 2002). Imprisonment may be simply another fact of day-to-day life and the social reaction in the home area depends on the community in which the family lives (Fishman 1990; Fishman 1988a; Kotarba 1979; Schneller 1978). That is not to say that *fear* of stigmatisation does not exist in prison-accustomed communities however: close relatives of prisoners may diminish their family ties and limit the information they disclose as a consequence of the stigma (Braman and Wood 2003).

The issue of community response is not uncontested. It has been argued that the broader socio-cultural context in which prisoners and their families are embedded stigmatises involvement in the criminal justice system (Arditti 2002, 2003) and that the loss of a family member as a consequence of incarceration seldom results in sympathy from others (Schoenbauer 1986). Yet these arguments run counter to other research which suggests that, depending on the nature of the offence, families may feel supported by their communities; it is when they visit the prison or deal with official bodies that they feel stigmatised. Where the prisoner is incarcerated as a consequence of what could be seen as a 'crime of principle' or conscience, such as in the case of political prisoners, then the community support for the families may be greater since they are the families of heroes (see McEvoy *et al.* 1999) or de facto 'prisoners of war'.

While the family's home community may be supportive, the effects of stigmatisation are most obvious when family members interact with official agencies. The police may pay the family more attention, because they have been redefined as a 'criminal' family (Davies 1980). Feelings of shame and stigmatisation may be most in evidence when visiting the prison. This can be the consequence of a range of factors, some linked to prison service attitudes and the facilities available at the prison. For example, the prison in the town where I live is in the town centre situated at a busy junction, and, until the opening of a specific visitors' reception and waiting area, families had to queue in full view of the passing traffic. Even now, the exposed and public entrance which prisoners' families have to go through makes privacy impossible. Although some prisons may be actively working to improve the experiences of family visitors, the difficulties of visiting and the feelings of humiliation, disrespect and hostility experienced by families is almost universally reported in the literature from the UK, the US and Australia amongst others: families often feel they are being made to feel like criminals themselves just for visiting a prison (Cunningham 2001; Cregan and Aungles 1997). Families can be made to wait, sometimes for hours, with no certainty as to when, if at all, they will be allowed in; this is especially the case if there are security concerns which are not explained to families. Megan Comfort, in her vivid account of waiting in 'The Tube' at San Quentin (Comfort 2003) describes the anxiety arising from the tyranny of 'the count', that is, a head-count of the prisoners, and the consequent lack of information and uncertainty of the families. Prisons may have restrictive rules on numbers of visitors, money and items which can be taken in, and in the US even on clothing. Depending on the jurisdiction, everything from denim clothing to underwired bras can be banned; of course, this poses a real problem for family members visiting for the first time who are unaware of the rules. These rules are not static but subject to change, so families visiting the prison, especially in the

US, face every possibility that the rules have changed again and they will not be allowed their visit. The same applies to other forms of communication, such as letters, parcels and so on.

A key concept in understanding the experiences of prisoners' families visiting prisons is that of 'secondary prisonisation': that is, they are in the physical and symbolic space of the prison and become defined and managed in relation to that (Comfort 2003). They become temporarily unfree people, a 'peculiar category of prisoner' (Comfort 2003: 79): in the perceptive words of one wife, quoted by Fishman (1988a): 'I got the real feeling that we're no different than those on the inside. We're just one more wing that they have to let in and out' (Fishman 1988a: 179). They become, 'quasi-inmates, people at once legally free and palpably bound' (Comfort 2003: 103). The role of prison staff is fundamental here; in Comfort's discussion of the women waiting to be admitted to visit at San Quentin, 'officials mark those forced to wait in the corridor as disgraced beings' (Comfort 2003: 102). Interestingly, family members may also feel shame at having to associate with other family members, fearing that they will take on their 'discredited status' almost by a process of contamination (Fishman 1988a). It is interesting to explore the willingness of these wives to distance themselves from the other family members: in Fishman's (1988a) study half of the women she interviewed felt 'contaminated' by these contacts with the other wives. These were mostly first-time visitors, who arrived with the assumption that the other wives 'must be suspicious, inherently discreditable and as committed to criminal activities as their husbands' (Fishman 1988a: 182). The role of prison staff is also fundamental here: attitudes of staff can make families feel at home, or, in contrast, profoundly unwelcome; in the words of Joyce A. Arditti on visiting a local jail in the US, officers treated family members 'as if they simply did not matter or were criminals themselves' (Arditti 2003: 126). The status of being a 'prisoner's partner' becomes the master status which overrides all others and removes the other cultural or social capital of the visitor (Comfort 2003), visitors being processed as a form of 'ceremony of belittlement' and what Comfort refers to as the 'abridgement of personhood' in the interests of prison security (Comfort 2003: 101). This, to some extent, is understandable. Prison staff are the public face of the prison, but are also responsible for security which, following the escapes from Whitemoor and Parkhurst, and the subsequent Woodcock (1994) and Learmont (1995) reports, have led to an increased emphasis on security, with prisoners and families at the time complaining about insensitive searching of visitors, especially children (Brooks-Gordon and Bainham 2004). Whilst it is undeniable that breaches of security occur by other routes, including via prison officers, the inflow of families represents an opportunity, in the eyes of prison staff, for security breaches including but not limited to the importation of contraband, including drugs and weapons. That said, there are different methods by which security could be enforced and some could be perceived to be more family-friendly than others. Strip-searching, for example, is a source of particular concern: although the demands of security may make it essential, it is still experienced as humiliating, especially, for example for women, who, in the UK, might be asked to remove sanitary towels. In the US strip-searches can be even more intimate. That said, concerns about the attitude of staff to children have led to some imprisoned parents being prepared to be strip-searched after visits if it meant their visiting children would be left alone (HMIP 2001).

Davies makes an interesting point about the stigma of being 'on welfare', which may not be a consequence of the crime but which may be a problem for a great many families (Davies 1980). It may be difficult to disentangle the stigma of imprisonment from the stigmas of poverty, or ethnicity, and subsequent social exclusion. However, the stigmatisation associated with visiting prisoners, and the fear of hostility, cuts across differences of class, ethnicity and so on: as Comfort (2003: 92) points out when discussing the visitors to San Quentin, 'although the majority of people lining up to enter San Quentin are low-income African Americans or Hispanics, the wealthy white women coming to see their loved ones endure the exact same conditions of waiting as everyone else'.

The impact on children

Whilst it is clear that a significant number of children and young people experience the imprisonment of a family member during their childhood, the precise number is unknown. Estimates suggest that somewhere between around 125,000 and 160,000 children in England and Wales currently have a parent in prison (Ramsden 1998; Gampell 1999; Prison Reform Trust 2007).[4] It has been estimated that up to half a million children and young people experience the imprisonment of their father at some time before they leave school (Brown *et al.* 2002; Laing 2003). There are, however, no estimates as to the number of young people who have a sibling or other relative in prison. In the US the number of children at any one time with an imprisoned parent is estimated to be around two million (Mazza 2002): this figure has risen by over half a million since 1991 (Hairston 1998; US Department of Justice 2000). It is similarly difficult to assess the number of children specifically affected by the imprisonment of their mother: in 2000 one estimate suggested 195,000 children in the US are affected by a mother's imprisonment, and even if those estimated to live with someone else prior to the mother's incarceration were excluded, the figure would stand at around 138,000 on any given day, with many more being affected at some point during their childhood (Young and Smith 2000). In the UK, around 66 per cent of female prisoners have a dependent child under sixteen, with over a third having a child under five (Prison Reform Trust 2007): a fifth of women prisoners are lone parents with dependent children (Social Exclusion Unit 2002). The reasons for the absence of more precise figures are a consequence of the invisibility of prisoners' families in official records, and the challenges and ethical issues raised by other methods of assessing the number of children affected by imprisonment. For example, in the context of schools, any attempt to ask young people to self-report their circumstances may result in inaccurate findings because it is commonplace for young people either not to be given any explanation for the absence of a parent or family member, or to be given some alternative explanation. In addition, it is possible that shame, fear and stigmatisation might result in young people concealing the whereabouts of their family member. Prisoners themselves may not disclose that they are parents for fear that social services could become involved. It could be argued that the actual statistics are unimportant: what is clear is that the number of children affected by imprisonment on any given day is significant, and the number affected by imprisonment at some point before the age of eighteen is extensive. The rising prison population, especially of women prisoners, means that more and more children are facing the challenges of the imprisonment of a parent at some point during their childhood and adolescence. For some young people the imprisonment of a family member offers important benefits for the family, as in the case of violent, abusive or neglectful parents, or parents with chaotic lifestyles. For other young people, however, any benefits may be outweighed by other consequences of the criminal justice process, their family members' absence, and their subsequent probable return.

In discussing the consequences of the imprisonment of a family member for children, it is difficult to disentangle the effects of the criminal justice process and the prison sentence from other life circumstances linked to poverty, deprivation and social exclusion. It has been argued that prisoners' children experience 'a range of negative outcomes' (Travis and Waul 2003a: 15) but it is difficult to assess whether the experience of these outcomes is a consequence of imprisonment or due to and interlinked with other socio-economic and social factors. It is difficult, and possibly impossible, to disentangle the specific effects of parental incarceration from other traumatic circumstances experienced by children: incarceration has been argued to increase the impact of other risk factors (Travis and Waul 2003a: 181); 'a cascade of risks for children follows from criminal justice practices that ignore family needs' (Braman and Wood 2003: 182). Golden (2005) is especially scathing about the effects on children of the imprisonment of mothers, referring to mothers as often the only 'anchor' which the children have; when the mother is imprisoned she refers to the children as being 'cast adrift'.

Although we know that the children of incarcerated parents experience an array of negative outcomes, it is difficult to assess whether these consequences arise from the prison sentence, or are related to other factors such as family life in the household, or broader socio-legal circumstances (Travis and Waul 2003a). It is fair to question how the experiences of prisoners' children differ, if at all, from those of children experiencing parental absence for other reasons, such as absence as a consequence of divorce, illness or work commitments; as Larman and Aungles (1991) sum it up, 'separation by imprisonment leads to the risk of experiencing the same problems, but in more extreme form, that any enforced and traumatic separation from a parent creates'. In discussing the responses of the children interviewed for her research study, Boswell (2002) asserts that 'these children's responses do not fit into neat categories' (2003: 23). Indeed, in reading the research literature it is fair to say that the impact of imprisonment on children does not fit into neat categories either. Different theoretical and analytical approaches have been used to document the impact of imprisonment for the children of prisoners: some studies adopt a chronological, criminal justice system-based approach and document and analyse the impact on children at every stage of the process from the offenders' arrest, through the trial and subsequent incarceration, to the challenges faced by the offender's re-entry to the family and the community. Some writers have adopted approaches based on the age of the children, this approach being especially relevant in the work emanating from a developmental psychological perspective, whereas others have documented the impacts category by category, assessing issues such as the problems of separation and keeping in touch, visits, stigma and shame, parentification, the challenges of lack of information, and sometimes, the either voluntary or coerced keeping of secrets. A key aspect of any discussion on the impact of incarceration on children is the variation in the circumstances in which children find themselves. A great deal depends on the substitute caregiving arrangements, the community response, and the opportunities to maintain contact with and to visit the imprisoned parent.

A substantial canon of literature has emerged, particularly in the last ten years, documenting aspects of the impact of imprisonment, from a range of perspectives but because of the practical and ethical issues involved, most of this research has not involved direct consultation, observation or interviews with the children of inmates (Johnston 1995). Rather, research has concentrated on studying prisoners' relationships with their children, or the experiences of prisoners' partners. There are, however, some important exceptions, where either the main focus of the research was on the children, as in Brown *et al.* (2001), or where children were specifically considered as a sub-group of interviewees who participated in a larger study (see Boswell 2002). The study by Brown *et al.* (2001) entitled *No-one's Ever Asked Me* is especially aptly named; the study interviewed or analysed questionnaires from a total of fifty-three young people aged between twelve and eighteen in an attempt to document the issues for young people experiencing the imprisonment of a parent or sibling, aiming to identify their needs and determine areas for future action. Boswell, with Peter Wedge, studied the children of imprisoned fathers (Boswell and Wedge 2001) but the interviews with the children were analysed and discussed in a separate article (Boswell 2002). This piece is striking in that it records some of the feelings of some very young children, some as young as three. These 'little people's voices' are often totally silent or silenced, even in the research literature ostensibly assessing the impact of imprisonment on young people; although scant, there is more research assessing the impact on teenagers and young adults (see Eddy and Reid 2003).

The extensive recent literature on the impact of parental imprisonment on children has documented the wide range of challenges negotiated by young people (Bernstein 2005; Robertson 2007). However, this literature has been criticised for focusing too much on the *problems* faced by children; Johnston (1995) makes the important point after a review of the literature that most of the studies have focused on the problems of prisoners' children and do not present a 'rounded' picture of their lives, even though, as she points out with reference to one of her previous research projects, amongst children specifically selected for study because of their behavioural, disciplinary or emotional difficulties, few had problems in every area, and 'all of the children were performing adequately in one or more areas' (Johnston 1995, referring to Johnston 1993).

Imprisonment as a dynamic process

Imprisonment is 'a dynamic process that unfolds over time' (Parke *et al.* 2003: 199). The effects of imprisonment on children begin before the period of the actual prison sentence, beginning with arrest and sometimes the refusal of bail, followed by the trial and the subsequent sentence. These effects do not automatically cease once their family member is released from prison: rather, the family must face new challenges in negotiating and coping with the familial, social and communal reintegration of a family member, or indeed, the consequences of not having contact with that family member if relationships have irretrievably broken down during the sentence.

Arrest

The initial process of arrest, especially if followed by refusal of bail and remand in custody, can be a time of extreme shock, stress, fear, confusion and instability for children, especially if the arrest is witnessed at home:

> Impressions of the arrest are burned on the child's mind and are likely to return at night: the violence of the police, the yelling and crying of the mother, the faces of curious neighbours and, above all, the way the father was removed in handcuffs or with a bag over his head, are sensations the child will never forget (van Nijnatten 1998: 82).

That is not to say, of course, that all arrests are like this: van Nijnatten was writing about arrests in the Netherlands, police arrest practices vary from jurisdiction to jurisdiction and are influenced by the nature of the offence, their knowledge of the offender, and issues such as public safety. Van Nijnatten's point is, however, valid: for many children, witnessing the arrest of a parent can lead to long-lasting trauma.

Children may not believe that their family member could be guilty (Cobean and Power 1978; Fishman 1983). Conversely, the child may feel guilt or responsibility, especially if the parent's arrest is as a consequence of a crime against the child. Children who are victims of parental crime have been referred to as 'double victims' (van Nijnatten 1998): first, they have suffered the violence, abuse, neglect or injury for which the parent is being arrested, and second because they then experience the negative impact of incarceration. It is important to remember that although this is not routinely the case in the UK, in jurisdictions where the police carry guns children may be exposed to fear of, or actual use of, firearms in an enclosed space. Children may not understand where their parent or other family member has gone, and may be disorientated by whatever arrangements are put in place for their temporary care. Some children may be alone for many hours before somebody assumes custody of them; Fishman (1983) argues that women may not reveal when arrested that they have children for fear that they may be taken into the care of social services and this has been found to be the case in recent research conducted in the UK.[5] The shock and confusion may be exacerbated by a lack of information being communicated to children, sometimes involving lies and half-truths told 'for their own good' (Mazza 2002) with the perhaps misguided intention of protecting the child from being distressed by the knowledge of the parents' alleged offence, or their detention on remand. Children may, if present during the arrest, witness the 'criminalisation' of their parent or family member through being handcuffed and taken away: Mazza (2002) perceptively likens this to the child witnessing the assault of a parent. According to Noble's UK study based on interviews with thirty families, one-third witnessed their father's arrest, often involving police dogs and several officers (Noble 1995). Young children may not be able to understand the nature of the process or the reasons why their parent has been apprehended and detained, so the whole process may appear unpleasant, possibly violent, non-consensual and unwelcome, and from the child's point of view can be experienced as witnessing an assault on the parent by a stranger, or witnessing family violence (Wilson 1996). Children at this stage may also lack support and individuals with whom they can discuss the situation (Mazza 2002). However, as the same author argues, if the child is absent at the time of the arrest, they may not understand where their parent has gone, or why. As one participant in Brown et al.'s study (2001) said:

The police raided our house to arrest my brother, but no-one was there … we got home to the house smashed up from the police raid. It was a mess, it was horrible. It's not a pleasant thing to find out about at all. It was all in the papers and on the news as well. They even put our addresses in, which was really out of order. It was really hard; I weren't sleeping, didn't know what was going on. It felt like it were a dream. (sixteen-year-old female with a brother in prison, quoted in Brown *et al.* 2001)

Brown *et al.* (2001) provides statistics on how teenagers in the study were informed of their relative's arrest: of the thirty-two interviewees seventeen were told by their mother, eight by the police, three by another relative, three by the prisoner, and one by a social worker. At this stage the key concerns for young people are being informed about what is happening, deciding whether or not to tell people, and concerns about people knowing about their situation. By not being fully informed, young people's feelings of shame, anxiety and isolation are compounded. Telling other people may involve a decision based on calculated risk-taking (Action for Prisoners' Families 2002); by revealing their situation they may be able to benefit from support by other people, such as teachers, youth workers and their peers, but there is also the fear of a negative and unsupportive response. It is important to remember that for a proportion of prisoners' children, the experience of their family member's arrest, bail and eventual imprisonment is not a 'one-off' experience but one which can occur more than once and sometimes frequently.

Imprisonment

Summarising the impact on children of imprisonment is no easy task. Categorisations vary, as do the experiences of children. In the published research literature, a range of different viewpoints of the impact has been taken, from the sociological to the psychological. The experiences of the children of prisoners have some similarities to those experiencing disruption of their family through divorce, whilst in other cases children can experience the imprisonment of a parent as a bereavement, and exhibit behaviours, emotions and attitudes linked to grieving (van Nijnatten 1998). The process of grieving by prisoners' children is rendered more difficult by their status as 'disenfranchised grievers', that is, where they are experiencing a sense of loss but 'do not have a socially recognised, right, role or capacity to grieve' (Hames and Pedreira 2003: 378; Doka 1995). In the closing paragraphs of their own chapter on the effects of the imprisonment of fathers, Boswell and Wedge (2001) write in the context of their own interviews with children from a range of age groups:

> [I]t is clearly difficult to put children's responses into neat categories. They differ in age, sex, family, school and life experiences and developmental stages. Some are old enough to have formed judgements of their fathers' behaviour and are dealing with the accompanying tensions, while younger children remain preoccupied with the emotions they feel for their absent parent. It nevertheless remains apparent that none of them is untouched by the loss of their father to imprisonment. All would prefer not to be in the situation in which they find themselves (Boswell and Wedge 2001: 79).

The negative outcomes which recur in the literature include psychological consequences such as depression, emotional withdrawal, anxiety, and 'acting in' or 'acting out' at home or at school (Travis and Waul 2003a; Johnston 1995; Jose-Kampfner 1995; Noble 1995). Assessing the psychological impact on children of parental imprisonment is no easy task. It is difficult – or impossible – to disentangle the effects of imprisonment from other forms of parental absence, or from other social and environmental factors.

Before exploring the negative consequences of parental imprisonment for children, it is important to reiterate that imprisonment can be beneficial for some children. Parental incarceration can lead to an increase in the quality of positive parenting, which might then have an impact on adolescent behavioural ('conduct') problems (Eddy and Reid 2003). For example, if the parent is a substance-abuser who regularly brings other substance-abusers into the home, and who also spends a lot of time out on the street rather than at home, if the children are moved to either a different family caregiver or the care of the local authority, conduct problems may not be significant (Eddy and Reid 2003). If the quality of positive parenting behaviours is decreased then adolescent conduct problems may be initiated or exacerbated (Eddy and Reid 2003). However, if parent and child have become estranged or lost contact prior to the sentence, then parental incarceration may have no impact at all (Eddy and Reid 2003). A UK study involving interviews with thirty-two teenagers found that for four of these there were no perceived familial effects as a consequence of their relative's imprisonment: the reasons given were that the family were not close anyway; it is the mainly the prisoner who has been affected because no-one trusts him anymore; the father is unaffected because he 'doesn't care about his kids', and because the young person is the only one who cares about the prisoner (Brown *et al.* 2001). Eddy and Reid (2003) stress the importance of parenting, and effective parenting by a non-parent caregiver 'can dampen the effects of parent criminality, parental transitions, and other stressful circumstances that adolescents experience' (Eddy and Reid 2003: 240). Of course, a great deal depends on the family situation prior to imprisonment. Children whose parents are incarcerated are already likely to live in difficult circumstances, including parental substance abuse, mental illness, poverty and criminality: thus, their problems did not begin with parental imprisonment (Travis and Waul 2003b; Johnston 2001). Imprisonment, while sometimes improving children's stability, more often leads to children feeling, in the words of Carl Mazza (2002) that 'the world fell apart'. The household equilibrium is 'severely shaken' and 'panic and confusion reign' (Mazza 2002). Children may not know or understand where their absent parent has gone, and they may experience lies and lack of information, or refusal to discuss the situation, from other relatives and caregivers. This can exacerbate anxiety and self-blame, children blame themselves for their parent's absence, especially if they are not present when the parent is arrested, since then they may feel a sense of abandonment (Mazza 2002).

Responsibilities and parentification

It is important to recognise that, at a time when a child may need additional support from non-imprisoned family members, those family members may be physically, emotionally and mentally unavailable to offer extra support. For example if a father is imprisoned then the child's mother may be coping with the practicalities of living as a de facto single parent, coping with the difficulties discussed elsewhere in this book, and also adapting to the absence of a partner, and the mixed and confused emotions often prompted by imprisonment (McDermott and King 1992). The mother may also be negotiating the formalities of visiting and coping with negative social reactions. Instead of receiving extra attention and support, children may take on additional responsibilities and become 'helpers' for the mother, possibly caring for younger children, taking on household chores, or, in the case of older children, bearing some of the emotional burdens of the mother (van Nijnatten 1998). This parentification is common in families coping with the sudden loss of a parent, or the failure of a parent to exercise parental responsibilities and duties. For example, children of alcoholics may have to care for younger siblings, and children of parents experiencing chronic illness often take on substantial, sometimes damaging, responsibilities. This reversal of roles, or 'promotion' of the child to the status of quasi-adulthood, can have profound psychological implications, and may in practice deprive children of the feeling of having a childhood. Linked to this is the phenomenon which van Nijnatten (1998: 87) refers to as having 'to bear the burden of their parental history'. That is, children become encouraged to fulfil parental expectations in terms of 'seeking the justice they never received', rectifying their mistakes or compensating for their failings (van Nijnatten 1998). In the same way as children growing up in dysfunctional families may exhibit symptoms of co-dependency, prisoners' children's identities, attitudes and behaviour may be inextricably tied to their parents' incarceration.

Keeping secrets

Linked to this is the web of 'secrets and lies' in which a substantial proportion of prisoners' children find themselves (Morris 1965; Shaw 1987). It is commonplace for parents to tell lies, half-truths or nothing at all to children and this 'conspiracy of silence' (Jose-Kampfner 1995) or 'forced silence' (Johnston 1995) can lead to increased anxiety and undermine children's ability to cope (Parke and Clarke-Stewart 2003). It is of course, important to recognise that parental deceptions – 'Daddy's working on an oil rig for the Government' or 'Daddy's on holiday' – may not be believed by children. After all, even relatively young children may be able to read the word 'prison' when visiting (Morris 1965) and they may be told the truth by other children. Children may feel bound to pretend they believe the parent in order not to upset them or to conceal the truth from other, younger siblings. Even if children are told the truth, it may become a family secret to be hidden from the outside world but this, however, can lead to children feeling isolated, alone and alienated from their friends. To reveal a secret to a friend can make a child feel like a traitor. This 'family secret', in which everyone in the family knows what is going on but nobody talks about it, is well illustrated by the 'elephant in the living room' example commonly used in the literature on dysfunctional families: the family lives its life around the elephant, clearing up after it and having to walk around it all the time, but never mentions it, even though it is immediately visible to an outsider (Hastings and Typpo 1984; Kroll 2004). Despite a common view that to tell children the truth might upset them, the research indicates that children cope better with their feelings if they are allowed to talk about them (Mazza 2002). Children need information to make sense of their situation, space to grieve the loss of the absent parent and support to cope with their changed circumstances (Parke and Clarke-Stewart 2003).

The psychological effects on children

A number of studies have found that children of incarcerated parents are more likely to display low self-esteem, depression and behavioural problems and evidence suggests that children of incarcerated parents are at a higher risk of future delinquency or incarceration (Johnston 1995; Eddy and Reid 2003). This may, however, be related to instability, poverty, poor caregiving or other aspects of criminal behaviour in which parents were involved prior to imprisonment. Children of different ages may experience different effects, and the length of the separation and community response can all make a difference (Travis and Waul 2003a). When a parent is imprisoned, it is argued that the child loses the benefits of a role model. This, however, assumes that the parent made a positive contribution to family life prior to the sentence (Laing 2003). For some children, imprisonment can simply remove the influence of negative role models. It is important to remember, however, that parental criminality does not mean that the parent is unable to provide any form of positive role model: a great deal depends on the parent's offending and their attitude to it. There are, however, some key principles which can be extracted from the literature, as discussed by Travis and Waul (2003a) and Wright and Seymour (2000). Children always experience the loss of a parent as a traumatic event. Developmentally, children may experience delayed or regressed development where their emotional energy is being diverted from developmental tasks. Children may develop sleep disturbances, enuresis and low self-esteem. They may regress, in the same way as children experiencing divorce, into old reaction patterns such as the need for special toys and security blankets, or bedwetting (van Nijnatten 1998). Situations characterised by uncertainty make it even more difficult for children to cope. Their reactions vary over time. Also, children experience the stigma of having a parent in prison and their needs are often not met in schools or in local communities (Ramsden 1998). The literature on prisoners' children echoes other research into parent–child separation: for example, Bowlby's classic theory of attachment (Bowlby 1973) underpins discussions of the importance of attachment and parent–child bonding and is highly relevant when discussing separating babies and infants from parents. When children lack regular and sustained contact with a parent, then their attachment to that parent can be prevented. Once that attachment has developed, the separation can result in adverse emotional reactions which, in turn, can interfere with the child's development (Parke and Clarke-Stewart 2003). A number of research studies of prisoners' children demonstrate that they experience a range of adverse outcomes which can be linked to separation and insecure attachments (Johnston 1995; Parke and Clarke-Stewart 2003). In terms of prison programmes, it is relevant that children who develop secure attachments to other adults, not necessarily parents, may experience this as compensatory to some extent, which is particularly relevant when considering provision for imprisoned mothers.

As Mazza writes, children may display 'acting in' or internalised behaviours, including anxiety, withdrawal, hypervigilance, shame and guilt. They may also externalise or 'act out', that is, through displaying anger, aggression and hostility. Mazza (2002) suggests that imprisoned fathers may unintentionally encourage acting-out behaviour, and children may believe that their parent is innocent and therefore being 'victimised' by the state and authorities. If prisoners repeatedly tell their children that they 'haven't done anything' or are innocent, this can make the children even more anxious because they may feel that they do not know which of their family members, including themselves, could be next to be randomly arrested and imprisoned without any cause. Girls are more likely to display internalised problems, boys more likely to externalise, although often these behaviours co-exist (Parke and Clarke-Stewart 2003; Cummings *et al.* 2000). Children can also be stigmatised; they may be viewed as 'a chip off the old block' or 'taking after their mother' in their behaviour, and so assume the label of being a 'problem child', a 'potential criminal' or coming from 'a bad family' (Mazza 2002). Mazza describes prisoners' children as 'a highly complex ... yet fragile population'. He stresses that they have 'had their trust, security and sense of consistency shaken' and may subconsciously be waiting for, or seeking to avoid, future abandonment or disappointment.

The future criminality of children

There is a strong intuitive acceptance of the assumption that parental imprisonment leads to an increased risk for children of imprisonment in later life, though the precise nature and extent of the link is disputed (Ziebert 2006). Some research, such as that by Bowlby (1946), has argued that there is a link between delinquency and parent–child separation in a number of forms and a substantial body of evidence has emerged supporting the view that children from so-called 'disrupted families' are at an increased risk of crime and delinquency than those from so-called 'intact' homes (Juby and Farrington 2001). Specifically, children who are brought up by parents who are offenders, particularly if they are imprisoned, have been argued to be more likely to go on to offend (Farrington *et al.* 1996). In addition, some studies have suggested that these children are at high (or higher than usual) risk of future criminality or anti-social behaviour (Johnston 1995; Eddy and Reid 2003). Research by Boswell (1996), a study of violent young offenders, showed that 57 per cent of their sample had experienced loss in childhood, mainly parental and often paternal. The long-running Cambridge Study in Delinquent Development has established a strong correlation between separation from parents, usually fathers, at less than ten years old, and conviction up to the age of thirty-two, with Farrington (1995) finding that 59 per cent of the boys in the study who had a convicted parent were themselves convicted up to this age. Some writers argue for the existence of a clear, firm link: others have interpreted the data in terms of 'risk' factors for offending.

The work of David Farrington and others (Farrington *et al.* 2001), drawing on the Cambridge Study, has tended to be quite assertive in its argument that crime could be said to 'run in families'. This can be linked to intergenerational transmission in exposure to multiple risk factors, that is, that this familial transmission forms part of a broader 'cycle of deprivation'. They have also considered questions of the environmental influence, genetic mechanisms, mutual influence and what they termed 'assortative mating', that is, people at risk of offending tend to become partners because of proximity or because people are attracted to people who are like themselves. Researchers have differed in their methodological approaches, some choosing quantitative methods and others adopting a more qualitative approach. Murray, for example, is highly critical of the methodology of many studies, arguing that the evidence on the impact on prisoners' children comes 'from cross-sectional studies using convenience samples, and without standardised measures, triangulation of sources or suitable controls'. He goes on to say that therefore only cautious hypotheses can be proposed about the specific effects of imprisonment on families and children (Murray 2005: 447). He points out that it is frequently

73

stated that the children of prisoners are six times more likely than their peers to be imprisoned but then says that there appears to be no documented evidence to support this claim (Johnston 1998, cited in Myers *et al.* 1999).[6] Murray also refers to the boy in Morris' study who was caught tampering with car locks who said he wanted to join his father in prison. Similarly, in my own fieldwork I interviewed a woman whose teenage son was so angry about his father's behaviour that he wanted to go and rob a bank 'to show his dad how it was done'.[7] Murray refers to Murray and Farrington (2005) as the only study which has prospectively examined later-life criminality among children who experienced parental imprisonment. Murray and Farrington found that of the London boys they studied 48 per cent of those who were separated between the ages of nought and ten because of parental imprisonment were convicted as adults, compared with 25 per cent of those who were separated for other reasons.

Murray and Farrington (2005) used prospective longitudinal data from the Cambridge Study. The study includes data on 411 Inner London boys and their parents. They compared boys separated due to parental imprisonment during the first ten years of life with boys in four control groups: those who were not separated, boys separated by hospitalisation or death, boys separated for other reasons, and boys whose parents were only imprisoned before their birth. Murray and Farrington's study claims a substantial methodological advance on previous studies, emphasising the high retention rate, use of well-validated measures and control of a wide variety of 'confounds'. They stress that children experiencing parental imprisonment during childhood are exposed to even more delinquency risk factors than children whose parents were only imprisoned prior to their birth. Murray and Farrington themselves recognise the problems of relating their sample group to today's prison population in which the proportion of those with long sentences has grown, as has the proportion of women and members of minority ethnic groups. Such findings are of limited value, and therefore to be of more widespread value need to be replicated for girls and in other social contexts, which Murray (2005) recognises. Murray is very critical of studies which have assessed psychosocial difficulties arising for children from parental imprisonment because, as he asserts, they have lacked the 'methodological sophistication' to distinguish the effects of parental imprisonment from other outcomes. The point about disentangling the effects is, however, an important one. For example, a key question is whether it is the absence of a parent which constitutes the risk factor, or whether the absence due to imprisonment creates an additional risk.

Dunlap *et al.* (2002), writing in relation to the transmission of conduct norms for drugs, violence and sexual exploitation amongst severely-distressed households in inner-city New York, have documented the intergenerational transmission of acceptance of heavy drug use, violence and sexual exploitation, where girls who have been desensitised to abuse and exploitation go on to model and replicate these conduct norms in the next generation. Drawing on Goffman's work (1961) Dunlap *et al.* (2002) vividly document the processes by which girls who grow up in households which not only tolerate heavy drug use, violence and sexual exploitation, but actively promote children's participation, react to these social environments through what Goffman terms the 'mortification of the self'. That is, they become 'inured to what comes next' (Dunlap *et al.* 2002: 2) and in the context of the constrained opportunities of growing up in an inner city, which Dunlap *et al.* liken to other forms of total institutions, go on to accept and replicate these conduct norms within their own families as adults. This work could support a view that children of offenders would do better without any contact with those parents, but this is not what Dunlap *et al.* suggest. They argue that the situation is complex and linked to the nature of the inner city experience of deprivation and social exclusion itself. As Dunlap *et al.* wrote, the people they interviewed

> live their lives within neighbourhoods that are only a few miles from the epicentre of global finance in New York City, yet are culturally light years away. What could be a short subway ride for these children and adults has become an impassable chasm to most of those embedded in this subculture (Dunlap *et al.* 2002: 18).

Dunlap *et al.* argue that to change the world of severely-distressed families in inner cities needs a cultural change, not merely provision of services. Although it is not explicitly stated in this article, one can deduce from other research that imprisonment is omnipresent in such communities and forms another aspect of the desensitisation of children to negative and damaging behaviours.

Considering the issue from a slightly different perspective, it is interesting to assess how many offenders come from backgrounds of parental crime and imprisonment. For example, Laing and McCarthy (2005) cite a report by the Prince's Trust (2001) which found that 60 per cent of 200 offenders interviewed came from families where at least one other person had a criminal record. Johnston (1991), working in the US, found that around 10 per cent of the teenage children of offenders were themselves incarcerated. It is useful, however, to remember the point made by Seymour (1998) and picked up by Laing and McCarthy (2005) that there have been no longitudinal studies following children through different phases of parental imprisonment and release. In the UK, although there has been some important research on prisoners' children, more is needed. The concept of agency is important here, but it is important to remember that many prisoners' children are experiencing multiple deprivations prior to parental imprisonment so their life choices are proscribed even without the impact of a prison sentence. Janet Walker and her team at Newcastle University (Walker 2006a) have explored the issues with reference to concepts of 'risk' and 'resilience' in relation to the likelihood of prisoners' children offending in later life. Their study aimed to examine the conduct and experience of parenting when one or both parents is serving a prison sentence; to explore the process of resilience, resistance and protection that might exist for a child who has a parent in prison; and to examine the connection between parental imprisonment and the risk of children engaging in criminal and anti-social behaviours (Walker 2006a). Part of this study considered the ways in which children and young people experience and negotiate risk. The core proposition under analysis was whether parental imprisonment places children at increased risk of offending behaviour and they found that it does, although there is no simple causal relationship. They found little evidence of cross-generational transmission of criminality. The majority of children in their study had not been in trouble with the police at all, and most of those who had been were already involved in what Walker (2006b) terms 'problem behaviours' prior to the parental imprisonment. They identified gender differences with boys more likely to have been excluded from school, to have been fighting and to have been negatively influenced by peers in terms of drinking and drug use. Of the thirty-eight young people they interviewed they found six had been in court or received a police caution and eight had exhibited 'behavioural problems' but had not committed offences. They noted variations between siblings in the same family who grew up in the same circumstances, as did Sampson and Laub (2005) who found that many young people who experience parental imprisonment during their childhood do not go on to offend.

This assumed linkage has led to arguments for policy development. Murray (2005: 443) writes: 'As Roger Shaw pointed out almost 20 years ago, "if we do not attend to the effects of imprisonment on children, we face the possibility of punishing innocent victims, neglecting a seriously at-risk group, and possibly causing crime in the next generation (Shaw 1987)." ' Murray and Farrington stress what they interpret as a clear link between parental imprisonment and future criminality, although their views present some problems for the informed reader:

> From a social policy point of view, it seems that imprisoning parents might cause antisocial behaviour and crime in the next generation, and hence contribute to the intergenerational transmission of offending. Clearly, extensive replication studies would be required to validate this hypothesis, but the issue cannot be ignored. If imprisoning parents does cause crime (or other adverse outcomes) among children, parenthood could be treated as a mitigating factor in sentencing, because of concerns about the child's welfare. Also, where parental imprisonment does occur, there could be an extensive range of family and child support services on offer (Murray and Farrington 2005: 1277).

Their statement poses more questions than it answers. Walker (2006a) found more evidence of intrafamilial transmission between siblings than between parents and children. It might be attractive to anyone concerned with promoting relationships between parents and their children to treat parenthood as a mitigating factor in sentencing but this totally denies the potential victim status of that child. For example, if a child is sexually abused by his or her father then it seems indefensible to argue that that parent's sentence should be mitigated as a consequence of their parenthood. Bluntly, parenthood has afforded the parent the opportunity to be in a close relationship with that child, and in a position of trust. Since breach of trust usually acts as an aggravating factor in sentencing it seems nonsensical and potentially highly unjust to treat parenthood as mitigation. The situation is much more complex than Murray and Farrington envisage. Similarly, if parenthood is treated as mitigation then arguably this discriminates against offenders who are not parents. The 'concerns about the child's welfare' which they mention may be profoundly important, and should be considered by the court, but Murray and

Farrington appear to deny the complexities of this multifaceted situation. They also refer to 'an extensive range of family and child support services'. To have family and child support services is clearly desirable but Murray and Farrington take no account of funding difficulties, the challenges faced by voluntary-sector bodies, and the often present atmosphere of negativity in society towards the families of prisoners. Thus although the sentiments within these sentences appear laudable, further examination shows that the issues have not been adequately thought through.

The challenge is to find a way of ameliorating the negative impacts of separation, especially from mothers, as documented in the psychological child development literature, at the same time as finding a way to insulate children from the negative effects of their parents' criminal behaviour. It is this 'breaking the chain' which is difficult, as some children of prisoners may model themselves on what they see their parents doing. Also where many family members and friends engage in crime, they may not only model themselves on what is around them but, as documented by Dunlap *et al.* (2002), may be actively encouraged to participate in potentially damaging and criminal activities. The nature of some families may not only be crime-tolerant but actively crime-promoting and in situations where children and young people have limited means of achieving status, recognition or parental approval, criminality may seem a normal and acceptable behaviour. Thus recognising the impact of imprisonment on families involves not simply identifying the immediate financial, emotional and social problems but also the broader challenges of the communities and families from which prisoners come and will usually return. It is not enough to simply document the harms, difficulties and immediate needs of families, but to actually document and ultimately challenge the intergenerational and intrafamilial continuation of these norms.

Conclusion

This chapter summarises the manifold and diverse consequences of imprisonment for families. There is not a 'one size fits all' summary of the impact of imprisonment on prisoners' partners and children. Rather, as the research indicates, families can experience some, any or all of a range of consequences. As we have seen, there are still major gaps in the literature and a need for further thorough and detailed research.

Notes

1 A number of American studies have considered the links between imprisonment and marriage rates, especially in the context of African American families, but I am not aware of comparable research on marriage rates which has been carried out in the UK.
2 For similar research findings from the US see Hairston (1991).
3 Morris is extremely judgemental in her commentary on the attitudes towards money of certain of the families in her sample, describing several as 'completely feckless' (pp. 154–155) and referred to some wives as 'less intelligent' for believing that if they received their National Assistance Board money on a Friday instead of a Monday they would have no financial problems.
4 The figure of 160,000 emerged during non-attributable discussions at the launch seminar of the report by Rose Smith and others (Smith *et al.* 2007) at King's College, London, 14 May 2007.
5 This issue was discussed during non-attributable discussions at the launch seminar of the report by Rose Smith and others (Smith *et al.* 2007) at King's College, London, 14 May 2007.
6 Note, however, that there is no reference given to Johnston (1998) in his bibliography, just Johnston (1995).
7 The account of this is taken from the unpublished fieldwork notes of interviews which later led to Codd (2000 and 2002).

Chapter 4

Prisoners' families and the law

In a recent conversation with a taxi driver on the way to a conference I was asked about my job and about the paper I was to present. I explained that I worked as a law lecturer and was to give a paper on 'prisoner's families'. His response was that that 'sounded more like social work than law'. On reflection this apparently throwaway comment reflects the situation of prisoners' families in relation to legal research in the UK. The needs and experiences of prisoners' families are more often categorised as questions of social work and welfare policy, rather than as raising important questions of law, rights and justice. That is not to say there has been *no* analysis; rather, that there has not been a great deal (see Brooks-Gordon and Bainham 2004; Codd 2004a, 2005b; Munro 2002; Tabib and Mole 2006).[1] The empirical research on prisoners' families has developed within the separate spheres of sociology, criminology, psychology and social work and there has been relatively little published socio-legal analysis. There is no such thing as 'prisoners' families' law' in contrast with the evolution of 'prison law' as a defined, recognised and specialist field, and the amount and quality of published research on issues related to prisoners' families varies depending on the context.

In contrast with prison law prisoners' families exist in the penumbra of the law. Legal decisions as to the rights of prisoners can, however, have a profound impact not only on prisoners but also on their family members. Prisoners' lives are governed by the Prison Rules, their experiences and opportunities regulated by statutes and case law; similarly, from day to day the lives of prisoners' partners and children are underpinned and shaped by law, which governs visits, correspondence, contact, the conditions in which the family member serves their sentence, and in most cases, eventual arrangements for release. More recently, the Human Rights Act 1998 has made it possible for breaches of the European Convention on Human Rights (ECHR) by public authorities to be dealt with in the domestic courts. Specific legal principles and legislative provisions affect particular aspects of the lived experiences of family members. For example, questions of contact between prisoners and their children can not only involve the application of the prison rules but also the principles underpinning the Children Act 1989. As we will see, the nexus between legal theory and practice here is a difficult one and can involve the courts in balancing rights and security. In addition, it is clear from the reported case judgments that legal decisions, like decisions in sentencing law, may also be influenced by actual or perceived public opinion.

As in other aspects of law, though, the most important issue may not be one of the adequacy of statutory and common law provisions for prisoners' families, but one of the extent of discretionary powers vested in the Prison Service, which has control over everything from the conduct of visits to whether to allow a prisoner access to facilities in order to father a child. It could be argued that in the UK context rather than guaranteeing rights to family members the law operates as a mechanism of checks and balances to promote accountability. This approach, however, means that the burden to object is put on family members, rather than certain things being guaranteed. Bearing in mind the social exclusion experienced by many members of prisoners' families, access to justice may not be readily available and family members may not realise that there may be legal mechanisms available to challenge official decisions, or may not have the resources, financial or otherwise, to do so.

In view of the breadth of issues involved, it is beyond the scope of one chapter to offer a summary of all the relevant legal issues. Rather, after briefly discussing the legal background, this chapter focuses on three aspects of prisoners' families interactions with the law which have been matters of current, or ongoing, social and legal controversy.

Prisoners, family life and the law

It is indisputable that imprisonment removes or limits some rights of prisoners, but it is also indisputable that prisoners do not automatically lose all rights either: the cases heard by the courts have explored *which* rights survive incarceration, and to what extent. As Deborah Cheney and others put it:

> It would be untenable to consider that human rights should be suspended at the gates of every prison and reactivated only when a prisoner takes that first step back to freedom (Cheney *et al.* 2001: 194).

The classic statement on prisoners' retention of rights is the following from Lord Wilberforce in *Raymond v. Honey* [1983] 1 AC 1, approved by the House of Lords in *Simms* [2000] 2 AC 115 recently discussed in the inaugural professorial lecture of Andrew Coyle, where he argued that this principle still applies and that its consequences are still every bit as important as they were in 1982:

> a convicted prisoner ... retains all civil rights which are not taken away expressly or by necessary implication (Coyle 2005).

The precise meaning of this, and its application, has occupied the courts since, as has the question of how to reconcile the rights of the non-imprisoned, i.e. family members, with the rights of convicted and imprisoned offenders. Where prisoners and their families wish to challenge the decisions of administrative bodies, a number of legal avenues are open to them. A number of cases during the last five years have raised questions of prisoners' rights in the UK, such as the decision in *Hirst*[2] on prisoners' rights to vote, *Re P and Q* on mother and baby units,[3] and the *Mellor* and *Dickson* cases on prisoners' access to facilities for artificial insemination. These cases all raise questions of judicial attitudes to prisoners and their families, and in some cases are not easily reconciled with the empirical research literature. A fundamental question remains: to what extent do prisoners' families maintain all their rights as citizens, and how and when can the abrogation of such rights be legally justified? How can the law balance the rights of families with the demands of prison security, especially in the context of an increasingly risk-averse culture of prison management? An analysis of the case law suggests that it could be argued that the question of balancing the rights of families with the demands of punishment and security cannot be satisfactorily resolved purely as a question of legal principles, rather, an understanding of the socio-legal context is essential.

The Prisons Ombudsman is not empowered to deal with complaints from families; however, judicial review and proceedings under the

Human Rights Act 1998 provide mechanisms for challenge, as does recourse to the European Court of Human Rights. In some situations, as happened at first instance in *Wainwright*, a case concerning the conduct of strip-searches, redress is sought through common law mechanisms such as the law of tort.

The primary piece of legislation governing prisons is the Prison Act 1952, although it does not make detailed provision for prison management; rather, it delegates authority to those who do. Under Section 47, the Secretary of State is given the power 'to make rules and regulations for the management of prisons, remand centres, detention centres and youth custody centres, and for the classification, treatment, employment, discipline and control of persons required to be detained therein'. The power to make delegated legislation under this Act has led to the Prison Rules 1999, which are subject to ongoing occasional amendment. It is important to note that breaches of the Rules are not themselves legally actionable; as Denning LJ pointed out in *Becker v. Home Office*,[4] they are regulatory directions only. However, the later case of *R. v. Deputy Governor of Parkhurst Prison ex p Hague, Weldon v. Home Office*[5] made it clear that the Rules do not give rise to any specific private law rights; that said, they would be potentially open to judicial review and also actions under the law of tort. The key principle is that prisoners do not have the right to bring an action for breach of statutory duty for breach of the Rules: this does not, however, mean that the actions of the prison authorities are not potentially subject to legal challenge and scrutiny.[6]

Contact between prisoners and their families is governed by a bundle of legal rights and privileges. For example, convicted prisoners are entitled to receive two visits in every four-week period but the Secretary of State may reduce this to one visit during that period. These 'statutory visits' can also be supplemented by 'privilege visits', the granting of which is in the power of the prison governor or the Independent Monitoring Board (Rule 35[6]). Additional visits can also be granted by the Secretary of State. Prisoners may also receive visits from legal advisers, priests and the like. Prisoners on remand may receive as many visits as they wish, within the limits and conditions set by the Secretary of State; that is, currently at least 90 minutes per week (Creighton *et al.* 2005).

Prison Rule 4(2) sets out that prisoners shall be encouraged and assisted in establishing and maintaining such relations with people and agencies outside prison as may best promote the interests of their family and rehabilitation. It is normally 'close relatives' who are entitled to visit. Others may visit but their visits are more likely to be stopped by the prison governor (Creighton *et al.* 2005). In *R (K) v. Home Secretary*[7] the courts refused to hold that the basic level of visits under the Prison Rules amounted to an unjustifiable interference with the right to family life under Article 8 of the ECHR.

The law on visits is a good example of the balancing act which exists between the preservation of family relationships and the demands of 'good order and security'. Rule 34(2) was amended in 2000 to respond to potential challenges under the Human Rights Act 1998, and stresses that restrictions imposed must be proportionate; these grounds for restrictions reflect those set out in Article 8(2) of the ECHR. Creighton *et al.* (2005) discuss the question of proportionality, suggesting that the power to exclude visitors should only be used to exclude close relatives in exceptional circumstances, but could be more widely available for other people. Although Prison Rule 73 allows for individuals to be banned from visiting, with the exception of legal vists and visits by Independent Monitoring Board members, Prison Service Order (PSO) 3610 sets out specific guidance as to the appropriate response when visitors are found to be supplying drugs. It is interesting to note that paragraph 9 of the PSO specifically includes references to Convention Rights; that is, Article 8 of the ECHR, Article 9(3) of the United Nations Convention on the Rights of the Child, if the prisoner is a juvenile and a ban would cause disproportionate harm to his or her right of access to a parent. Broadly speaking, the demands of security can usually be met by the imposition of closed visits, rather than an outright ban, as suggested in *R (Wilkinson) v. Home Secretary* in relation to the passing of contraband.[8] Linked to this is the issue of searching of visitors, which can be extremely stressful. Governors have a general power to search prisoners in their custody as they deem necessary and Creighton *et al.* (2005) suggest it is increasingly common for searches to take place before and after visits. Prison Rule 7 appears to set out a higher threshold of suspicion to justify the searching of visitors and the searching of visitors was disapproved by the European Court of Human Rights in *Wainwright*, as discussed later.

The Wainwright case and the legality of strip-searching visitors

Prior to the decision of the European Court of Human Rights,[9] the response of the courts in the case of *Wainwright* raised serious issues of concern for anyone interested in the rights of prisoners' families, as the case related to the strip-searching of a prisoner's mother and half-brother. Until it reached the European Court of Human Rights the case was viewed and analysed primarily in relation to its impact on the law of privacy, although it raised important questions about the family life of prisoners and the legal status of their family members (Codd 2005b).[10] It is important to remember that the incident took place before the Human Rights Act came into force. It raises fundamental questions of the rights and dignity not only of prisoners, as do many of the cases, but of their partners and family members who may experience hostility and be put in humiliating and stigmatised situations whilst visiting prisons, justified on the grounds of 'security'.

The facts of the case

A prisoner, Patrick O'Neill, was remanded in custody in Armley Prison in Leeds, awaiting trial for murder. His mother, Mrs Wainwright, and her son, Alan (O'Neill's half-brother) went to visit him. Alan had cerebral palsy and learning disabilities. The prison authorities suspected Patrick O'Neill of dealing drugs in the prison, so under the Prison Rules required his visitors to be strip-searched on entry to the prison. The strip searches were governed by the prison's internal code of practice, which set out that:

1 searches had to be held in a completely private room;
2 the visitor should not be asked to take off all their clothes at once, but expose first the upper-half and then the lower-half of the body, and not to be completely undressed;
3 no part of the visitor's body could be touched apart from hair, ears and mouth;
4 a consent form should be signed in advance.

Mrs Wainwright and her son consented reluctantly, and went to separate rooms and were searched. Alan, the son, alleged that the person who searched him had touched his penis to lift the foreskin. Mrs Wainwright believed that she could be seen by people in the block opposite, since it was dark outside and the blinds were not pulled down; she was stripped naked with her knickers around her ankles and her vest above her breasts (Lester 2004). They were not asked to sign the consent forms until afterwards and were told that if they did not consent to the search they might not be allowed to make their visit. Nothing was found during the searches. None of the prison staff could remember the incident. They proceeded with their visit but Mrs Wainwright went to the toilet and cried and vomited about four times, and Alan Wainwright was shaken, nervous and upset. They did not stay for the full length of the visit. Mrs Wainwright complained of the infliction of emotional distress, including exacerbation of existing depression and unpleasant memories; Alan claimed to have suffered post-traumatic stress disorder as a result. The medical evidence demonstrated that the severe upset had exacerbated her existing depression, and that Alan had suffered from post-traumatic stress disorder and depression as a result. During a subsequent visit, he saw some of the officers who had strip-searched him and became very frightened. Mrs Wainwright did not visit Mr O'Neill again for a further four months.

The County Court Judgment

In the initial County Court trial it was accepted by the judge that the prison staff had not set out to humiliate them, and that any deviation from procedure was 'mere sloppiness'. He accepted the claimants' arguments that the searches could not be justified as a proper exercise of the authority's powers under the Prison Rules, and held the searches to be disproportionate and unnecessary, because the prison could have searched the prisoner after the visit, rather than the visitors. Alan was awarded £4,500 for trespass against the person.

The Court of Appeal Judgment

On appeal by the Home Office, the Court of Appeal disagreed that the searches were unnecessary, set aside the ruling in respect of Mrs Wainwright and reduced Alan's damages by £750 (Hewson 2003). The Court of Appeal found that the tort of trespass to the person required intention or recklessness as to the causing of harm, which had not occurred. Second, the Human Rights Act could not be used to construe the Prison Rules consistently with Article 8 of the ECHR since that would involve applying Section 3 of the Human Rights Act retrospectively. Third, it was said that since the Human Rights Act was not in force then the judge should not have become involved in issues of proportionality, but even if the Human Rights Act had applied the strip-searches had been necessary and proportionate and would have been lawful had it been properly conducted. Mummery LJ added that there was no tort of invasion of privacy at common law. The claimants then appealed to the House of Lords. Their appeal was dismissed because first, their Lordships agreed with the Court of Appeal on the trespass point, namely that any tort based on the case of *Wilkinson v. Downton*[11] that would provide a remedy for distress not amounting to psychiatric injury required actual intention or recklessness as to the causing of harm. The officers' failure to observe the rules for searches amounted to 'sloppiness' and not intention to cause distress. Second, they rejected arguments for the existence of a general tort of the invasion of privacy. Third, Lord Hoffman rejected arguments that if the English courts did not create a tort of invasion of privacy then the European Court of Human Rights would find a violation of Articles 3 and 8, involving the prohibition on inhuman and degrading treatment and the right to respect for private and family life respectively. Lord Hoffman argued that 'the conduct of the searches came nowhere near the degree of humiliation' required for a breach of Article 3.[12]

The House of Lords Judgment

The key issue in the House of Lords was whether Mrs Wainwright had a cause of action in tort; following the precedent from *Malone v. Metropolitan Police Commissioner*[13] it was not enough for her to argue that the searches were conducted without statutory authority. With the exception of the actual battery to Alan, there had been no tortious conduct, and thus no liability.

Subsequently, several case notes assessed the decision mainly in relation to privacy and human rights issues (Lester 2004; Morgan 2004). Reading the House of Lords Judgment from a more socio-legal perspective is quite shocking. Alan and Mary Wainwright experienced humiliation at the hands of prison officers in a situation which, as the empirical research demonstrates, is often a source of great stress and anxiety in itself. However, since the prison staff claimed they could not remember the searches, this could be taken to mean that either they were lying or that the procedure was not unusual. In his judgment Lord Hoffman (paragraph 50) pointed out that the Wainwrights 'were upset about having to be searched but made no complaint about the manner of the search', pointing out that Mrs Wainwright 'did not ask for the blind to be drawn over the window or to be allowed to take off her clothes in any particular order'. This seemed to partially ascribe fault to Mrs Wainwright, and took no account of their status as visitors to a prison. Empirical research has described the feelings of fear, anxiety and powerlessness as experienced by prisoners' families, especially in relation to prison visits, yet only Alan's vulnerability appeared to have been recognised.

In his perceptive article Jonathan Morgan (2004) suggested that the House of Lords' decision amounted to a refusal to allow recovery for distress; both Lord Hoffman and Lord Scott seemed to view distress as 'a trivial kind of harm'. Although characterised by Morgan as 'a glaring example of degrading behaviour by a public authority' (Morgan 2004: 395) Lord Scott said:

> The issue of importance in the present case is whether the infliction of humiliation and distress by conduct calculated to humiliate and cause distress, is without more, tortious at common law. I am in full agreement with the reasons that have been given by Lord Hoffmann for concluding that it is not. Nor, in my opinion, should it be. Some institutions, schools, university colleges, regiments and the like (often bad ones) have initiation ceremonies and rites which newcomers are expected to undergo. Ritual humiliation is often a part of this. The authorities in charge of these institutions usually object to these practices and seek to put an end to any excesses. But why, absent any of the traditional nominate torts such as assault, battery, negligent causing of harm etc., should the law of tort intrude? If a shop assistant or a bouncer or barman at a club is publicly offensive to a customer, the customer may well be humiliated and distressed. But that is no sufficient reason why the law of tort should be fashioned and developed with a view to providing compensation in money to the victim.

For the reader familiar with the literature on prisoners' families, this was nothing short of bizarre. Was Lord Scott arguing that what happened to the Wainwrights was a form of initiation ceremony after which they would become a member of some kind of group? How many shop assistants or barmen (or even night club door staff) require customers to submit to a strip-search? It could be argued that there are indeed similarities between the experiences of the Wainwrights and those who experience 'initiation' rituals, in that one person's initiation is another person's bullying: the 'rough horseplay' cases of Jones and Aitken are not without their critics.[14] The law of privacy seemed ill-fitted to respond to the experiences of the Wainwrights, but there was no alternative ground on which they could seek legal redress for their experiences.

The Wainwright case in the European Court of Human Rights

The Wainwrights argued that Article 3 and Article 8 of the ECHR had been violated. That is, the right not to be subjected to torture or to inhuman or degrading treatment or punishment and the right to respect for private and family life. Although the Human Rights Act was not in force at the time the events took place, the House of Lords had considered whether if the Act had been in force, breaches of the Convention could be made out. The Lords argued that there had been no breach of Article 3, and disagreed as to whether there would have been a breach under Article 8, Buxton LJ arguing that they would have had a strong case for relief and Lord Hoffman arguing against.

The applicants argued that Article 3 had been contravened as they were members of the public and not suspected of a criminal offence, and that the experience was highly distressing and constituted degrading treatment. The applicants also argued that Article 8 was engaged as they were seeking to visit a member of their family, although the Government, in response, argued that they had been given a choice as to whether to be searched in order to see their relative and that they had not been subject to any threats or coercion. In addition, the Government argued that the searches were proportionate in terms of preventing crime and protecting the health of prisoners.

The court concluded that ill-treatment must attain a minimum level of severity if it is to fall within the scope of Article 3 of the ECHR and the assessment of this minimum level of severity is on all the circumstances of the case, such as the duration of the treatment, its physical and mental effects and, in some cases, the sex, age and health of the victim. In considering whether a treatment is 'degrading' within the meaning of Article 3, the court will have regard to whether its object is to humiliate and debase the person concerned and whether, as far as the consequences are concerned, it adversely affected his or her personality in a manner incompatible with Article 3. The suffering and humiliation must go beyond the inevitable element of suffering or humiliation connected with a given form of legitimate treatment or punishment, as in, for example, measures depriving a person of their liberty, but of course the family members here were not the subjects of the punishment.

The court had already had occasion to apply these principles in the context of strip and intimate body searches and held that a search carried out in an appropriate manner with due respect for human dignity and for a legitimate purpose may be compatible with Article 3. However, where the manner in which a search is carried out has debasing elements which significantly aggravate the inevitable humiliation of the procedure, Article 3 has been engaged. Similarly, where the search has no established connection with the preservation of prison security and prevention of crime or disorder, issues may arise. The court noted that although there was a regrettable lack of courtesy there was no verbal abuse by the prison officers and, importantly, there was no touching of the applicants, save in the case of the second applicant. That aspect was found to be unlawful by the domestic courts which gave damages for the battery involved; the second applicant cannot claim any longer to be victim of this element and it is excluded from the court's assessment. The treatment undoubtedly caused the applicants distress but did not, in the court's view, reach the minimum level of severity prohibited by Article 3. The court found, however, that the case fell within the scope of Article 8 of the ECHR and which would require due justification under the second paragraph of the Article, which allows for the right to be interfered with by a public authority only if certain justifications are made out.

The court held that the searches pursued the legitimate aim of fighting drug use in the prison. In these circumstances the court considered that the searching of visitors may be considered as a legitimate preventive measure but emphasised nonetheless that 'the application of such a highly invasive and potentially debasing procedure to persons who are not convicted prisoners or under reasonable suspicion of having committed a criminal offence must be conducted with rigorous adherence to procedures and all due respect to their human dignity'.

The court, however, was not satisfied that the searches were proportionate to that legitimate aim in the manner in which they were carried out:

> Where procedures are laid down for the proper conduct of searches on outsiders to the prison who may very well be innocent of any wrongdoing, it behoves the prison authorities to comply strictly with those safeguards and by rigorous precautions protect the dignity of those being searched from being assailed any further than is necessary. They did not do so in this case.

In addition, the court found a breach of Article 13; that is, the right to an effective remedy in the national courts. The judgment of the European Court is significant in that it foregrounds the fundamental dignity of persons in this context and recognises that prisoners' family members are not to be treated as if they were themselves prisoners. This issue is also at the core of the recent cases both in the UK domestic courts and in the European Court of Human Rights in relation to prisoners' access to artificial insemination facilities, which will be discussed at length later in this chapter.

Mothers, children and babies

The backdrop of any exploration of the law in relation to babies and young children and prisons is the growing awareness of children's rights: children are being recognised as 'an important minority group with rights of their own' (Fortin 2003). The Human Rights Act 1998 has challenged adults' perceptions of the status of children and Fortin (2003) argues that the concept of children as rights-holders is no longer contested. In the international arena, UK state obligations under the United Nations Convention on the Rights of the Child are increasingly being recognised, discussed, disputed and explored (Fortin 2003; Friends World Committee for Consultation [Quakers] 2005a, 2005b; Tabib and Mole 2006).

Contact between children and their imprisoned parent(s)

Little research literature has explored the legal questions arising from contact between prisoners and children. There are specific regulations governing prisoners' visits from children where the prisoner is assessed as posing an ongoing risk to children (see Creighton *et al.* 2005), and governors can exclude visits to or from persons under eighteen if it is felt that this would not be in the best interests of the visitor or the prisoner. It has been argued recently that the rules on children visiting have become more stringent (Creighton *et al.* 2005); for prisoners convicted of or charged with a offence against a child or with a previous conviction for such offences then contact will be limited to children in their immediate family or the children of a partner where they were living together as a couple prior to imprisonment. For the prisoner to have contact with any other child then the governor has to agree that this would be in the best interests of the child and a risk assessment would have to be completed, along with other relevant checks, in order to comply with the principle that the welfare of the child is paramount. This tightening of the rules, and ongoing concern about contact between prisoners and children, reflects not only concerns about prison security but also, more specifically, concerns about child protection following the Ashworth Inquiry which, *inter alia*, discussed a situation in which a father had taken a female eight-year-old child to a high-security special hospital to visit a man with a history of violent sexual assaults on girls (Fallon *et al.* 1999). The girl was undressed by the man and allowed inappropriate physical contact with him and the inquiry found that the girl was being 'groomed' for sexual abuse (see Brooks-Gordon and Bainham 2004). Interestingly, Brooks-Gordon and Bainham (2004) suggest that the increase in the numbers of sex offenders in prison, linked to concerns around the deficiencies of the Mental Health Act 1983 in relation to those diagnosed as having 'psychopathic disorder', has meant a lower proportion of the prison population being allowed contact with children.

Judicial responses to questions of contact between prisoners and children differ from the 'usual' contact disputes, often as a consequence of divorce and relationship breakdown, which customarily occupy the courts. When, for example, one parent leaves the family home on separation, it is usual, as recognised in both the Convention on the Rights of the Child and the European Convention on Contact Concerning Children, to emphasise the need for the child to maintain regular and direct contact, except where this would be beyond the child's best interests (Fortin 2003). It has long been assumed by the judiciary in this non-prison context that it will almost always be of benefit to children to have as much contact with their non-resident fathers as possible.[15] The Court of Appeal appears to assume that, in all cases except those involving domestic violence or which may involve harm or risk of harm to the child there is 'sufficient scientific knowledge' to justify the courts assuming that contact with a father is, for a child, beneficial in all other circumstances.[16] However, this view has not gone uncriticised, and simply assuming that contact will be beneficial does not fit with complex contact disputes, where contact may not always be achieved happily. Interestingly, the research on whether or not it is good for children to maintain contact in less than happy circumstances is ambiguous and the question of whether biological ties entitle parents to ongoing relationships with their children is contested. Enos (2001) considers mothering as a position, a relationship and an activity, a key question is therefore whether parenting is simply a matter of biology, or whether in the eyes of the courts an ongoing parent–child relationship must be earned. This is highly relevant in the context of prisoners, where the question is whether parents possess a relationship with their children purely on biological grounds, or whether there are other hidden 'qualifiers' which may be taken into account in deciding what contact is permitted.

There has been some discussion in the family law child contact literature of the contact questions raised where there has been domestic violence. The case law is of especial value in the context of prisoners' family relationships, since violence within the home can be the reason for the prisoner's imprisonment. The case of *Re L* (a child) stressed that courts dealing with contact disputes should take proper account of the impact of the father's violence on the family and the potential psychological risk to children in enforcing contact in such cases.[17] Rather than dismissing mothers' accounts of resistance to contact as hostility, the courts must now make findings of fact where domestic violence is alleged and, if established, should take full account of its impact on children, and the reasons why contact is being sought. Avoidance of danger to the mother and child is fundamental, however, this does not mean there is a presumption of non-contact. These cases can be directly relevant to prisoners who are imprisoned as a consequence of intrafamilial violence.

One case, however, is especially disturbing in the context of prisoner–child contact. The courts, in their zeal to promote contact, can order what is termed 'letter-box contact'. This may be especially applicable to prisoners because other forms of indirect contact, such as the use of contact centres, are not available as options for prisoners. The case of *Re G* involved the court in ordering indirect contact via cards and presents at birthdays and Christmas, even though the father had killed the mother when the child was three years old and was serving a four-year sentence for manslaughter, the father had no understanding of the child's needs and the child was frightened of him and reluctant to see him.[18] This is another example where it is essential to listen to children, and respect their views (Munby 2004a, 2004b). Similarly, the presumption of contact no longer applies where there has been sexual abuse, or allegations of sexual abuse.[19] Fortin (2003) is forceful in her assessment of the potential danger to children of continuing a relationship with an abusive parent, in that it may promote the continuance of a relationship which, even though it may not be sexually abusive, may be emotionally abusive and put pressure on children. More specific research is needed, but it could be argued that the additional rules governing children's visits to jailed sex offenders offer more protection to children than is available where sexual abuse allegations have been made as part of civil contact disputes, where there has been no criminal trial or incarceration, or where the father is no longer in prison (Macaskill 2002).

For prisoners and the families the issues are not so much about availability of any contact time, as may be the case with reluctant parents after separation/divorce, and more a question of the nature and context of the contact time available to children in a prison setting. For example, children may be able to visit, but if the parent is on a closed visit, for example, then the child may feel this interferes with their relationship. The recent attempt at judicial review in *X v. Secretary of State for the Home Department & ors* (QBD) [2005] EWHC 1616 (Admin), a case before the Queen's Bench Division Administrative Court, is interesting because it involves a parent seeking to harness the rights extant under Article 8 of the ECHR to challenge a Prison Service decision to deny her release on temporary licence (ROTL) in order to see her children, even though she had previously been granted that facility. The case involved a woman sentenced to ten years for importation of cocaine, who had previously been allowed ROTL but as a consequence of (later quashed) findings that she had been involved in violence and intimidation involving other prisoners and her consequent transfer to another, higher-security prison, involved the woman in contending that she had allowed her children to visit her at the prison up until she believed they could understand where they were; she had always told them that she was in hospital. The applicant argued that her rights under Article 8 had been infringed, but this was rejected by the court on the grounds that the usual mechanism for parent–child contact was via the children visiting the prison, and if the mother chose not to have her children visit, for whatever reason, then her rights were not being denied by the public authority i.e. the Prison Service, but rather by her own choice. She also unsuccessfully argued that, as the children's mother, she was the person best placed to know what was in the best interests of her children, but again this was rejected by the court.

When viewed from the perspective of a commitment to children's rights, it could be argued that the full potential of the Human Rights Act in promoting and preserving children's interests in relation to their imprisoned parents has not yet been fully explored or realised. Munby J (2004a, 2004b) has stressed the importance of adequate representation of children's interests, and also of listening to children themselves. There appears, however, not to be a great deal of case law on this point. This reflects the marginalised location of prisoners' families within the discourses of law and criminology: prisoners' rights are recognised, and prisoners are given rights to minimal numbers of visits, and so on, but this is not conceptualised in relation to the rights of either partners or, perhaps more persuasively, children.[20] It is difficult to reconcile dangerousness with parenthood, but it is important to remember that not all individuals who have, for example, behaved violently, have been, or are likely to be, violent in all contexts. It is uncontroversial to suggest that, if a parent has been convicted of the physical or sexual abuse of their child then they should not be allowed to contact with that child, but dilemmas are posed by, for example, a parent who has responded well to an in-prison treatment programme or by a child who expresses a legally-competent and informed wish that despite the abuse they still wish to see their parent. The blood tie is not everything – and indeed in some situations it may mean nothing – but in some situations it may not be easily dismissed. It could be argued that an honest, listening approach to prisoners' children is needed, with greater input of, and representation of, children's own views in deciding what kind of contact, and contact programmes, are to be developed and made available.

Imprisoned mothers and babies

The situation in relation to mothers who wish to keep their babies with them in prison is potentially more encouraging in terms of recognition of the rights of the children of prisoners (Munro 2002).[21] Under the Children Act 1989 the court is legally bound to consider the best interests of the child as the paramount consideration; as the European Court of Human Rights said in *Yousef v. The Netherlands* [2003] 1 FLR 210 at para. 73: 'If any balancing of interests is necessary, the interests of the child must prevail.' This 'best interests of the child' criterion offers an apparently clear focus for the court's decision-making. However, this apparently clear approach can be deceptive, the thorny question being that of how these 'best interests' can be assessed and determined. After all, one view is that it is in the best interests of a child to be with their mother, albeit in a prison setting, whereas a contrasting view is that it is better for a child to be separated from a convicted parent mother and to be cared for outside the prison. One Quaker report, in discussing whether it is better for children to remain with their mothers in a prison setting, or to remain outside, summed up the difficulties. It is 'not a question of choosing between a good option and a bad option, but between two bad options' (Nari 2000, cited in Friends World Committee for Consultation 2005b). The problems of this binary choice are especially visible in the UK context, where we do not have the same alternative approaches as are available in some jurisdictions, such as community units and half-way houses.

In *Re P and Q* the Court of Appeal had to consider a challenge brought by two serving prisoners against the policy of the Prison Service [PSO 4801] which prohibited babies from remaining with their mothers in prison after they had reached the age of eighteen months.[22] It was held that the Prison Service was entitled to have a policy of this kind, but was not entitled to operate this policy in a rigid fashion. The court reached this conclusion for two reasons. The first was because the policy's own declared aim was to promote the welfare of the child. The second ground was that, on the proper application of Article 8, there might be rare exceptions where the interests of mother and child coincide and outweigh any other considerations arising from the fact of the mother's imprisonment and the implications of any relaxation in the policy on the individual prison and the Prison Service generally. Since this decision, however, there have been several judicial review applications challenging the exercise of the discretion, one of the most publicised being that of Claire Frost in *CF v. Secretary of State for the Home Department and another*.[23] In this case, the Prison Service had initially decided to separate the mother from her baby, Lia-Jade, at the age of nine months, rather than move them both to a different mother and baby unit until the baby reached eighteen months, having taken the view that separation was better 'earlier rather than later'. The report of the judicial review decision indicates what can only be described as a shocking lack of professionalism on the part of the social worker who was responsible for representing the baby's interests at the separation board: she only became involved with the case on the day of the meeting, had not seen any relevant papers prior to arrival at the prison, and was described by Munby J as being 'woefully unprepared for the task in hand'. Munby J took the view that, in this situation, the Prison Service should have adjourned the hearing.[24] Munby J stressed the procedural unfairness in the decision-making process and quashed the decision to remove the baby at nine months, ruling it was a matter for the Prison Service to reconsider, and stressing the need for appropriate representation of the interests of the child. As a consequence, the baby was sent to live with her grandparents in May 2004 when she was sixteen months old: Claire Frost was subsequently transferred to Askham Grange, the prison to which she had initially requested a transfer so the baby could stay with her up to the age of eighteen months.

The case is significant because the judgment stressed both procedural issues and also the requirement of individualised responses to planning for the needs of babies amd their mothers in prison. Munby J offered further reflections on his decions (Munby 2004b), when he reiterated the central important of the obligation of the Secretary of State not only to permit the representation of the baby's interests but also to ensure that the baby was properly represented and that this representation was adequate to the gravity of the matter in hand (Munby 2004b). In his public lecture to the National Youth Advocacy Service he stressed that, in order to comply with the ECHR, the Prison Service, or any other administrative decision-maker, has to ensure that the child's interests are adequately represented, describing Article 8 as 'fundamental to everything we do as professionals concerned with children and their families' (Munby 2004a, 2004b). Although the Court of Appeal is not a family proceedings court, as Munby J points out, the court is required to make a decision of equal importance regarding the welfare of a child: that is, because a decision is taken administratively rather than by a court is not of itself any reason why a child or parent should not be adequately represented. There is a distinction between the emphasis on the representation of children in judicial hearings, which stands in stark contrast to that in administrative decision-making, but he identifies promising indicators that change could be possible via, for example, centralised planning in the Prison Service, and the potential role of the Prisons Inspectorate.

In a later case a pregnant woman who had pleaded guilty to acting as a courier for the importation of cocaine and was sentenced to three and a half years imprisonment was placed in an ordinary prison then transferred to a mother and baby unit prior to the birth.[25] As a consequence of behavioural problems she was transferred from the unit and was separated from her baby. The baby was placed with one of her friends.[26] She applied for judicial review and the decision was quashed on the grounds first that the letter setting out the decision did not refer to the child's best interests, which had probably been given inadequate consideration by the decision-maker. Second, in terms of proportionality the Prison Service had failed to assess the risk to the child arising from separation, in the context that the first step was to assess the risk posed by the mother to others, especially other babies, in the mother and baby unit and to consider whether this risk could be reduced or managed by measures short of separation, such as increased support, disciplinary measures or a move to a different mother and baby unit. Then, the risk to the child from the separation should be assessed and, if possible, reduced. Finally the risk to others had to be weighed against the detriment suffered by the child. On a procedural level, the mother had not been given the opportunity to answer the allegations and to make representations.

The mother and baby cases demonstrate the beginning of judicial recognition of the voices of family members in prison decision-making. The Children Act requires the interests of the child to be paramount (see Brooks-Gordon and Bainham 2004). It is possible, therefore, that in the future, issues of the impact of Prison Service decisions on prisoners' children may be more readily brought to court. It is encouraging to read the text of Munby J's public lecture (Munby 2004a, 2004b) in which he reiterates the importance of listening to children. These cases have procedural as well as substantive components: it is not simply a question of what decision is made, but of how it is made, and how the interests of parents and their children are represented. The decision in the *CD* case builds on the emphasis in Re *P & Q* on an individualised rather than universal approach to mothers and their babies, but it is interesting in that, although there are set procedures governing admission to a mother and baby unit, the case report explains that there are no similar procedures governing this kind of decision to exclude and separate.

The PSO 'The Management of Mother and Baby Units' sets out circumstances which may justify temporary or permanent exclusion or separation but the Order does not address the procedural aspects. As Kay J explained in his judgment, not only is it to be regretted that the Prison Service did not have a set procedure to be followed where exclusion and separation were to be considered, but that it was not right, as happened in this case, for the decision-maker to proceed on the basis of 'a one-sided presentation of the facts'. In this case, these facts involved disciplinary issues related to the mother's behaviour and also undocumented allegations relating to an ongoing disagreement with another prisoner. Expert reports supported the reunion of mother and child in a different mother and baby unit, as a matter of urgency; delay could cause long-term psychological harm through attachment disruption. The expert was critical of the way mother and baby were separated, and although the baby's substitute carer appeared to be doing very well, the expert argued there was insufficient contact with local social services and little opportunity to assess the potential substitute carer. There was an ad hoc review after the decision, but Kay J considered that this did not amount to 'a procedural corrective', because, again, there was no representation by the applicant or her solicitors and the reviewers again accepted the original allegations at face value: thus this did not remedy the initial flaws. Thus the application for judicial review was successful. Rather than ordering a restoration to a mother and baby unit by means of a mandatory order, however, Kay J took the view that since it was the Prison Service which made a flawed decision it was for the Prison Service to reconsider the decision. He then went on, beyond the pure decision to explain what he envisaged as the correct approach, which should include procedural fairness:

> The greatest difficulty facing the Prison Service decision-maker is that he is rightly enjoined to treat the best interests of the child as 'the primary consideration' but must also keep in mind at all times that the context is one of a prison which has a profound need fort the maintenance of good order and discipline.

Bearing in mind that the decision-maker in this case had said that taking this decision was not a task with which he felt comfortable, Kay J said in cases where it was not obvious what the best interests of the child might be, then the decision-maker should seek assistance from appropriate experts. Since the number of cases such as this were small on an annual basis, Kay J suggested that the burden of creating and applying a policy for all mother and baby units would not be too onerous for the Prison Service.

These cases indicate that in relation to judicial review applications the courts are demonstrating recognition of the need to identify the particular needs of children, and to ensure that they are represented in their own right. Reading these cases from a perspective based purely within the UK legal system, these cases apparently demonstrate a significant recognition of the rights of children, which is to be applauded. However, this raises the metaphor of goldfish not having a word for water because they are in it all the time. These cases, and the vociferous recognition of the importance of listening to children displayed by members of the judiciary such as Munby J and Baroness Hale, are encouraging for the reader because from the point of view of the existing law and the UK criminal justice system, the

Prison Service has been given a clear message that blanket policies for dealing with children as if they are all identical are inappropriate. From a more critical perspective, however, there are broader questions of the age limit in this country for residence in mother and baby units: in some other countries, children may stay with their mothers for longer (EUROCHIPS 2006). The binary nature of the decision does not take account of alternative approaches to sentencing which do not face decision-makers with the straight 'prison or separation' choice. Since most female prisoners have not been imprisoned for violent offences (Prison Reform Trust 2007), public protection may be differently nuanced. Clearly, the public and the community's economic interests need to be protected from theft and fraud, but if the interests of children are to be paramount, then this needs to be recognised. There are, however, dilemmas in adopting arguments based on motherhood and parenting responsibilities. It is possible to ask why there are no father and baby units, but this has been justified in relation to the biological demands of parenting small babies and issues of maternal bonding and breast feeding and also in terms of lack of demand. That said, it would be interesting to assess the response of the courts to a new father who wished to care for his baby during his sentence.

Prisoners and not-yet-conceived children[27]

In January 2007 the Grand Chamber of the European Court of Human Rights began considering the case of *Dickson v. The United Kingdom*. This case concerns the controversial questions of whether prisoners and their partners should be allowed access to facilities for artificial insemination and whether the denial of access to such facilities contravenes Articles 8 and 12 of the ECHR.[28] The court published its judgment on the case in April 2006, and it was subsequently referred for the consideration of the Grand Chamber. The prior judgment raises not only issues of human rights, reproductive autonomy, the nature and purposes of punishment and the role of the state in family life, but also involves consideration of the status and rights of an as-yet-unconceived child. The judgment of the Grand Chamber was published in December 2007.

The question of whether long-term male prisoners should be allowed to attempt to father children, or, conversely, whether female inmates should be allowed to attempt to become pregnant, is an emotive one. Although it is a controversial issue, to date it has received relatively little public or media attention in the United Kingdom with the exception of brief newspaper articles reporting on the *Mellor* and *Dickson* cases and a low-budget comedy film.[29] This relative invisibility stands in stark contrast to the situation in several other jurisdictions. For example, in the US the constitutional challenges raised in the *Goodwin* case and in the so-called 'procreation by FedEx' case of *Gerber v. Hickman* have led to a deluge of published academic articles debating the issues (Bozzuti 2003; Roth 2004).[30] Sperm smuggling, in which prisoners smuggle semen out of prisons so that their partners can attempt to become pregnant, first came to the widespread attention of the American public in 2002 when the *New York Post* reported that a prisoner and his partner, who were ineligible for conjugal visits, had allegedly bribed guards to smuggle sperm out of a prison and into a fertility clinic, as a consequence of which their daughter was conceived and born (Kadison and Weiss 2002). Sperm smuggling has since formed part of a storyline in *The Sopranos*.[31] Prisoners' access to artificial insemination is also currently a matter of debate in Israel, where the partner of the man convicted of the murder of Prime Minister Yitzhak Rabin has been caught attempting to smuggle sperm out of his jail (Sunday Times 2006). Despite the relative lack of publicity, however, the legal situation in the UK is more complex than in the US. In the UK, there is no provision for conjugal visits for prisoners and their partners. If a prisoner and his or her partner wish to conceive a child together, unless the prisoner is permitted ROTL then the prisoner has no alternative but to seek access to facilities for artificial insemination. As Sutherland (2003) writes, 'unlike the position in the United States, the right of prisoners to procreative freedom in the United Kingdom is not removed at the prison gates'. In contrast with the US, where there is a blanket ban, the decision as to whether to grant a prisoner access to such facilities is made by the Family Ties Unit, part of the Prisoner Administration Group of the Prison Service.[32] Judicial review and proceedings under the Human Rights Act 1998 provide valuable mechanisms for challenging the decisions of the Unit, as does recourse to the European Court of Human Rights.[33] It is, arguably, the discretionary nature of this decision which makes this issue more thought-provoking in legal terms than if there were an outright prohibition on access to these facilities.

The starting point for the decision as to whether to allow a prisoner access to artificial insemination facilities is that, in the words of the Secretary of State, such requests 'are carefully considered on individual merit and will only be granted in exceptional circumstances'.[34] Several challenges have been brought by dissatisfied prisoners, including that by Gavin Mellor several years ago and more recently those by Kirk and Lorraine Dickson.[35]

The Mellor case

In *R. (on the Application of Mellor) v. Secretary of State for the Home Department*,[36] the Court of Appeal upheld a judgment dismissing an application for access to artificial insemination facilities from a prisoner serving a life sentence. His wife, whom he married in prison in 1997, would be 31 when the tariff element of his life sentence expired. Mellor was challenging the Home Office policy and claimed that the refusal to allow him access to artificial insemination facilities breached his right to respect for private and family life under Article 8 of the ECHR, and his right to marry and found a family under Article 12. The court rejected Mellor's claim, stating that one of the purposes of imprisonment was to punish the criminal by depriving him of certain rights and pleasures which he could only enjoy at liberty, including the enjoyment of family life, the exercise of conjugal rights and the right to found a family. In his judgment, Lord Phillips argued that a policy which generally accorded prisoners the right to conceive children by artificial insemination would 'raise difficult ethical questions and give rise to legitimate public concern'. He also discussed the difficulties of creating a de facto single-parent family, contending that it is both legitimate and desirable that, when considering whether to have a general policy of facilitating artificial insemination for prisoners or the wives of prisoners, the State should consider the implications of children being raised in those circumstances.

This case was brought by a prisoner in relation to his *own* rights, not that of his partner, but of course prisoners' partners also have a right to found a family.[37] Depending on how 'founding a family' is defined, if a male prisoner is denied access to facilities for artificial insemination, then in order to exercise her own rights his partner would either have to have sex with someone other than her husband, or conceive through formal or informal artificial insemination by donor (AID), and thus bear a child of whom her husband would not be the biological father. Thus the partners of prisoners denied access to artificial insemination are themselves eligible to challenge the policy on the grounds that their *own* rights are being infringed, although to date only one prisoner's wife, Lorraine Dickson, has attempted this.[38]

The Dickson case

Lorraine Dickson, herself an ex-prisoner, befriended Kirk Dickson, who is serving a mandatory life sentence for murder, via the prison penfriend scheme. They married in a prison ceremony in 2001. Lorraine Dickson has now been released from prison. Her husband will not be eligible to apply for release on licence until 2009, by which time she will be 51 (Hull Daily Mail 2003). Mr Dickson has no children; Mrs Dickson has three children by other relationships. In October 2003 Kirk Dickson's application for access to artificial insemination facilities was refused. In his letter the Secretary of State set out his policy for responding to such requests, which was very close to that considered by the court in the earlier *Mellor* case.[39] The letter explained that particular attention is given to several considerations:

- whether the provision of artificial insemination facilities is the only means by which conception is likely to occur;
- whether the prisoner's expected day of release is neither so near that delay would not be excessive nor so distant that he/she would be unable to assume the responsibilities of a parent;
- whether both parties want the procedure and the medical authorities both inside and outside the prison are satisfied that the couple are medically fit to proceed with artificial insemination;
- whether the couple were in a well-established and stable relationship prior to imprisonment which is likely to subsist after the prisoner's release;
- whether there is any evidence to suggest that the couple's domestic circumstances and the arrangements for the welfare of the child are satisfactory, including the length of time for which the child might expect to be without a father or mother;
- whether having regard to the prisoner's history, antecedents and other relevant factors there is evidence to suggest that it would not be in the public interest to provide artificial insemination facilities in a particular case.

In the Dicksons' case, the Secretary of State recognised that Lorraine Dickson would be 51 at the earliest possible date of release; however, the refusal was justified on the grounds that the relationship had not been tested in the normal environment of daily life; there was insufficient provision in place to provide for the material welfare of any child which might be conceived and that there was no immediate support network in place for the mother and child. The child would also be without a father for an important part of its childhood, and in the light of the violent nature of Kirk Dickson's crime there would be legitimate public concern that the punitive and deterrent elements of his sentence were being circumvented if he were allowed to father a child by artificial insemination.

A subsequent application for leave to apply for judicial review was unsuccessful: Pitchford J said that the Prison Service was justified in refusing access, and in taking into account the factors described.[40] Lorraine Dickson already had three children by other relationships, and the judge refused to accept that the couple's desire to have a child 'trumped all other considerations'. The Dicksons then sought permission to appeal this earlier decision, and asked for an extension of time in which to do so. In September 2004 the Court of Appeal refused the Dicksons leave to apply for judicial review, stressing the validity of the Prison Service policy, and describing the Home Secretary's decision to refuse artificial insemination facilities as 'an exercise of discretion and proportionality'. The Dicksons took their case to the European Court of Human Rights, arguing that the refusal of access to artificial insemination facilities breached their right to respect for private and family life under Article 8, and also that the refusal breached their right to found a family under Article 12.

In their submission to the European Court, amongst other things the applicants argued that the aim of the restriction had to be punishment, since there was no security or other physical or financial barrier, but if this were the case then it would be incoherent to admit exceptions. Indeed, the starting point of the policy was wrong *ab initio* and the policy should be that they had a right to conceive children unless there were compelling reasons against.[41] They also maintained that the social factors underlying the policy and the Secretary of State's response to them were not factors contemplated under paragraph 2 of Article 8 which permits interference with the right to respect for private and family life on certain grounds, including public safety, the protection of health and morals or the protection of rights and freedoms of others. They argued that there were insufficient reasons to justify this restriction in their case, and submitted that the refusal of access to artificial insemination would for them mean that their right to found a family would not merely be delayed but would be extinguished, making the point that even if Kirk Dickson had forfeited some of his rights on imprisonment, the same could not be said of his wife. The applicants also challenged the Secretary of State's conclusion as to the financial implications, pointing out that they would pay for the facilities themselves and that Lorraine Dickson owned significant assets. They contended that 'moral considerations were not a matter for the government when considering the effectiveness of human rights' (p. 9).

In response, the Government argued that the restriction was a punishment, the consequences of which 'were not disproportionate to the aim of maintaining a penal system designed to punish and deter' (p. 7). It also submitted that the policy was consistent with relevant ECHR case law because it allowed for examination of each application on its individual merits. It was submitted that the policy was justifiable on the grounds that the loss of the opportunity to conceive children was an ordinary consequence of imprisonment; that public confidence in the prison system would be undermined if prisoners could conceive children while serving long sentences for serious offences; and that the inevitable absence of one parent for a long period would have negative consequences for the child and for society as a whole. In the Dicksons' case, the fact that they would not be able to conceive children at all was overcome by the other reasons relied on by the Secretary of State. The Government argued that they should be allowed a wide margin of appreciation, and that there did not appear to be any European consensus in favour of the provision of artificial insemination facilities to prisoners (Proctor 2003).

The court published its judgment in April 2006, and held by four votes to three that there had been no violation of either Article. The majority agreed that prisoners do not forfeit their Convention rights upon imprisonment, but that imprisonment entails limitations and controls on the exercise of Convention rights and, in this context, on the possibility of begetting a child. It was held that the restriction, however, does not limit a general entitlement already in place but involves the State's refusal to exceptionally allow something, and thus in complaining that access to artificial insemination was refused the applicants were complaining that the State failed to fulfil a positive obligation to secure respect for private and family life. The court held that contracting states enjoy a wide margin of appreciation in relation to such areas as conjugal visits. In relation to the underlying aims of the policy of the maintenance of public confidence in the penal system and the welfare of any child conceived as a result of artificial insemination, the court accepted that the maintaining of public confidence in the penal system has a legitimate role to play in penal policy within prisons and also that the State 'has positive obligations to ensure the effective protection and moral welfare of children' (p. 12). Particular importance was attached to the fact that the policy was not a blanket policy. In relation to the Dicksons' situation, the court stressed that careful consideration of their circumstances was given by the Secretary of State but concluded that other factors outweighed the unlikelihood of conception after release; namely, the nature and gravity of Kirk Dickson's crime and the welfare of any child who might be conceived. In conclusion, it was held that in these circumstances and having regard to the wide margin of appreciation afforded to national authorities, the decision to refuse artificial insemination facilities was not arbitrary or unreasonable nor did it fail to strike a fair balance between the competing interests. It was thus held that there was no breach of Article 8 or, subsequently, of Article 12.

Judge Bonello agreed with the majority but for slightly differing reasons, giving less prominence to the State's margin of appreciation. The overall tone of his judgment is one of negativity towards single-parent families generally, exacerbated by Kirk Dickson's status as a prisoner. In his concurring judgment he argues that

> The concept of 'family' enshrined in Article 8 and Article 12 ... requires more than the mere forwarding of sperm from a distance in circumstances which preclude the donor from participating meaningfully in any significant function related to parenthood (p. 13).

Bonello's judgment discusses the wife's situation but argues that there must be a balance between 'her natural craving to found a family' and 'the rights of the child she desires to generate' and concludes that allowing the Dicksons to have children would not be fostering the best interests of the child; indeed it would be 'injurious to the rights of others':

> I am far from persuaded that kick-starting into life a child in the meanest circumstances, could be viewed as an exercise in promoting its finest interests. The debut of life in a one-parent family, deprived of the presence of the father and a father-figure, offspring of a life prisoner convicted for the most serious crime of violence, would not quite appear to be the best way of giving a child-to-be a headstart in life (p. 16).

He implies that the State would have to bear some of the financial burden of the child's upbringing because the wife had not adduced evidence to disprove the Government's arguments about the 'seeming insufficiency' of material resources. He goes on to discuss the circumstances of the parents' meeting and relationship, contending that 'the union of the applicants still remains that engendered in a dysfunctional ambience, where restriction and control are the rule and liberty the dream' (p. 16). Although, he contends, it is argued that children are regularly allowed to be born in similar or worse circumstances, in the Dicksons' situation the State would be an active accomplice and participant and a responsible State is right to require standards of iteself 'higher than those beyond its control in the free procreation market' (p. 16).

The dissenting opinions are interesting and thought-provoking. Judges Casadevall and Garlicki argue that the majority erred in its classification of the nature of the prohibition of artificial insemination, in assessing the UK's general policy, and in assessing the particular circumstances of the case. In particular, they consider that the Dicksons' case is highly exceptional and what is at stake is not a temporary limitation of the right to procreate but its 'full and irrevocable destruction'. They do not consider that the Secretary of State's reasons were sufficiently serious to justify this and argue that the arguments were too paternalistic: 'it is not for the State to determine who may have children and when' (p. 18). They reject arguments that the refusal was necessary to maintain public confidence in the penal system. The dissenting judgment of Judge Borrego Borrego goes further and, significantly focuses on Mrs Dickson, to whom he refers as 'the "forgotten person" in this case'. He vividly asserts that in an artificial insemination process 'the man's role is essential but rather limited' whereas the woman's role is more complicated and potentially painful. He argues that denial of the right based on the gravity of Kirk Dickson's offence is not a punishment imposed by a court and is absurd, because after 2009 or his release date, he could attempt without hindrance to become a father: it would seem to imply that after 2009 'the nature and gravity of the crime' would have ceased to exist whereas in fact it would be his wife's ability to conceive which would have ceased to exist. In addition, he argues that the potential mother's role in the first years of a child's life has been forgotten and that the refusal was paternalist, if this is the case then the same arguments could be used to argue against the conception of a child where one parent has a life-limiting illness. In concluding with his express hope that the judgment be examined by the Grand Chamber, he says that there could still be a chance for Mrs Dickson to conceive, saying: 'It really would be regrettable if a real problem became, through the passage of time, a purely theoretical one. The Convention guarantees rights which are "practical and effective", not "theoretical or illusory"' (p. 20).

On 4 December 2007, the Grand Chamber of the European Court of Human Rights handed down its decision in *Dickson v. United Kingdom*, holding by a 12:5 majority that there had been a violation of Article 8, but that it was not necessary to examine the complaint under Article 12.[42] Despite attempts by the UK Government to suggest otherwise, the Grand Chamber held that Article 8 was applicable in that the refusal of artificial insemination facilities concerned the applicants' private and family lives which notions incorporate the right to respect for their decision to become genetic parents. The court referred to the judgment in *Hirst*, which concerned a prisoner's right to vote, stressing that prisoners in general continue to enjoy all the fundamental rights and freedoms guaranteed under the Convention save for the right to liberty, where lawfully imposed detention expressly falls within the scope of Article 5 of the ECHR. A person thus retains his or her Convention rights on imprisonment, so that any restriction on those rights must be justified in each individual case. Significantly, the court said that this justification cannot be based solely on what would offend public opinion. The court saw the key issue as being the balance between conflicting public and private interests. In response to the government's submissions, the Grand Chamber agreed with the Dicksons, stating that 'whilst the inability to beget a child might be a consequence of imprisonment, it is not an inevitable one, it not being suggested that the grant of artificial insemination facilities would involve any security issues or impose any significant administrative or financial demands on the State.' The court, as the Chamber, reiterated that there is no place under the Convention system where tolerance and broadmindedness are the acknowledged hallmarks of democratic society, for automatic forfeiture of rights by prisoners based purely on what might offend public opinion but accepted that public opinion may have a role to play in the development of penal policy. The court also highlighted the evolution in European penal policy towards the increasing relative importance of the rehabilitative aim of imprisonment. The court accepted that the welfare of a child to be conceived was indeed legitimate but 'that cannot go so far as to prevent parents who so wish from attempting to conceive a child in circumstances like those of the present case, especially as the second applicant was at liberty and could have taken care of any child conceived until such time as her husband was released.' The Grand Chamber held that the policy as set out in *Mellor* placed an inordinately high 'exceptionality' burden on the applicants when requesting artificial insemination facilities. The Grand Chamber held that a fair balance between the competing public and private interests involved was not struck and that accordingly there had been a violation of Article 8.

This is a surprising but very positive result bearing in mind that the Dicksons had been unsuccessful at every previous stage. It remains to be seen what changes in prison policies and practices will result, but this case represents a real recognition in the European legal context of the rights not only of prisoners but also their partners. That said, all the media reporting of the decision in the UK subsequently has focused on the question of prisoners' rights and almost without exception the decision has been vehemently criticised. Indeed, Wilson (2007) writing in the Daily Mail called it a 'perversion of human rights', referring to Kirk Dickson as a 'jail thug', a 'wicked man', 'a moron' and 'murderous cretin'. From the point of view of somebody concerned with the rights of prisoners' partners, however, the decision is of the utmost significance and is to be warmly welcomed.

The *Dickson* case raises fundamental questions about the nature, impact and purposes of imprisonment, highlighting the ongoing process of interpreting the rights of prisoners and their families under the ECHR. More philosophically, and of potential significance for medical law, the case highlights the question of whether the State has a legitimate interest in regulating the creation of the children of offenders and appears to argue that unconceived children can be considered in legal decision-making.

Human rights, families and punishment

One of the core issues in both *Dickson* and the previous case of *Mellor* is the question of whether the right to procreate is lost as a collateral consequence of imprisonment, not only for offenders but also for their partners. It is indisputable that imprisonment removes or limits some rights of prisoners, but it is also indisputable that imprisonment does not automatically result in the forfeiture of all rights at the prison gate. The cases have explored *which* rights survive incarceration, and to what extent. Andrew Coyle reiterated that the classic formulation of prisoners' rights laid down in 1982 in *Raymond v. Honey*[43] and subsequently approved by the House of Lords in *Simms*[44] still applies and that its consequences are every bit as important as they were in 1982 (Coyle 2005); that is, in the words of Lord Wilberforce 'a convicted prisoner ... retains all civil rights which are not taken away expressly or by necessary implication'.

Professor John Williams (2002) challenged the loss of the right or opportunity to procreate as a 'natural consequence of imprisonment', and explored the court's reasoning in *Mellor* concerning the welfare of the child and the problems of guaranteeing equal treatment for male and female inmates. He contended that the explicit denial of prisoners' rights to have children appears to have no authority and contradicts Prison Rule 4. Of course, if prisoners were allowed conjugal visits then there would be no need to seek access to alternative means of conception, but it has been argued that the necessary privacy required could endanger the security of the prison. The same, however, is not true of artificial insemination.

These cases prior to the Grand Chamber judgment attracted a great deal of criticism. John Williams (2002) referred to the policy of the Secretary of State as 'the constructive sterilisation of prisoners' and argued that it does not provide the appropriate level of respect for prisoners' rights. He is dismissive of the court's reliance in *Mellor* on concerns that it would be inherently problematic to grant access to male inmates because then such access would have to be granted to women, arguing that 'to deny a right to somebody simply on the basis that another person may be denied it does not rationally further the cause of equal opportunities'. This view of the *Mellor* decision is shared by Owen and others, who refer to it as 'a particularly regressive approach to prisoners' legal rights', arguing that 'the level of deprivation which is legitimated by a sentence of imprisonment is considerably harsher [in the UK] than in other countries in Europe' (Owen *et al.* 2003). Indeed, these policies controlling access to artificial insemination have been referred to as 'the new eugenics' (Sutherland 2003).

The *Dickson* case differs from *Mellor* in that the application and the subsequent legal decisions explicitly addressed the wife's rights as well as the prisoner's. This is a significant development in the UK context, where the gendered impact of the regulation of prisoners' reproductive choices has hardly been recognised in the research literature. This can be contrasted with the situation in the US where writers such as Rachel Roth (2004) have assessed critically the impact of law and policy in relation to offenders and their partners, both in the prison context and also in relation to parole and probation, arguing that such policies have a disproportionately gendered impact on women. Research into the collateral consequences of imprisonment for prisoners and their families has documented the stigma and social exclusion of prisoners' family members, especially prisoners' partners.

As the research literature documents, it is tempting but too simplistic to argue that since they are not convicted prisoners themselves, prisoners' partners and family members retain all the same rights as other citizens. It is not easy to explain why the partner of a prisoner can lose her own right to found a family as a consequence of being married to a prisoner, since prisoners' partners have not been convicted and imprisoned. It is, however, well established in the criminological research literature that prisoners' family members are frequently treated as 'guilty by association', stigmatised and taking on a share of the 'spoiled identity' of the imprisoned family member. Both Gavin Mellor and Kirk Dickson were serving mandatory life sentences and it seems that the courts were drawing a distinction between those convicted of murder and those convicted of other offences.[45] As Judge Borrego Borrego pointed out, however, it seems bizarre that there is nothing to stop life sentence prisoners fathering children once they are released on licence, or even out on temporary licence. In the *Mellor* judgment, Lord Phillips cited the 1975 case of *X v. UK*,[46] a case concerning the denial of conjugal rights, and concluded that 'a lawfully convicted prisoner is responsible for his own situation and cannot complain on that account that his right to found a family has been infringed'. The courts appeared to be applying the same principle of voluntariness to prisoners' partners, offering an implied judgment on the wisdom or otherwise of having a relationship with a prisoner. In both of these cases the women married serving prisoners, and for both couples the judges referred to the fact that their relationships had not existed outside the prison. The policy suggests that the situation would be different if the marriage had existed prior to the period of incarceration. In the decisions in both *Mellor* and *Dickson* prior to the Grand Chamber judgment there is an undercurrent of negativity towards the women and the rejection of the possibility that they could provide a responsible and loving family environment for a child, reflecting a narrow view of the nature of the desirable and appropriate family. The decisions in these cases can be contrasted with the acceptance that sperm consensually donated by husbands who have subsequently died can be used to conceive despite the fact that the resultant child would not only be deprived of a father for a long period of time, as in the case of some prisoners, but for life. The courts appear to be displaying a sentimentalised view of tragic death and also adopting a perspective that it is better to have a dead parent than a parent in prison, even if that parent may well subsequently be released and then never reoffend.

The persistence of the welfare principle and reproductive autonomy

The future welfare of children to be conceived by artificial insemination was a key consideration in *Mellor* and was reiterated in *Dickson*. The adoption of these welfare considerations in this context reflects the principle embodied in Section 13(5) of the Human Fertilisation and Embryology Act (HFEA) 1990 which provides that, in relation to fertility services, a woman should not be provided with treatment services unless account has been taken of the welfare of any child who may be born as a result of the treatment (see Diduck and Kaganas 2006). The welfare of children has been of fundamental importance in legal decision-making in family law for many years; however, as Emily Jackson points out, the welfare principle enshrined in the HFEA 1990 differs from previous formulations such as that under the Children Act 1989 in that it purports to make a child's best interests relevant to a judgment made prior to that child's conception. It is clear from reading the judgments in *Mellor* and *Dickson* that a version of this welfare principle operates in the decision-making process of the Prison Service even though the HFEA itself does not apply in this context.

This application of a welfare principle to pre-conception decision-making in relation to assisted reproduction has been vociferously challenged and less convincingly defended (Jackson 2002; Laing and Oderberg 2005). In an insightful article challenging the primacy of the welfare principle, Emily Jackson (2002) argues that the inclusion of welfare considerations in the decision in *Mellor* was misguided and that to consider the future welfare of any child a prisoner may conceive is 'too speculative a consideration' in this context. In referring to the 'best interests of the unborn child' the Court of Appeal and the European Court in *Dickson* hit a complex philosophical issue head-on, that is, the 'non-identity problem', i.e. the person protected never benefits from this interpretation of their best interests because they are never born (Sutherland 2003). As Sutherland (2003) perceptively points out, whilst it is undisputed that the state has obligations to children already born, in terms of promoting their welfare and protecting them from harm, 'in denying the opportunity to procreate it is going a great deal further by policing access to parenthood itself'.

Intuitively one may argue that it is undesirable for someone who has offended to be allowed to conceive a child especially if they have offended against a child; however, it is difficult to convincingly argue that it is in a child's best interests not to exist. To disallow certain 'unfit' individuals from conceiving is, it could be argued, a eugenic principle, whereas child protection is a legitimate function of government. Medical lawyers such as Emily Jackson have expressed concern that in his judgment Judge Bonello was treating a child who has not yet been conceived as a person who has rights which are protected by the ECHR. As Emily Jackson points out in a brief commentary on the case (Jackson 2006):

> [T]o give an unborn, and indeed as yet unconceived child 'rights' under Article 8(2) runs counter to the assumption that foetuses, who do at least exist, do not have any rights under the Convention, so that, for example, lawful abortion is not incompatible with the right to life under Article 2. There would obviously be enormous practical difficulties if as yet unconceived children were to enjoy enforceable rights against public bodies.

The approach to procreation embodied in these cases sets a higher standard of proof of potential adequacy as parents for prisoners than most putative non-imprisoned parents usually have to attain before conceiving a child. Couples who cannot conceive naturally are subject to having to satisfy a higher standard of proof to become parents than those who can conceive without assistance, the prisoners' cases prior to the decision of the Grand Chamber confirming that such a standard also applies to detained prisoners. This 'policing of procreation' is experienced by non-imprisoned couples seeking fertility services, and has been vigorously opposed by critics who argue for greater decisional privacy or, as it has been termed. 'decisional liberty' (Jackson 2001, 2002; Harris 1998). Roger McIntire (1973) discussed that one does not require a licence to be a parent. By its very nature, the current process of the requirement of a formal application for artificial insemination facilities to be granted removes any possibility of decisional privacy. It could be argued that the fact of imprisonment removes any right to autonomous decision-making as to conception, in that imprisonment entails many manifestations of the loss of privacy; however, it is philosophically and legally difficult to justify the extension of this loss of autonomy to prisoners' unconvicted partners. This could be tenable if there were significant public resource implications, but it is important to distinguish artificial insemination from IVF and to consider whether, as is often argued, artificial insemination can be achieved as simply as by a prisoner handing over a filled receptacle to his partner during a visit.

It has been argued that 'we should each have the liberty to shield certain personal decisions from public scrutiny' (Jackson 2002). Perhaps most worryingly for those concerned with human rights, the decision as to whether the welfare test is satisfied is made not by clinicians acting under the guidance of HFEA but by an administrative department of the Prison Service. That is not to say that if doctors were to make these decisions the situation would be unproblematic. Jackson (2002) has vociferously challenged the application of any welfare principle in relation to the conception decision, arguing that individuals should have the right to privacy in relation to their decision to conceive. If the application of a welfare principle is to be accepted in relation to decision-making for prisoners' applications for artificial insemination facilities, then there are grounds for arguing that, it is inappropriate for this decision to be taken by civil servants.

In the current penal climate it is unsurprising that the courts chose to interpret the rights of prisoners and their families in this way (see Pratt *et al.* 2005). Even though the Dicksons have now won their case the judgment in *Dickson* fails to adequately grapple with questions of the rights of a non-imprisoned partner, and does not adequately analyse the complexities or relevance of a test based on the 'best interests of the child yet to be conceived'. Even if in the future it is held that the right to the opportunity to procreate continues to exist during a prison sentence, further questions need to be explored as to the precise nature and operation of such a right. This issue is nowhere near settled in legal, penal or philosophical terms.

Themes and conclusion

A socio-legal critique of these cases, which draws on the extensive published research literature on prisoners and their families, identifies a number of themes. First, although it is tempting to argue that there is a clear distinction between prisoners who are detained according to the due process of the law, and their family members, who are free citizens, this distinction is often blurred. When family members seek to engage with the prison system, such as by visiting, they then enter liminal space. Prisoners' families undergo 'secondary prisonisation' upon visiting: that is, they are within the physical and symbolic space of the prison and become defined and managed in relation to that, becoming, 'a peculiar category of prisoner', 'quasi-inmates, people at once legally free and palpably bound' (Comfort

2003). In legal terms, the rights of prisoners' family members are inextricably intertwined with those of prisoners, and the law responds to them in some situations as if they have a status which differentiates them from individuals who are not associated with prisoners. Second, current legal avenues for responding to the needs of prisoners' family members are not always appropriate or effective. Whilst Articles 8 and 12 of the ECHR are useful in some contexts, the response of the domestic courts in the *Wainwright* case demonstrated the difficulties of responding to prisoners' families through existing legal categories. In contrast, for example, with Germany, where the constitution guarantees an inviolable right of human dignity (Jones 2004), the humiliation experienced by Mrs Wainwright was difficult to recognise as in breach of any existing UK law. Third, where children are concerned the Children Act 1989, combined with the Human Rights Act 1998, offers great potential for preserving the rights of prisoners' children, although the cases illustrate the complexities of implementing the principle of the 'best interests of the child' in decision-making within the context of the current prison system.

Notes

1 For a discussion of the law in relation to consideration of the impact on the family and other personal circumstances at the sentencing stage, see Piper (2007).
2 *Hirst v. United Kingdom* (74025/01) Times, 8 April 2004 (ECHR). For a commentary on the case, see Foster (2004).
3 *R (P) v. Secretary of State for the Home Department, R (Q) v. Secretary of State for the Home Department* [2001] 1 WLR 2002.
4 [1972] 2 QB 407.
5 [1992] 1 AC 58.
6 For many examples of such challenges see Creighton *et al.* (2005).
7 [2003] EWCA Civ 744.
8 [2002] EWHC 1212 (admin.).
9 *Wainwright v. The United Kingdom* (12350/04) Judgment, 26 September 2006.
10 *Wainwright v Home Office* [2001] EWCA Civ 2081: *Wainwright v Home Office* [2003] UKHL 53.
11 [1897] QB 57.
12 For an interesting discussion of Article 3, see Foster, S. (2005).
13 [1979] Ch 344.
14 *Jones* (1986) 83 Cr. App. R., *Aitken* [1992] 1 WLR 1066.
15 See *R. v. O.* (contact: imposition of conditions) [1995] 2 FLR 124, pp. 129–30.

16 See *Re L* (a child) (contact: domestic violence) and other appeals [2000] 4 All ER 609, cited in Fortin (2003: 203).

17 *Re L* (a child) (contact: domestic violence) [2000] 4 All ER 609.

18 *Re G* (domestic violence: direct contact) [2001] 2 FCR 134.

19 This can, however, put mothers in a difficult position: see Hale J. (1999: 385).

20 A San Francisco Group has published a proposed Bill of Rights for Prisoners Children, which is worthy of further consideration. See San Francisco Children of Incarcerated Parents Partnership (2005).

21 For a discussion of the rights of a mother not to be separated from her child, see *Togher v. UK* (1998) 25 EHRR. CD99.

22 *R(P) v. Secretary of State for the Home Department, R(Q) v. Secretary of State for the Home Department* [2001] 1 WLR 2002.

23 [2004] EWHC 111 (Fam).

24 The lecture to the National Youth Advocacy Service by the Honourable Mr Justice Munby entitled 'Making Sure the Child is Heard', took place on 5 February 2004 and has since been published as Munby (2004a) and Munby (2004b). For further discussion of the views of the children of prisoners, see Brown *et al.* (2002).

25 *R (on the application of CD) v. Secretary of State for the Home Department* [2003] 1 FLR 979.

26 For a commentary on this case see Bailey-Harris (2003).

27 Some of the ideas in this section are explored in Codd (2007b).

28 *Dickson v. The United Kingdom* (Application no. 44362/04) Judgment, European Court of Human Rights, 18 April 2006.

29 *R (Mellor) v. Secretary of State for the Home Department* [2001] 3 WLR 533: *Dickson v. The United Kingdom* (Application no. 44362/04) Judgment, European Court of Human Rights, 18 April 2006. The film *Baby Juice Express* was released in 2004 and stars Nick Moran, more well-known for his role in *Lock, Stock and Two Smoking Barrels.*

30 *Goodwin v. Turner* 702 F. Supp. 1452 (W.D.Mo.[1988]); *Gerber v. Hickman* 273.F.3d 843 (9th Cir.[2001]).

31 I am grateful to Glyn White for bringing the *Sopranos* storyline to my attention.

32 This provision applies to male prisoners. As far as I am aware no similar applications have been made by female prisoners.

33 Note that the Prisons Ombudsman is not empowered to deal with complaints from families.

34 Letter from the Secretary of State, 28 May 2003, cited in the judgment in *Dickson v. The United Kingdom* (Application no. 44362/04) Judgment, European Court of Human Rights, 18 April 2006.

35 *Dickson v. The United Kingdom* (Application no. 44362/04) Judgment, European Court of Human Rights, 18 April 2006.

36 [2001] 3 WLR 533.

37 Article 8 appears to protect de facto family life: under Article 12, it could be argued that, following the decision of the ECHR in *X & Y v. Switzerland*, if the applicants are married they have therefore founded a family. See Williams (2002).

38 *Kirk Dickson, Lorraine Dickson v. Premier Prison Service Ltd., Secretary of State for the Home Department* [2004] EWCA Civ 1477: *Dickson v. The United Kingdom* (Application no. 44362/04) Judgment, European Court of Human Rights, 18 April 2006.

39 *R (Mellor) v. Secretary of State for the Home Department* [2001] 3 WLR 533.

40 He killed a man in a fight.

41 In support of this the applicants cited the judgment in *Hirst v. the United Kingdom (no.2)* (no. 74025/01) ECHR 2004.

42 *Dickson v. United Kingdom [2007] ECHR 44362/04* (Grand Chamber, 4 December 2007).

43 [1983] 1 AC 1.

44 [2000] 2 AC 115.

45 Other inmates serving long sentences have been granted access to artificial insemination on the grounds that their wives would be too old to conceive on their release, including in one case, a drug smuggler serving a 17-year sentence (see *Sunday Times* 2002).

46 (1975) 2 D&R 105, cited in the *Mellor* Judgment (supra).

Chapter 5

Imprisoned women and their families

I have been dismayed at the high prevalence of institutional misunderstanding within the criminal justice system of the things that matter to women and at the shocking level of unmet need. Yet the compelling body of research which has accumulated over many years consistently points to remedies. Much of this research was commissioned by government. There can be few topics that have been so exhaustively researched to such little practical effect as the plight of women in the criminal justice system (Corston 2007: 16).

The rise in the female prison population

The number of imprisoned women in England and Wales has more than doubled during the past decade (Commission on Women and the Criminal Justice System 2004) and a high percentage of imprisoned women are responsible for children (Prison Reform Trust 2007). This dramatic expansion in the female prison population has been mirrored in the US and women prisoners have been described as the fastest growing group of prisoners worldwide (Sudbury 2005). It is commonplace for articles on imprisoned women to begin with a summary of this drastic growth in the female prison population which, in the US, has heavily focused on the incarceration of women from minority ethnic groups and has been linked to mandatory minimum sentencing policies and the 'war on drugs' which has led to harsher penalties for drug users (Solokoff 2005; Golden 2005). Similarly, in Canada and Australia this growth has disproportionately affected indigenous women (Cameron 2001; Monture-Angus 2002). This increase has led to some of the most graphic manifestations of the impact of policy changes on families and communities in a number of jurisdictions including the UK and the US. The increased imprisonment of mothers has meant that many children face disruption in their living arrangements and emotional support networks.

This rise in women's imprisonment has been explained with reference to a lower custody threshold especially in relation to 'get tough' policies in relation to drug offenders. The increased shift towards the criminalisation of users of drugs such as heroin, cocaine and ecstasy has meant that, in both the US and the UK, more and more women have been swept into the imprisonment net. Whereas earlier policies focused on higher level importers and dealers, an ample body of literature has explored the impact of the 'war on drugs' as a 'war on women', especially women members of minority ethnic groups. Women who act as drug couriers (so-called 'mules') often receive substantial custodial sentences from the courts, as evident in the population statistics for Holloway and Styal prisons.

There has also been a dramatic increase in the use of short custodial sentences by magistrates: as Medlicott (2007) points out, quoting Carter (2004), the chances of a woman receiving a custodial sentence in a magistrates' court is seven times greater than it was in 1991 and there has been a general increase in severity in the sentencing of women. There is also anecdotal evidence which suggests that the 'domestic discount' where childcare was assumed to be a key characteristic in keeping women out of custody may no longer operate routinely to mitigate a custodial penalty. Rather, it appears more likely now than previously that courts adopt an assumption that a female offender is by implication a bad mother by reason of her criminality and her children would be better off without her. This approach is well illustrated by the report in my local newspaper of the woman who was jailed for three years for supplying heroin. She was described as having smoked heroin in the same room as her baby son and was found to have supplied drugs to an undercover police officer when in a main street with her infant son in a buggy. The tone of the newspaper article implies that the presence of her child aggravated the seriousness of the offence (Lancashire Evening Post 2006b). More research is needed, but in the current penal climate it seems too easy and too glib to suggest that women are at a lesser risk of custody because they have childcare responsibilities.[1] Ideologies of appropriate motherhood and appropriate femininity may mean that this only applies to some women, not all women.

Research into the families of imprisoned women

Despite the expansion of research documenting and analysing the experiences of women prisoners surprisingly little is known of their family relationships. Research into the experiences of prisoners' families has, with few exceptions, considered the heterosexual female partners of imprisoned men. In the research into prisoners' families and the collateral consequences of imprisonment, we often see women in roles as caregivers of others, that is, as female partners of imprisoned men; as imprisoned mothers; as carers for the children of both male and female prisoners. In the UK literature there is nothing, to my knowledge, which considers the needs and experiences of the male partners of female prisoners, and equally nothing on pre-existing same-sex relationships. Men are portrayed as prisoners, not outside caregivers, and although women are also portrayed as prisoners most of the research focuses on their role as mothers and does not explore other aspects of women's relationships. For example, female friendship may be an important source of support to incarcerated women, especially in the absence of a supportive male partner who can 'keep the home fires burning' as expected of female partners of imprisoned men. Again, however, this is not covered in the literature.

Frances Heidensohn argued in her pioneering research into women and crime (Heidensohn 1985), that women criminals are often invisible and when they do appear they are portrayed in narrowly stereotypical ways. Whilst women are visible in research as the female partners of imprisoned men, we know little of women prisoners' own families, and equally little of women as prisoners' mothers or as same-sex partners. Men who support female prisoners are equally invisible, although this may reflect the simple fact that men are less likely to care for female prisoners' children and less likely to remain involved with female prisoners. Women in prison are held further away from home than men and are more likely to have children under the age of 16 living with them at the time of their sentencing (Prison Reform Trust 2007). When men are imprisoned children usually continue to be cared for by their partners, usually mothers, but women have to rely on substitute caregivers, and this may pose difficulties for women in re-establishing or continuing relationships with their children after release (CASC 1999; Richards and McWilliams 1996). Although the number of women in prison has increased rapidly in the last decade, we have not witnessed a corresponding increase in the number of men supporting female prisoners from the outside. Although it is possible that there has been an increase, this population is almost invisible in the literature. Indeed, the literature suggests that instead of an increase in the number of men, for example, caring for the children of women prisoners, instead we are witnessing a burgeoning number of grandparents taking on caring responsibilities. Around one-third of female prisoners lose their homes during their sentence (Corston 2007). Men in prison are more likely to assume that women, be they partners or mothers, will maintain the house and family, so during their time in prison they are more likely to be concerned about themselves; in contrast women are concerned about life 'out there', particularly in relation to children (Home Affairs Committee 2005). Not much is known about imprisoned women's other caring responsibilities outside the prison, such as caring for parents and other family members, but clearly this could also cause distress and concern when women are unable to fulfil these obligations.

A range of ethnographic and sociological academic studies has documented and analysed the centrality of women prisoners' relationships both with family and friends outside prisons and also within prisons, and more recent work such as that by Kelly Hannah-Moffat (2007) has linked relationships to strategies of governance. Many of these accounts focus on women's relationships with children and in comparison less is known of relationships between women and their other family members and friends. For example, although there is a plethora of publications analysing and documenting the importance of prison visits for male prisoners, and the experiences of women visiting imprisoned men, we know little of who visits women prisoners, and their views and experiences are almost entirely unresearched.[2] Although feminist criminologists and penologists have challenged the silencing and invisibility of female prisoners, we still do not know who visits women, how often and what challenges they face. Similarly, where women do not have visits we do not know whether this reflects a lack of social support and absence of actual or fictive kin relationships. We also do not know whether, for women prisoners, letters and telephone calls can operate as a form of maintaining family contact of equal importance to visits, but for the 22 per cent of the female prison population who are foreign nationals, these may be the only means of keeping in touch (Prison Reform Trust 2007).

In terms of who visits, and how often, the study of women in Drake Hall conducted by Action for Prisoners' Families (Action for Prisoners' Families 2007) showed that the most common, and frequent, visitors to the women prisoners were described as 'all of [the prisoner's] children', followed by mothers and then partners.[3] A wide range of other family members, including cousins and in-laws, also visited, and some of the women described 'friends' as family members. Of the respondents, 86 per cent received visits from family members with nearly half receiving visits more than twice a month. Over a third of respondents, who received less frequent visits, felt that this was because the prison was too far away for the family to travel and financial constraints were also a matter for concern. The report identified particular difficulties in relation to poor transport links, with no scheduled bus services and a taxi to and from the prison from the station costing around £26.

The report also highlighted several areas of concern in relation to the procedures for booking visits; difficulties experienced by disabled visitors and dissatisfaction with the visiting experiencing ranging from concerns about security to the costs and unreliability of the vending machines in the visits area. Some prisoners reported that their visitors were often hungry, and suggested that there could be a canteen facility for visitors run by prisoners which would provide work opportunities and also a valuable service. The children's visits sessions were valued although the limited number of children allowed to participate each time was seen as too low; many women felt that the play facilities and activities were limited and that there should be more child-friendly facilities. Focus-group participants found it difficult that they had to remain seated and were not allowed to get up and play with their children, and argued that this was inconsistent with the prison's semi-open status. Several foreign national women received no visits and had to rely on telephones and letters for contact, which was stressful and distressing. There also seemed to be confusion about children's visits with one woman reporting that she had been in prison for nearly three months and had not known about them, and many women reported that their child had had to take a day off school sick to attend a visit.

Under half of the respondents said they had received information with regards to how to keep in touch with their family; how items could be brought in from the outside and how to get visiting orders for families. On being asked to rate their information needs in order of importance, the need for information as to how to maintain family relations was ranked as the most important. There was little awareness of prison-based or community-based support services such as the Prisoners' Families Helpline. This study is significant in that it provides at least some insight into imprisoned women's own views of visiting and also provides useful data in terms of participation in and frequency of visits. The responses of the participants also reflected dissatisfaction with the operation of the extended visits programme for prisoners' children, which clearly demonstrates that it is not sufficient for an institution simply to arrange extended visits without giving detailed thought, consideration and to some extent, investment, to rendering the environment suitable and the activities beneficial and enjoyable. This study emphasises the key role played by mothers in visiting prisoners, as could be intuitively predicted from what we already know about women's caregiving behaviour in relation to male inmates. It is significant because so little information on these aspects of the lives of women prisoners is currently available.

Relationships and the 'pains of imprisonment'

Autobiographical accounts of women's imprisonment reflect the central role of family relationships as a core concern, and also, along with loss of the privacy and prison discipline as the greatest source of stress and anxiety (Wyner 2003; Peckham 1985). The 'pains of imprisonment' (Sykes 1958) for women most often include separation from family and concerns especially in relation to children. Indeed, for women with children concern about their well-being as well as emotional stress and upset at separation are dominant features of the experience of imprisonment (Boudin 1998; Enos 2001). As one women poignantly said:

> The hardest thing about being out there doing your time is your children and who is looking after them and it goes through your head, you know, did he fall down and get hurt? Who is hugging him when he cries? (interviewee quoted in Maidment 2006: 99).

The 'pains of imprisonment' for women have been argued to differ from those experiences by men because women are more relational in their attitudes and needs (Bloom *et al.* 2004). A number of recent reports such as those undertaken under the aegis of the Fawcett Society, chaired by Vera Baird (Commission on Women and the Criminal Justice System 2004) and Baroness Corston (Corston 2007), have reiterated that women in prison experience prison differently from men, and have different needs. Research into criminogenic risk factors has found differences between the significance of criminogenic risk factors for men and women: for women, family and marital status, accommodation, companions and relationships, alcohol and drugs and emotional and personal factors were more significant for women than men. Women may have been coerced by men into crime, or experienced relationships which create pathways into crime. Worryingly, in the community motherhood seems to protect women from suicide but this is not the same in prisons, where women are either denied the chance of childbearing or experience separation from their children (Corston 2007).

The prison experience is significantly different for women as they are far more likely to be primary carers for their children. As Baroness Hale perceptively put it, in the context of the prevalence of women's self-definition in relation to familial roles, and also similar societal definitions, 'to become a prisoner is almost by definition to become a bad mother'; for a woman 'separating her from her family is the equivalent for many of separating a man from his job' (Hale 2005). For most women prisoners their incarceration was the first time they had spent any significant period of time separated from their children (Prison Reform Trust 2007). According to the Corston report 60 per cent of women in prison are single, compared with 17 per cent in the general population, and 34 per cent are lone parents. Caddle and Crisp (1997) found that 61 per cent of female prisoners were mothers living with their children before their sentence, with around a third having child under five. In contrast with the large numbers of women partners who care for the children of male prisoners, the children of women prisoners are far more likely to be cared for by other female relatives, as many as 25 per cent being cared for by grandmothers (usually maternal grandmothers) and 29 per cent by other family members or friends. Only 9 per cent of the around 18,000 children estimated to be separated from their mothers by reason of imprisonment are cared for by their fathers; 80 per cent of women in prison lose the support of their partners and only 5 per cent of prisoners' children remain in their own home once the mother has been sentenced.

Corston is particularly shocked by the finding of the Revolving

Doors Agency survey which found that of 1,400 first-time prisoners interviewed in Holloway, 42 per cent had no idea who was looking after their children. This statistic is indeed shocking but for several reasons. These women may not have known who was caring for their children. Conversely, they may have known but denied knowledge, or even denied having children, so as to protect the children from intervention by social services and child welfare organisations, for fear the children would be taken into local authority care (Smith *et al.* 2007). That women feel the need to conceal their children's whereabouts is indeed shocking, but perhaps also reflects the links between disrupted childhoods and imprisonment; 20 per cent of female prisoners in England and Wales have been in care themselves compared to 2 per cent of the general population (Commission on Women and the Criminal Justice System 2006).

Statistics published in 2004 demonstrated that women were held on average 62 miles away from their homes, in comparison with 51 miles for men, but this is likely to have changed due to the re-roling of Brockhill and Bulwood Hall to take men (Corston 2007). This is another example of women being treated as second-best in relation to men: that men's imprisonment is increasing the fact that women may need to remain closer to families appears to have been a consideration of no relevance. It is difficult to ascertain exact numbers of women who have children who receive visits, although Corston (2007) cites an earlier report of the Chief Inspector of Prisons which stated that only half of women who had lived with their children or been in contact prior to imprisonment had received a prison visit. Women are also less likely to have a family life to go out to which has continued throughout their sentence: women may try to hold the home together for men to come out to but the same does not apply to women and many come out to uncertain accommodation and family circumstances, especially as 30 per cent of women in prison lose their accommodation during their sentence (Corston 2007). Foreign national prisoners often experience higher levels of anxiety and stress due to the extreme problems of having family members, children and friends in other countries.

For foreign national women the problems of contact with family members may go beyond those experienced by non-foreign national women, and vary depending on the woman's 'home' country (Prison Reform Trust 2004). For example, women from some countries may fear that their children end up homeless on the streets, vulnerable to abuse and prostitution. One organisation, Hibiscus, has recognised that the Prison Service has come a long way in its response to foreign national women, who make up a higher proportion of the total female population than that contributed by foreign national men (HM Prison Service 2007). At the beginning of the 1990s Nigerian women formed a siginificant proportion of the foreign national women imprisoned in the UK for drug offences, hence the office of Hibiscus in Lagos, then through the 1990s Jamaicans became the dominant group. More recently, as a consequence of stricter anti-drug measures at Jamaican ports and stricter visa controls, more and more non-Jamaican women from the Caribbean are being detained (Prison Reform Trust 2004). Three-quarters of foreign national women in 2003 were serving sentences of four years or more, so the problems of separation from family members are not short-term temporary disruptions (Prison Reform Trust 2004). Family contact has been identified as one of three 'primary' problems in relation to foreign national prisoners in England and Wales, along with immigration and language (HM Inspectorate of Prisons 2006).

Imprisoned women and their children

It has been argued that women in prison experience high levels of role strain in trying to reconcile their role and status as mothers with their status as offenders who are denied the opportunities to engage in many of the socially-constructed expected behaviours inherent in mothering. The question of role strain is complex and in the US has been linked to race, sentence length and whether women had children living with them prior to their sentence, but a study of 109 women in a minimum-security setting discovered that women in prison experience significantly less role strain if they are allowed to engage actively in mothering activities, thus stressing the importance of the distinction between 'mothering as action' as opposed to simply 'motherhood as status' (Berry and Eigenberg 2003).

However, in contrast with the large number of studies assessing the experiences of male prisoners in relation to familial separation, visits and experiences of visiting, where women prisoners are concerned we know very little. Indeed, although autobiographical accounts demonstrate that separation from family and friends is one of the hardest aspects of imprisonment for women, we know little of who visits, how often and how both visitors and the imprisoned women experience these visits (Casey-Acevedo and Bakken 2002). Where women are mothers we know that visits from children can be a 'bitter-sweet' experience, providing the chance for much-needed contact but also provoking profound sadness once the visit is over, and re-emphasising the agonies of separation (Corston 2007). Visits may also reinforce women's feelings of lack of control over their children's lives, in that they may hear of problems their children are experiencing in relation to friends, schools, and even sexual experiences, and mothers may feel powerless to help (Casey-Acevedo, et al. 2004).

One study carried out in the US attempted to assess visitation at a maximum-security prison for women, collecting data on 180 women who between them averaged 22 months of incarceration (Casey-Acevedo and Bakken 2002).[4] During their imprisonment 79 per cent of the women received at least one visit from a friend or family member. Of those women who received visits the most frequent visitors were friends, both male and female, not family members. Some 61 per cent of the women who were mothers did not receive any visits from their children. After male and female friends, mothers were the most frequent visitors. In relation to children 158 women had 285 children between them. In contrast with other research, in this study just over half of the children had lived with their mothers prior to their imprisonment, with a higher proportion in foster care than estimated in previous studies (Beckerman 1989). However, this may reflect the fact that the prison studied was a maximum-security institution and the nature of the women's offending or previous criminal lifestyle could mean that, in contrast with research into local jails, a higher proportion of their children were already under some kind of child welfare supervision. Younger women were more likely than women over 33 to receive visits from their children; this might reflect that older women may be more likely to have older children who may choose not to visit. The relatively low number of women receiving visits from children may reflect the many purely practical challenges of visiting prisons a long way from home, and the associated costs. It may also reflect the relationship between the mother and the caregiver. That said, although inmates said they were sad after visits, the women looked forward to them, especially visits from children, and both prisoners and wardens believed that visitation was a positive experience (Kitzinger 1997).

However, research has also suggested a link between disciplinary adjustment by women in prison and visits from children. The same study (Casey-Acevedo et al. 2004) gave rise to a quantitative analysis which evaluated the impact on women's disciplinary behaviour of children's visits. This research question drew on earlier research by Holt and Miller (1972), who found that inmates who maintained contact with family members were less likely to commit disciplinary infractions, and conflicting research which found a link between visits and violent behaviour in the prison (Ellis *et al.* 1974). However, as pointed out by Casey-Acevedo *et al.* (2004), these studies focused only on men and their relationships with their wives and other adults, whereas their study focused on women and, specifically, on visits to mothers by their children. Casey-Acevedo *et al.* (2004) perceptively make the point that visits from their minor children are qualitatively different from visits from other adults and may have a more significance impact on mothers' behaviour, pointing out that

> the atmosphere in women's prisons encourages concern about children, and contact is expected and encouraged. Even women who did not have contact with their children prior to incarceration begin to show interest in their children when imprisoned (Casey-Acevedo *et al.* 2004: 420).

They concluded that the women who received visits had a higher probability of engaging in both violent and serious infractions in the prison. In contrast, women who did not receive visits were less likely to commit infractions and where they did they tended to be minor. This could imply that women who receive visits from their children experience profound strain and stress and also are less likely to become 'acclimatised' into the prison, in the sense that they are regularly being reminded that they have 'other lives' outside the walls. Casey-Acevedo *et al.* also point out that the emotional impact of visitation may lead to women either over-reacting to minor events or self-medicating with drugs or alcohol to cope with the emotional pain of separation. However, Casey-Acevedo *et al.* caution against the argument that visitation should be banned, as there are many other benefits, not least to children. From my own point of view, their work emphasises once more the centrality of the mother–child relationship for women prisoners and invites the development of new approaches and indeed a rethinking of imprisonment itself which does not by definition punish women and their children simultaneously.

The work of Casey-Acevedo *et al.* (2004) is significant because it is one of the few studies which specifically focuses on visitation. Other research has reiterated the double-edged nature of visits for women, especially from children, and also the dilemmas for women of desperately wanting contact with their children but not wanting them to see them in a prison environment.

Mothering from inside prisons has been the specific focus of research emanating from the US (see Bloom 1992; Baunach 1985; Enos 2001), but UK research has explored women's experiences of imprisonment quite broadly (Bosworth 1999) or has focused on the needs and experiences of particular groups of offenders, as exemplified in Wahidin's work on older female prisoners (Wahidin 2004) and that of Mary Corcoran (2006) on women political prisoners. The work of Sandra Enos (2001) is significant because unlike other research into the lives and experiences of imprisoned women, Enos focuses specifically on mothering. In many cases, mothers in prison must arrange and subsequently manage care of their children, unless of course their children are in local-authority foster care or, as is common in the US, being freed for adoption under the Adoption and Safe Families Act 1997 (Gentry 1998). Women try to continue as mothers of their children through their caretakers, although of course substitute caregivers also have a huge day-to-day impact on children. This creates conflict, especially where caregivers have stepped in prior to the period of incarceration either as a consequence of asking for help or as a consequence of believing that a mother is not appropriately performing her role; for example, when children are being neglected to due to their mother's criminal behaviour or substance abuse. In such situations not only are the caregivers looking after children and trying to influence their behaviour, but may also be attempting to influence the imprisoned mother. Many such informal arrangements emerge, involving negotiations amongst all concerned, and often, at least in the US, it is only when these informal arrangements break down or become unsatisfactory that formal child support services become involved.

Relationships between caregivers and imprisoned women vary and can be harmonious and also challenging for all concerned. Fathers in prison are visited more frequently by their children than mothers in prison. When mothers are in prison, the nature and quality of the mother–child relationship is heavily dependent on the quality of the relationship between the mother and their child's carer and visiting is unpredictable and sporadic. Mothers have to work harder at maintaining contact with their children than fathers and children in care rarely visit their parents in prison (Walker 2006b).

Another concern is that of demonstrating fitness as a mother (Enos 2001). Because this is linked to residence, or in many ways perceived 'ownership' of children, imprisoned mothers seek to prove that they are, or can be, good mothers. For imprisoned women, having arranged good, stable childcare may allow women to define themselves as 'good mothers' doing their best for children despite their imprisoned status, which tends by implication to bring with it the label of 'bad mother'. However, caregivers can be competent and experienced or, instead, incompetent and incapable, and where substitute childcarers are elderly, such as grandparents, then they may become exhausted. Similarly, where children go to prisoners' sisters, friends or other family members, caregivers have to cope with the strains of having extra children to care for when they may already have several children of their own.

As Enos demonstrates, the negotiation of caring is ongoing and, in her research in the US, reflected cultural differences and constructs of familial obligation. For women who are using drugs or living chaotic lifestyles prior to their incarceration, imprisonment can give them a form of 'time out' or breathing space in which they can try to rebuild or renegotiate a positive relationship with their children which may have come under challenge or even have been destroyed by the mother's previous behaviour. As Comfort (2007) argues, for women, imprisonment of their male partners can give women back some control over their lives, the prison acting as the only reliable source of help in an era of welfare cuts; in a sense the same can be said of prisoners' children, although because there is so little empirical research which has been carried out directly with prisoners' children it is difficult to argue whether this is the case or not. However, it seems intuitively uncontroversial to argue that the absence of a chaotic, unpredictable and perhaps unstable or erratic parent may allow children a period of respite, and allow women a chance to rebuild relationships in a limited and managed sphere without the day-to-day challenges of practical motherhood. That is not, and is in no way to be taken to mean, that imprisonment is to be advocated as a good method for rebuilding relationships; rather, that in some cases it can allow children respite and also enable mothers to identify their children as important to them.

In the US, levels of financial support vary but most states provide low levels of support for mothering (Ferraro and Moe 2003). When linked with figures on poverty in the state in which they carried out their study (Arizona) it is not difficult to see why some of the women explained that they had commit crimes in order to financially support their families; that is, not in contravention of the appropriate role as mother but in support of it. For some women, 'life was so arduous and precarious that incarceration was actually perceived as an improvement' (Ferraro and Moe 2003: 23), particularly for women living in abusive relationships. Another woman in their study perceived the prison as offering a better environment for her pregnancy in terms of healthcare. For some women, however (Enos 2001) they took the view that mothering in prison was impossible; that they maintained their status as a mother by reason of giving birth but could not, because of their incarceration, claim to have been mothering, that is, performing as a mother, while they were in prison. The expectations of being a 'fit mother' may be particularly difficult for imprisoned women to fulfil, as the nature of imprisonment limits opportunities for them to perform 'mother work' through which they could otherwise prove their abilities and commitment. This has been argued to amount to double punishment of women; that is, by holding women to standards of motherhood which it may be difficult for even for non-imprisoned mothers in the community to meet, women in prison also have their imprisonment used as evidence of 'unfitness' (Beckerman 1994).

Enos (2001) identifies this as one of the obstacles facing women who are engaged in legal challenges to regain or maintain legal custody of their children. The same challenges face women in the UK whose children are in local authority care: women in prison may need to 'prove' that that are 'good mothers' but the nature of imprisonment and the opportunities afforded to women do not make this easy and indeed it is sometimes impossible. This leads to challenges once women are released, not least of which is the social housing problem. If women are single and without children they are not a priority for the provision of social housing. However, without a stable address women may not be granted residence of their children (O'Brien 2001). It is important, however, to recognise that not all women who would like to have their children to live with them have the physical, emotional and other resources to provide appropriate care, and it is important not to over-romanticise women's own desires to have a 'real family' after their release, when due to substance abuse, mental health issues or other concerns in fact women are not able to provide a stable environment for their children.

Women prisoners who wish to 'mother' their children in a setting in which the opportunities for 'mothering' are limited face complex challenges. For women, criminal behaviour is inextricably linked to being 'bad' in one way or another. That is, being a 'bad girl', a 'bad mother' or a 'bad woman'. The dominance of these stereotypes of appropriate femininity have been documented in the literature from more than twenty years ago and more recently can be considered in conjunction with the research by Kelly Hannah-Moffat (2007) into how these ideologies of motherhood can become strategies of governance. Understanding mothering in prison cannot be separated from understanding the gendered dynamics and challenges of mothering on the outside. Women are assumed to be able to dispense love, care and resources for children, and in many ways to sublimate their needs and desires to those of their children in ways in which men are not. It seems contradictory that where women have offended for financial gain, in order to provide for their children, or have fulfilled gender expectations of supporting male partners or relatives in criminal enterprises, such as in the case of women who sell goods which have been stolen by their partners, or women who participate in their male partners' drug-dealing, these women find themselves then defined socially as bad women, and particularly as bad mothers. This is clearly seen in the profoundly negative reaction of sentencers to cases involving women who have committed criminal activities with their children present, or appropriated aspects of children's activities and goods as a 'cover' for their offending, as in the case of women who hide stolen goods in pushchairs while shopping, or buy drugs with their children present, or sell drugs from park benches while watching their children playing. That is not to seek to repaint these women as perfect women or even as 'good enough' mothers, but clearly some may be. The social reaction to female offending however, even over twenty years after the feminist challenges brought by writers and activists such as Pat Carlen and Chris Tchaikovsky (see Carlen *et al.* 1985), is still one which inextricably binds criminality together with gender to reassert the assumption that a good woman and a good mother is not a criminal.

Motherhood can exist as a means of prison management control of women, particularly where mothering activities are linked to extra privileges such as, for example, extended visits or family days. It can also operate as a site of resistance; as an identity for which women can fight and which allows them to retain some sense of themselves as women with lives outside the prison walls. While motherhood can clearly pose many difficulties and challenges for socially excluded women, especially those in prison, it can offer women a ground from which they can challenge structural and individual sources of oppression (Ferraro and Moe 2003). Motherhood in prison may lead to despair at separation from children but also promote hope and a sense that a woman's life is not over; that she is a valued person even if the only person viewing her in that way is the child. They can provide motivation and strength for women. Women can display photos of their children, and cards and letters, as a means of proclaiming that they have an identity and a life beyond that of merely being a criminal or a prisoner. The reiteration of motherhood also allows women to reassert their womanhood in an environment in which adult women are infantilised, referred to as 'girls' and treated rather as if they are faintly disobedient teenagers (Carlen 1983; Bosworth 1999; Carlen *et al.* 1985). To reassert an identity as a mother is to reassert one's status as a woman with adult responsibilities, even if one is not yet technically over the legal age of majority.

Family relationships can also provide for exchange and relationships between women prisoners. Although in the past some non-feminist researchers have been accused of being obsessed with women prisoners' (mainly sexual) relationships we know little as to the nature and processes of women prisoners' friendships amongst themselves. Peckham (1985) recounts in her autobiographical account how younger women kept food for her at mealtimes to make sure that by the time she got to the front of the queue that there was some left for her, as she was older and less likely to rush and push than the other much-younger women. Wyner (2003) discusses her cautious friendship with another woman developed during gardening. 'Family talk' or 'mother talk' can provide a shared verbal currency of exchange and friendship amongst women, many of the experiences of motherhood cutting across boundaries of difference.

Mothers and babies

The question of whether mothers should be allowed to have their young children with them in prison is not easy to answer, and prompts many further questions of, if so, for how long and in what conditions. At the time of writing, in England and Wales there were seven mother and baby units, and if it is judged to be in the baby's best interests then a baby may be allowed to stay with his or her mother up to an agreed maximum age. At New Hall and Holloway babies can stay with their mothers up to the age of nine months; at Peterborough, Bronzefield, Eastwood Park, Styal and Askham Grange the maximum is eighteen months. As was explored earlier in this book the precise timing of the separation is a matter for the discretion of the relevant prison-based panel. The justifications for endeavouring to allow women to keep their babies with them are based on research into the fundamental importance of bonding and attachment during a child's early years and is often linked to the work of John Bowlby (1946, 1973), who is most well-known for his work assessing the relationship between the mother and child as essential to a child's psychological and emotional development. Against this are the problems of children growing up in the restricted environment of a prison, where they may be exposed to women who have committed violent crimes and come into contact with behaviour, language and attitudes which would not be recognised as beneficial to a child's well-being. For example, some toddlers in prison have been reported to be using prison slang.[5]

In contrast with discussions in the UK about how long prisoners should be allowed to keep their children with them, and ways of ameliorating the worst aspects of the prison experience for babies, in many other countries it is more circumstance and custom which has led to assumptions that children go to prison with their mothers, sometimes up to the age of five or six, or sometimes even older (EUROCHIPS 2006). A recent report on women and their children in Indian prisons (Pandey and Singh 2006) has documented the serious problems raised by the presence of children. Children have to share the food supplied for their mothers; have to live in poor quality accommodation and may not have adequate facilities for education, recreation and medical care. In addition, they are cared for entirely by their mothers as there are no specially-trained staff available to care for the children. In some cases children as old as eight or nine find themselves living with their mothers in prisons in India in the absence of children's homes, although in Pandey and Singh's study of the 885 children living in prisons with their mothers, they were all aged under six, and half were under two. Alongside practical concerns go concerns in relation to the impact on the child in the future of being denied what the report's authors refer to as a 'normal environment' of a family life and instead are exposed to 'criminal elements' which may make a 'permanent imprint' on their outlook on life (Pandey and Singh 2006: 18).

In Jamaica, for example, there are no separate facilities for mothers and babies and until babies have to leave prison at the age of six months they live in the same dormitories as other prisoners (Henry-Lee 2005). Indeed, it is important to remember that the presence of children in prison with their mothers was one of the key issues addressed by the work of Elizabeth Fry, which, whilst controversial in many ways, went some way towards removing children from the damaging environment of the prison. Thus in many other countries, especially developing countries, research and campaigns focus more on removing children from prisons than on encouraging and enabling them to stay.

An interesting way forward is that of 'half-way houses' as are used in some European countries (EUROCHIPS 2006). Here the women live in community-based accommodation where they have to be locked in at night but which allows them to access prison education, training and support whilst their children are at nursery in a non-custodial setting. The challenge in relation to mothers and babies is to minimise the harms of separation but also ensure that the negative impact of the prison setting is minimised.

One of the longest-running initiatives is that of the Children's Home ('Mutter-Kind-Heim') in the Preungesheim Prison in Frankfurt, Germany, which celebrated its 30th anniversary in 2005 (Hessisches Ministerium der Justiz 2005). Having been initially built in 1975, the current Home was opened in 1998 (Glasser 1993; Douglas 1993; Boudouris 1996). Within the prison complex there are places for five mothers and their children in 'closed' conditions and for eighteen in 'open' conditions. The women in 'closed' conditions work within the prison complex during the day, and those in open conditions work outside the prison and return at 5pm. During the day the children are cared for by trained staff. After 5pm women in open conditions can leave the prison with their children until 8pm or, if appropriate care is arranged, the woman can herself go out again until 10pm.

Women, relationships and reoffending

In contrast with imprisoned men there is much less emphasis in official policies on the importance of family relationships in preventing women's reoffending. Indeed, it cannot necessarily be assumed that the same factors which can contribute to desistance in men apply equally to women. For men, much of the research demonstrates that a strong intimate bond, such as that with a spouse or stable partner, plays a central role in preventing reoffending, but men may play a significantly different role in female desistance than that played by women in relation to men (Leverentz 2006). As Laub and Sampson (2003) discovered, in their sample criminally-involved men married pro-social, non-criminal women who then increased their bonds to conventional life. In contrast, especially in urban America, the likelihood of a female ex-offender becoming involved with a non-offending man is much lower than that for a man coming into contact with a non-criminal woman.

In her interesting and thought-provoking study of forty-nine women who were, or had been, involved with a halfway house for female ex-offenders in Chicago, Leverentz (2006) noted how the regime of the house, with its emphasis on recovery, discouraged romantic relationships and also challenged the prevailing assumption that a partner with a criminal offending history could not necessarily be a pro-social partner. In contrast, she documents how for some couples a shared understanding and experience of offending could lead both of them into desistance, as sometimes happens with people recovering from addictions, thus supporting each other in their recovery. Leverentz also considered same-sex relationships, an aspect of the discussion of the links between relationships and desistance which has almost always been invisible in the research. Significantly, Leverentz also discussed the strategy of relationship avoidance adopted by 40–50 per cent of the women she interviewed, with some viewing this approach as temporary and others viewing it as more permanent. For these women who had been abused and whose relationships had indirectly or directly contributed to their offending, avoiding relationships was a way of avoiding the resultant strain. For some of these women, independence offered them a real chance of a non-offending life, although at first glance this runs counter to arguments such as that by Covington (2003) that women need relationships and connection. As Leverentz suggests, woman can find these relationships in a non-romantic form, particularly in recovery communities. This reflects, as perceptively identified by Leverentz, the difference between men and women in the relevance of relationships with the opposite sex in their offending; for women, in contrast with men, men often play a central role in women's offending and thus avoidance can become a strategy of prevention of future offending which, in this case, was encouraged as part of the therapeutic approach of the halfway house. It is important to reiterate that pro-social relationships are limited to those with no history of offending whereas in contrast Leverentz identified the value of mutual understanding and benefit through shared experience. Leverentz also argues that relationships are social processes and not static facts, which move and change over time.

This study is important as it illuminates the dominance of a particularly selective interpretation of the concept of pro-social relationships which is more visible in relation to criminal men than criminal women and also by implication stresses that the same assumptions as to the role of romantic relationships in desistance cannot be assumed to apply to women in the same way as men. Although in the UK the importance of relationships in encouraging desistance has been stressed again and again in relation to men, little has been discussed in terms of how women's relationships contribute to, or damage, the prospects of successful resettlement. Although women's lives are interpreted much more in terms of relationships than men's, this has not trickled through to work on desistance, and whilst a stable marriage may increase a man's chance of desistance the same cannot necessarily be said of women. Indeed, we hear little of the potential role of men in assisting in resettlement, whereas recent policy documents cast women in relationships with imprisoned men as co-workers in the process of release and successful re-entry. The research on women's lives after imprisonment is more limited than that for men (O'Brien 2001; Eaton 1993), and Maidment (2006) found that very few women in her study had supportive family relationships even prior to their imprisonment, as a consequence of sexual abuse by family members, dissolution of kinship relations on entering foster care and then the breakdown of family relations linked to entering prisons and other institutions. Some women, but very few, reported supportive intimate relationships as a major source of assistance through their prison term, in contrast with male prisoners as considered in much of the published literature. That said, for the small number of women she studied who had strong and supportive family networks these were 'an invaluable source of support at all stages of their criminalization, especially when it came to "making it" on the outside' (Maidment 2006: 115). These supportive family relationships were a major factor which differentiated those who successfully made the transition from prison to the community and those who continued to go back into prison and other institutions. For those, however, whose institutionalisation was longstanding the absence of family support and positive role models was significant. Thus, it is clear that family relationships are immensely important for female prisoners, but that family support is more likely to be in the form of support from mothers and other family members, with male intimate partners seeming less significant.

Thus in considering the families of female prisoners we see lots of contradictions. There is an emergent body of work on grandparent caregivers. In the US this has been linked to the impact of a combination of AIDS, the 'war on drugs' and subsequent increasing incarceration of women, and is most prevalent in African-American communities. There is not much data in the UK, in the same way as there is no real comparable data on the 'collateral consequences' of imprisonment for communities in the UK. Although sometimes in the 1950s and 1960s male prison researchers seem to have been obsessed with prison lesbianism far less is known about women in prison and pre-existing same-sex relationships.[6] We know that men often do not maintain relationships with imprisoned women, in contrast with Corston's comments about women 'keeping the home fires burning', but we do not know if this is what is done by women in relationships with imprisoned women. Do the same-sex partners of women prisoners support them, care for their children and visit? Similarly, women are often analysed in the prison context in relation to their relationships, sexual or otherwise, with other prisoners, and there is an ongoing debate in the US about whether the nature of women's relationships in prison is changing especially in the context of the gang subcultures which are so dominant in prison research on male prisons. Although not discussed in the same way in the UK, US prison research has considered dyadic 'couple' relationships between women and 'pseudofamilies' where groups of women take on identifiable, and sometimes named, family roles.

Conclusions

With the exception of imprisoned mothers, we know that relationships are important to women and loss of contact with family and friends seems to be a key 'pain of imprisonment for women' but there are huge gaps in our knowledge. For researchers such as myself who have been interested in women's imprisonment since it was commonplace for university criminal justice courses to omit to mention women entirely, it seems counter-intuitive to argue that not much is known about women prisoners' families. After all, it is tempting to think, that thanks to the research of Pat Carlen (1983), Mary Bosworth (1999), Barbara Owen (1998) and others, we know far more about the day-to-day lives of women prisoners. However, research into the 'outside the wall' aspect of imprisonment has focused on women caring for imprisoned men, and so subsequently very little is known about the families who are affected by women's imprisonment. There is thus a need for research into the diverse relationships of female prisoners, and an assessment of the processes by which men do care for women in prison, even if this number is very small. As it is, when we discuss the relationships of female prisoners this is constituted in the research primarily in terms of motherhood. Whilst this is indeed a central concern of women prisoners, it narrows the recognition of the scope of the many possible aspects of women prisoners' relationships. Even though feminist research has rendered visible the women partners of imprisoned men, and the problems faced by imprisoned mothers, we still only have a partial picture of the impact of the imprisonment of women. With the exception of the children of women prisoners, we have little idea of their other relationships. This demonstrates an ongoing androcentricism which continues to dominate, and which portrays women primarily in terms of their relationships with men, or as mothers.

Future research needs to recognise the many aspects of the relationships of female prisoners, and consider the collateral consequences of imprisonment in this context. For example, if the main carers for women prisoners' children are other women, then this gendered impact can be a core feminist concern. Alongside this goes the question of why men, even if they are in relationships with imprisoned women at their sentence, do not tend to 'wait around' and maintain the relationship. This may be linked to the stigma of being in a relationship with a female prisoner, or an interpretation of imprisonment as something which terminates a relationship. Men may not be able or willing to work hard to maintain contact in the face of challenging circumstances, especially as women are often held a long way from home. When men are working it may be hard for them to take time off work to visit. In contrast with the romanticised image of 'standing by your man' there is no equivalent of that expectation in terms of 'waiting for your woman'. Indeed, caring for the children of a female prisoner, or maintaining a monogamous relationship in their absence, may be interpreted as 'unmanly' and the absence of the woman may be interpreted as an opportunity to escape familial ties and obligations and live a single life again, unfettered by the demands and expectations of a partner or children. Since women prisoner's children are less likely to be cared for by their fathers than male prisoners children are to be cared for by their mothers, the male partners of imprisoned women may view the sentence as an opportunity for a free life without responsibilities. The other possibility, which again has not really been explored in the literature, is that if female offending is often linked to male offending, and imprisoned women are more likely to be in relationships with criminal men than male prisoners are to be with criminal women, then the male partners may be unable to offer support simply because they are incarcerated themselves.

Notes

1 The argument here is not that women are never treated more leniently due to their childcare responsibilities, but that this should no longer be

considered as a routine, strong factor for women in influencing sentencing decisions. For a discussion of the legal situation, see Londono (2007).

2 One of the very few pieces of research on this topic is that conducted by Casey-Acevedo and Bakken in the US (2002).

3 The responses from twenty-nine female prisoners from Drake Hall were collected and a focus group was conducted within the prison involving twelve respondents, ten of whom were white; one black and one mixed race.

4 The study was based on 222 women but for forty-two women visitation data was missing.

5 See the judgment in *Regina (P) v. Secretary of State for the Home Department and another: Regina (Q and another) v Secretary of State for the Home Department and another* [2001] EWCA Civ 1151, [2001] 1 WLR 2002.

6 One exception to this invisibility can be found in Maidment (2006) which mentions a woman interviewed after leaving prison, who describes the positive support she receieved from her non-imprisoned same-sex partner and says she could 'never have done it without her' (Maidment 2006: 118).

Chapter 6

Supporting prisoners and their families

Having spent most of the preceding chapters documenting the manifold negative consequences of imprisonment for families, and the mixed response of law and legal mechanisms, this chapter offers an opportunity to adopt a more positive note by assessing good practice in supporting prisoners and their families and suggesting strategies for challenging the selective visibility of families in policy-making.

Sources of support for families

Support for prisoners' families can be formal or informal, direct or indirect. The partners and children of prisoners often receive practical, emotional and financial help from their relatives and friends although such support is not automatic and where the offence has been intra-familial or has harmed the community the offender's immediate family may be shunned. The same can happen where the offence has been of a shocking nature, such as sexual offending against children: previous friends may withdraw their friendship and relatives may withdraw their support. In contrast, relatives, friends and neighbours may 'rally round' and help families cope by providing babysitting and childcare during visits; providing transport to and from prisons; providing money including helping with bills and rent or mortgage payments and help with dealing with official agencies.

The support provided by relatives, friends and communities can be immensely important in enabling a prisoners' partner to cope with the sentence. In earlier decades the probation service played an important role in supporting families of prisoners (Morris 1965) but shifts in penal policies and changes in the role and responsibilities of probation officers away from work with 'uncoerced clients' towards a new conception of officers as 'offender managers' has meant that prisoners and their families are dependent increasingly on not-for-profit or voluntary sector organisations for information, support and assistance. Beyond the immediate help which can be provided within families and communities, direct support for families can be provided 'by family members for family members' in support/self-help groups. Prisoners' family members receive different support and help from a range of sources sometimes including faith-based organisations such as churches and religious groups (Braman 2004).[1]

Support and self-help groups

Most help given to prisoners' families is currently provided by organisations within the not-for-profit sector. Since the 1960s a number of support or self-help groups have evolved, usually from small groups of women meeting together on an ad hoc basis to share their experiences and offer mutual support. Some of these groups are specifically aimed at helping prisoners' families, whereas others may focus on particular kinds of social problems where imprisonment is common: for example, ADFAM provides information and support to prisoners' families as part of its work in relation to drug dependency. Other groups focus on offenders or the criminal justice system more broadly, but offer help to families as part of their work.[2] As will be explored further later in this chapter, most participants in these groups are, and from their inception have always been, women, who support not only their own imprisoned family members but also other families (Codd 2002; Howarth and Rock 2000; Condry 2007).

In recent years many of these non-statutory not-for-profit organisations have begun to work jointly with prisons to develop services and projects for families, such as children's visits. For example, POPS (Partners of Prisoners and Family Support Groups), based in Manchester has been established for over fifteen years and is a good example of the growing importance of 'third sector' organisations working in partnership with official agencies and institutions. It began as a support group established by and for the partners of prisoners, and now has a number of paid staff and runs visitors' centres in a number of prisons in the North/West, working in partnership with the Prison Service. Although in the beginning there was some suspicion of the POPS staff as being 'on the side of the prisoners', this relationship seems to have improved and prison staff recognise the benefits to them of POPS undertaking responsibility for dealing with queries from families which would have previously taken up officers' time (POPS 2003).

Qualitative research with members of such groups has identified the many benefits of membership (Condry 2007; May 2000; Codd 2002). Family members can draw on the experience of others who have been in the same situation, and this can be especially useful in the early days of a sentence when partners may not know how to obtain relevant information, how to claim benefits and assisted visits, what prison rules are, and many other issues. Since lack of information is a real concern of prisoners' partners, support groups can help family members access other agencies who may be able to help. The groups provide not only practical but also emotional support and an environment which, to families experiencing social stigma or fear of stigma, may feel like a genuinely safe space in which it is acceptable to express emotions and concerns to others who will not judge. As one participant in a qualitative study said, 'it's like a family' (Codd 2002). Support groups can also empower family members to maintain a positive identity when their own social status and identity may have been tainted by their relationship with a prisoner. In an earlier piece of research I suggested that my qualitative interviews with a number of older prisoners' partners had indicated that, in the context of the social, gendered rules and expectations about appropriate female caring behaviour, family members felt that through their involvement in a support group they could maintain a positive female identity as a giver of care and not as a recipient, and thus maintain a positive gendered identity as a women. In contrast, research by Condry (2004) suggested that the women she interviewed were already heavily involved in caregiving, sometimes to an extreme and burdensome extent.

For many support and self-help groups operating in the UK funding is a constant source of worry and uncertainty. Their role, however, can be of fundamental importance, and as has been discussed, some prison visitors' centres are managed and staffed by members of self-help groups. Such groups offer advice, support and sometimes practical help. Such groups can be especially valuable for families of offenders who feel stigmatised as a consequence of the offending, as instead of being ostracised and not being accepted, all the family members are experiencing similar difficulties. Rachel Condry (2004, 2007) has explored the importance of the role played by one now defunct group, Aftermath, in assisting prisoners' family members to cope with the trial and subsequent sentence, and also to cope with the challenges of maintaining a positive self-identity and coping with stigma. These groups, run by and for families, can provide a range of services and also encourage social activities for parents and children, including Christmas parties and day trips.

These organisations clearly have the most experience and expertise in helping families, but there are, of course, limits to the services that voluntary agencies can provide, and not all families seek the help of a support group. Some commentators are uneasy that these organisations are having to assume responsibilities which are arguably the functions of the public sector (Codd 2007a). Recent policy initiatives have done little to demonstrate a commitment by state agencies to helping prisoners' families (Mills and Codd 2007). For example, the Reducing Re-offending: National Action Plan includes 'Children and Families' as one of seven pathways to support the rehabilitation of offenders (Home Office 2004), but was criticised as a 'missed opportunity for positive change' as it failed to tackle the chronic lack of services and support for prisoners' families (Action for Prisoners' Families 2004). It did not provide any additional resources to maintain and strengthen family relationships or meet the needs of prisoners' families nor encourage families' potential resettlement role. Instead, the plan focused on existing available help for prisoners' children such as Sure Start and Connexions.[3] These programmes are not specifically designed for prisoners' children and at the moment provision of Sure Start schemes varies nationally. This kind of approach is of little relevance to those prisoners and families who do not have children. It also suggests that the intention of such proposals is neither to support families through the sentence nor to reduce reoffending by ex-prisoners by strengthening their family ties, but to prevent future criminality amongst prisoners' children. The plan does not address the issue of statutory responsibility for prisoners' families. As in many areas of social policy in recent years, it appears that partnership and joint working between the public and not-for-profit sectors will continue to dominate practice and, in a policy speech to the Prison Reform Trust in 2005 the then current Home Secretary, Charles Clarke, reiterated the key role to be played by voluntary sector agencies in relation to prisoners and their families (Clarke 2005).

Although published research has identified the fundamentally important role played by support groups, many prisoners' family members do not join such groups, partly because family members do not know about such groups or they do not know that some groups are national in their scope (Codd 2002). At a time when family members are feeling alienated, confused and vulnerable it can be of immeasurable assistance to be able to discuss the situation in a non-judgemental setting. Support groups maintain that their strength lies in shared experience. That said, in some groups more and more members are developing professional skills in, for example, counselling. Rachel Condry's (2007) work has discussed the role of support groups in relation to identity. In the support groups the role of gender is highly visible: most members of such groups are the female partners of male prisoners, and therefore in addition to caring for their male partners they also care for other female partners (Codd 2002).

In the national arena, Action for Prisoners' Families provides an active campaigning voice, and has undertaken valuable research into the needs of families. Action for Prisoners' Families is the main 'umbrella' organisation working on behalf of the family members of people in custody in England and Wales, with Families Outside fulfilling a similar role in Scotland (Loucks 2004). Action for Prisoners' Families co-ordinates the free Prisoners' Families Helpline, launched in July 2003, which is run by a consortium including POPS and the Ormiston Children and Families Trust. Action for Prisoners' Families has created an annual awards programme, the Daisy & Tom Awards, which recognises and rewards prisons for initiatives that lead to significant improvements in family ties. Action for Prisoners' Families is also a member of EUROCHIPS, the Europe-wide network working on behalf of children separated from a parent by imprisonment, which has regular conferences and which, amongst other activities, encourages the dissemination of good practice in working with the children of prisoners (EUROCHIPS 2006). The launch of the national helpline for family members marked an important milestone, and Action for Prisoners' Families provides a focal resource for those seeking information and assistance.[4] However, the focus of Action for Prisoners' Families on prison-based programmes and initiatives as exemplified by the Daisy & Tom Awards has led to criticism (No More Prison 2006).

Broad-based not-for-profit agencies

Some not-for-profit organisations focus specifically on prisoners' families whereas others have a broader criminal justice or prisoner-focused remit. A good example of this latter kind of organisation is the Criminal Information Agency, based in Liverpool, which offers many services to those who have been convicted of a crime or served a prison sentence. Not only do they staff a 24-hour helpline but they have an outreach team working in schools and communities; have teamed up with an insurance broker in order to offer insurance to ex-offenders; can recommend a mortgage broker who could help an ex-offender get a mortgage, and can also recommend solicitors. They also have a comprehensive and useful website.

Prison-based initiatives

Families may also receive support, or family relationships can be preserved or promoted, by means of prison-based initiatives.[5] Some such initiatives specifically focus on families and contact during the sentence, whereas other schemes, such as parenting courses, have their focus on relationships after the sentence. Some schemes, such as the activities of Relate in prison, aim to maintain and develop family relationships for humanitarian and relationship-based reasons whereas others reflect more directly the research evidence which links strong family ties to a decreased risk of recidivism after release. Murray and Farrington (2006) discuss evidence-based programmes for prisoners' children, and point out that it is important that the effects of imprisonment be isolated and separately identified from the effects of other forms of social exclusion. They then hypothesise that if certain links were found then certain related initiatives should be developed. However, they do not identify or discuss any specific programmes.

Reading projects

The DfES has funded several reading-based projects involving prisoners and their children under the auspices of their work on offenders' learning and skills. These projects can also benefit children, as sharing books has been linked to children's language development and later educational progress (Wells 1986). Offenders' learning and skills are linked to improved prospects of employment after release, and to reducing reoffending. Schemes may involve book-sharing, which may also include tapes of inmates reading the stories along with a personal message, and may be run in conjunction with librarians based both locally and also in the prison library (Newnham 2002). One of the most well-known reading-based projects is the Big

Book Share (BBS). This scheme aims to enable parents in prison to contribute to their children's reading development, to enable parents to play an important part in family life outside prison and to build closer links between families of prisoners and public libraries. The scheme is co-ordinated by The Reading Agency and has evolved from a pilot phase run in HMP Nottingham in 2000–2 to seven prisons and, more recently, to at least fourteen involving pilot and associate projects. The focus has been on partnership working between libraries and prisons, in conjunction with publishers. The BBS encourages imprisoned parents to contribute to their children's reading development. Children's librarians run sessions in prisons during which prisoners can discuss, then choose, childrens books which either they or a librarian can read on tape for their children. Prisons also run family visit sessions at which prisoners can give books and tapes to their children. The most recent phase of the project aims to focus on work with the whole family, and to develop patterns of library use and support when offenders leave prison.

The Reading Agency publishes a handbook and other resources for use by those involved in running the scheme and also provides training. Evaluation has been integral throughout. The range of positive outcomes has included improved opportunities for prisoners to connect with their families and improved communications between them, increased parental awareness of children's books and libraries and increased parental confidence in choosing and reading books and in making up stories. Amongst other outcomes the projects have helped to improve the literacy skills of the prisoners involved and have helped prisoners develop increased social and interpersonal skills. The evidence reflects enjoyment by both prisoners and their children. This and other linked reading schemes offer benefits on a number of levels, both in terms of literacy for offenders and their children and also in reinforcing family contact.

A possible related effect follows from increased awareness of public libraries, as public libraries usually hold information on a range of issues including welfare benefits and support groups. Thus, increased awareness of libraries by family members may lead to increased access to information and also access to electronic resources via open-access IT facilities. This would allow prisoners' partners in particular, who may not be able to afford IT facilities at home, or who feel that they do not possess the relevant skills, to access the range of useful web-based resources for family members including websites such as that of Action for Prisoners' Families but also bulletin board sites such as Prison Chat UK.

The BBS is probably the most well-known, but a number of other projects have developed incorporating reading, creative writing and discussion of books, and the Literacy Trust offers a valuable overview of these, pointing out that, in the words of one prisoner, books are harder to obtain in prison than heroin (Literacy Trust 2006).

'Storybook Dad' and 'Storybook Mum'

The award-winning 'Storybook Dad' scheme, which resembles schemes such as 'Aunt Mary's Storybook' run in the US, has been successfully implemented in England at a number of prisons following its development at HMP Dartmoor in 2002.[6] The scheme does not simply involve a prisoner reading a story onto a tape for a child. Prisoners are recorded telling the story, which is recorded then downloaded onto a computer for editing. A fifteen-minute story may lead to three hours of editing time. During the editing process sound effects and music are added, mistakes are edited out, and the final version is put onto a CD. The editing process means that prisoners who do not read well, or who do not read at all, can still produce the CD, since prompts and help from mentors can be edited out. HMP Dartmoor now has two editing suites, and the additional benefit is that some prisoners can be selected to train as editors and gain skills and qualifications in sound and audio production. Other prisons can utilise the editing expertise available at Dartmoor, by recording stories using a minidisk recorder and a microphone, with the recordings being sent to Dartmoor for editing.

At the time of writing, more than 1,700 prisoners had taken part and the programme was running in more than twenty-five prisons. Due to the expansion of the scheme and the growing numbers of prisoners participating, other prisons are now building editing suites and carrying out the editing process. More recently, the programme has included women's prisons under the name of 'Storybook Mum' (Kirsch 2005). From its inception the scheme has sought feedback to monitor its impact, and identifies many benefits including prisoners developing self-confidence, recognising the value of reading and storytelling for children, improved self-esteem as a parent and happiness that family links are being maintained. Some prisoners choose to write their own stories, which can lead to IT skills, a sense of achievement and improved writing skills. Parents involved in any aspect of the programme may wish to develop their own literacy and creativity further, or develop their parenting skills, and thus seek greater involvement in prison education and activities.

For children, the scheme can confirm their importance to the absent parent and challenge the problems of separation. They are encouraged to engage with storytelling and develop their imagination. Since the CD is a permanent medium they can play it again and again whenever they want to, and may be proud of their parent who has made it for them. More research is needed into the scheme, especially in relation to resettlement outcomes, but feedback from prisoners, partners and children has, on the whole, been very positive. Such schemes offer a positive contribution by the imprisoned parent to the family, offer a direct link between prisoners and their children, does not raise security issues for the prison and also have significant linked benefits for prisoners in terms of the development of literacy and parenting skills. It may also encourage children to explore books more, and encourage them to read.

The potential role of books in the lives of prisoners' children is significant, and is reflected in the attendance of representatives of 'Bookstart' for young children at 'Grassroots Family Days' in Lancashire. Books may provide a means of contact between imprisoned parents and children, as in the storytelling and book-sharing projects, but may also enable children to cope with the stresses and anxieties of imprisonment. Their experiences have been likened to those of grieving and the positive role of books has been identified (Hames and Pedreira 2003). A number of books are available for children of all ages which deal with aspects of criminality and imprisonment. These can be useful for prisoners' children in helping them to cope with and understand the situation, and can also be useful in school settings to develop an understanding and awareness of imprisonment more generally.

Time for Families

Time for Families runs education programmes for those who find their relationships with their partners, their parenting skills and their family budgets adversely affected by their custodial sentences. The courses give hope to prisoners and a future of stability to their families on release.' The charity works, or has worked, in around twenty prisons and run accredited relationship education programmes which include discussion not only of emotional and interpersonal relationships but also practical relationship concerns such as budgeting, debt and money. Their course work is supported by long-term mentoring.[7]

Relate

Since 2002 Relate has been working in three prisons, Ashwell, Acklington and Winchester, running workshops, and they also have a video. They offer a range of prison-focused courses which can be made available, including a course called 'Reconnect' which aims to facilitate the successful return to a relationship after release. Relate also offer a workshop, 'Inside Out' which lasts a day and which prisoners and their partners undertake together, and a course focused on helping prisoners' partners to reduce the harmful effects of prison on their family, focusing on children.

Parenting courses

Reading the literature, especially on prisoners as parents, it is tempting to assume that when a person is imprisoned they lose responsibility for the care of dependent family members such as children. In one sense this is true, in that they no longer reside with their children and are not directly concerned in their everyday lives, not having to get them up in the morning, get them ready for school, and so on. However, in most cases imprisonment does not stop somebody being a parent and viewing themselves as a parent: they are simply not able to undertake all the activities and responsibilities of a non-imprisoned parent. Parenting classes are available in many prisons and most youth offending institutions (Jarvis *et al.* 2004) and are also common in other jurisdictions (Pollock 2002). These appear to have positive results in the sense that the participants have acknowledged changes in their attitudes to parenthood and parenting over time and appear to have retained the information learnt (Jarvis *et al.* 2004; Dennison and Lyon 2001). These courses run not only in male but also female prisons. These course are of especial significance where, as in the case of many prisoners, the prisoner him- or herself has not grown up in a supportive and loving home environment.

The work of Jarvis *et al.* (2004) offers an illuminating case study of the methods and impacts of a parenting course in one youth offending institute (YOI). They evaluated the 'Parentcraft' course run at Aylesbury YOI, which ran for sixteen weeks of three-hour sessions, leading to a validated Open College Certificate, depending on the level and type of assessment undertaken. The significance of the qualification is not to be underestimated as for some prisoners it may be the first qualification which they have ever achieved. The course included consideration of contraception and sexual health, pregnancy and birth, child development to the age of five, the role of adults in supporting child development, listening to children, behaviour management and parental responsibilities. Many of the young offenders were fathers themselves. The course also addressed the relationship between a father and the child's mother.

The research discovered that many of the young men knew little about child development and the fundamental role of adults in encouraging children's development. Many were surprised by what they learnt; as one young man said, 'I didn't know kids were so clever' (p. 24). The course looked at the importance of play and encouraged the students to play with toys themselves and to think about how these toys could be used with young children. Many of the young men had limited memories of ever having played with toys and games as children themselves, and so they needed 'hands on' practical experience of how to play and what to play with. Similarly in relation to the use of books in the Aylesbury project, it was important for the young men to engage with books, using them and practicing telling stories. The course raised many issues for the young fathers, including the thorny topic of masculine identity and the showing of affection; for some young men, childcare is seen as a 'feminine' activity. The course encouraged participants to consider the points of view of other people, including their children. Although there was no guarantee that the students would put what they had learnt into practice, the young men also learnt positive discipline and behaviour management strategies, in contrast to the violent discipline which many of them had experienced as children. It is important to note that there was explicit recognition in the course of the diversity of conceptions of what it means to be a father and the emphasis was on sharing experiences and opinions rather than on promoting one view of appropriate fathering. As in previous studies, such as those by Evans (2002) and Boswell and Wedge (2001), the participants appreciated the emphasis on sharing, stressing that it made them feel 'human' (Evans 2002: 119). These courses have been shown to affect attitudes and some partners of men who have undertaken these courses have reported positive effects (Boswell and Wedge 2001).

Of course, parenting courses are not a 'magic wand' and it has been argued that there needs to be more follow-up after release since, although ex-students on such courses have reported good intentions on leaving prison, Dennison and Lyon (2001) found that six months after release some were back in custody and some had limited child contact (Jarvis *et al.* 2004). The Aylesbury evaluation discussed by Jarvis *et al.* (2004) provides an insight into how such a course is run and the relative strengths and weaknesses. The benefits of these courses are multifaceted and include potentially improved literacy for both prisoners and their children where reading or journal keeping has been involved; greater intimacy between parents and children; and improved interpersonal skills.

One of the most well-known initiatives is the accredited 'Family Man' course developed by Safe Ground alongside their 'Fathers Inside' programme. 'Fathers Inside' focuses on parenting; Family Man focuses on relationships. The 'Family Man' course is now running in many institutions. The courses utilise drama, role play, storytelling and video and were developed with inmates at three prisons. The courses are skills-mapped into the adult literacy, key skills and life skills curricula. After being tested at one prison the materials were piloted at nine other prisons (Halsey *et al.* 2002) with staff being given materials allowing them to deliver the course. The prisoners involved in the development reported positive outcomes, as did those involved in the trials. The use of drama and the video was important because it made the course accessible to all regardless of literacy and the prisoners reported feeling that they had a better understanding of family relationships and parenting; that they felt more committed to their families; that they had developed improved team working and communication skills; greater understanding of the needs and perspectives of others; and more positive attitudes to education. Some prisoners felt that a greater awareness of others, and how they may be affected by offending could have a positive impact on offending behaviour.

It is interesting to note that family members confirmed many of these outcomes and effects were still in evidence three to four months after the courses were attended. While not specifically working with family members, the course can have a clear positive impact on families and may also go some way towards lessening the anxiety felt by family members about how things are going to be after release, although this is pure conjecture. For families under strain, or where the offender's previous behaviour has not reflected a positive commitment to family life, the course may signal a new determination to undertake a new identity and to be a better partner or father. Parenthood can offer an opportunity for offenders to develop a new, non-offending identity and offer a prompt for positive change.

Prison visits programmes

Prison visits are the lynchpin of contact between prisoners and their families, and provoke joy and unhappiness in almost equal measure.

They provoke joy at being – briefly – reunited with a parent, partner, child or friend and also anxiety, stress and sometimes unhappiness prompted by, for visitors, difficult travel arrangements, complex prison policies, or simply an unhappy or difficult meeting with the prisoner. Little, however, is known of prisoners' experiences of visits.

Visits have been linked to positive resettlement outcomes, such as an increased likelihood of a job or accommodation after release, although one should be cautious in asserting that there is a direct causal relationship (Mills and Codd 2007; Niven and Stewart 2005a, 2005b Shafer 1994). They may act as an indicator of a resourceful, strong support network (Niven and Stewart 2005a; Shafer 1994). The 2003 Home Office resettlement survey found that those who received at least one visit during their imprisonment were more likely to have accommodation and employment arranged on release, which may partly explain the lower reoffending rates among those with active family ties. The chances of having accommodation arranged on release were nearly three times greater for prisoners who received family/partner visits during custody. The likelihood of having an education, training or employment (ETE) place arranged on release was more than doubled if a prisoner had received at least one visit from a family member or a partner, and the frequency of visits also increased the likelihood of positive ETE outcomes. Of those receiving visits at least once a month 40 per cent had ETE arranged in comparison to 27 per cent of those receiving visits less often (Niven and Stewart 2005a). As the authors of this study conclude, 'efforts to improve resettlement for prisoners might be facilitated through more attention to the ways that partners and families can more effectively participate in this process' (Niven and Stewart 2005b: 23).

However, the use of visits as a measure of strong family ties (Niven and Stewart 2005a, 2005b) should also be treated with caution (Mills and Codd 2007). These studies have focused on frequency or number of visits, rather than adopting a qualitative assessment. There are many reasons why families do not visit and it is not easy to equate a lack of visits with a lack of family support. For example, if a prisoner decides to 'do hard time' for the sake of his or her family as he or she does not want them to experience the stress of visiting or to see him or her incarcerated, this may be the consequence of a profound commitment to the family. Prisoners whose families live a long way away from the prison, or prisoners from abroad, may not receive visits because of practical and financial considerations but will receive supportive letters (Niven and Stewart 2005b). There has been little research on the meanings and impacts of non-visit contacts for prisoners in the UK, although there is a wealth of anecdotal evidence in support.[8]

Visits are essential in maintaining relationships, yet the number of non-legal prison visits has fallen by a third during the last five years despite a rise of more than 20 per cent in the prison population (Prison Reform Trust 2004; Broadhead 2002). Research has suggested wide variation in the attitudes of penal establishments to families, some prisons being perceived as profoundly unwelcoming by visitors (Codd 2003), leading Broadhead (2002) to contend that many prisons view family visitors as a 'nuisance'. In contrast, during the last ten years some prisons in the UK have established innovative, imaginative visits programmes aimed at encouraging the maintenance of relationships between both male and female inmates and their children. The age of the prison does not necessarily relate to the adequacy of the facilities or the attitude of officers; in her address to a joint meeting of two parliamentary groups, Lucy Gampell (2004) described the facilities at HMP Bronzefield, which at the time she was writing was one of the newest prisons. The visitors' centre has been designed and built with what she described as 'bus shelter seating' and the information leaflet available to families was a reprint of one which was thirteen years old (Gampell 2004). Families at Bronzefield reported difficulties booking visits, especially where designated pre-booking telephone lines were either engaged for days, very busy or, as in one instance, taken out of service so the line could be used for a fax machine instead (Gampell 2004). Although the Woolf Report (1991) envisaged improved family links, family members visiting prisons report hostility and negative attitudes from officers and it appears that, during the last decade, the increasing demands of prison security have led to increased suspicion of families (Brooks-Gordon and Bainham 2004). There seems to be some mismatch between prison service rhetoric and what actually happens 'on the ground', leading to the paradox that at the time the prison service is allegedly encouraging family ties, the number of visits to prisons is falling.

The experiences of children when visiting can be particularly problematic, as the environment and the security concerns of the prison may frighten children or simply not adequately respond to their needs. That said, most prisons have some kind of toy area or toy box, and some have crèche facilties such as those run by the Mothers' Union. The Ormiston Trust provides crèche facilities as part of its visitors' centre provision allowing children to be taken to join their parents part way through the visit. This is important as it prevents children becoming bored and allows adults valuable time together to discuss important issues (EUROCHIPS 2006).

Some prisons have been running a variety of extended or innovative visits scheme for some time. The 'Sunday Brunch' scheme at HMP Altcourse, whereby prisoners could pay for family members to have brunch with them on Sundays, has evolved into an extended visits scheme. Some prisons have 'family days' or child-centred visits. HMP Holloway pioneered day-long visits for mothers and their children although more recently the scheme was reduced from day-long visits to two-and-a-half-hour visits every two weeks. This was due to staffing difficulties and concerns from the prison management that a day-long visit placed too much pressure on the mother. Perhaps more worryingly, the number of children has dropped dramatically in recent years, with some mothers saying they did not want their children to come inside the prison (EUROCHIPS 2006).

The Grassroots Family Days and Support Project run by the Blackburn Diocese of the Church of England is a pilot hybrid project which includes both prison-based extended visits, called family days and also community-based support for family members. In May 2005, the Blackburn Diocese Board of Social Responsibility was granted funding from the Invest to Save Budget (ISB) to run a three-year pilot project designed to offer support to prisoners and their families.[9] Initially, four Lancashire prisons have been involved in the pilot: HMP Preston, HMP Wymott, HMP Lancaster Castle and HMP Kirkham. Project staff are based in both the prisons and the community, and activities are delivered using a combination of paid employees and volunteers. The project aims to maintain links between prisoners and families, to support individuals who are affected by the imprisonment of a family member, and to facilitate improved resettlement outcomes for prisoners, thus reducing reoffending (Grassroots 2006). In East Lancashire the project is linked to pre-existing family support projects including the operation of a child contact centre, and families may receive different kinds of support at different times, including focused support for prisoners' families if a family member is imprisoned.

The project has hosted a number of family days at prisons, where prisoners have been able to spend several hours with their families in relaxed surroundings with a buffet and activities provided. Paid staff and volunteers have provided activities ranging from face painting, card making, biscuit decorating, table tennis and others, and representatives from 'Bookstart', welfare benefits advice and other people such as deaf awareness trainers have also been present. The emphasis of the family days has been on informality as far as possible, with prison officers on first-name terms with inmates and their families, and with children able to run around and play with the toys made available.

A typical Grassroots family day was held at HMP Preston in August 2006, and the image of a baby cooing happily for nearly an hour in the arms of a female prison officer, with the baby face-painted to look like a cat, is one which is not easily forgotten but is too easily contrasted with usual visits. Dads were able to spend time playing with and talking to their children and the informal atmosphere allowed prisoners and their partners to relax together in a more 'normal' setting than in a visits room. The extended length of the visit allowed for more relaxed conversation and less of the tension than on a usual visit. The family day at Preston also benefited other prisoners because the provision of the buffet, which was not only for the participating prisoners and their families but for other invitees including the Governor, allowed prisoners learning catering skills the opportunity to learn and practice food preparation and presentation skills suitable for a high-class buffet, rather than prison meals. The project is being evaluated by an experienced research officer and although the formal evaluation process is ongoing anecdotal evidence suggests that families have found the family days really enjoyable and beneficial, with many expressing informally the view that there should be more visits like that.

In the first year of the project, 345 prisoners and their families asked for support, and in November 2006, ninety-six families were being supported. The number of families being supported, however, far outweighs the number who are able to participate in the family days, with prisoners involved in the project only being eligible to participate once and others denied participation due to security considerations or simple lack of available space to host the event. The community-based support of families distinguishes this project from those which are purely prison-focused, in that although the number of prisoners who can participate in extended visits is limited, their families are still eligible to receive support from 'satellite' Grassroots teams based in their local communities. It is important also to note that although the project has its base in the Church of England, the activities of the project are non-religious and open to all.

Some other countries have extended private visits or conjugal visits. Conjugal visits tend to be between a prisoner and his partner (Smith 2006). In some jurisdictions this must be marital partners

(Bandele 1999). These visits began in Mississippi in the early part of the twentieth century and at the time were aimed at black inmates as an incentive to work harder (Hopper 1969). There is much, however, to be criticised about the aims, implementation and inherent racism of this early programme, which involved access to prostitutes and assumptions that black inmates were less able to control their sexual urges than white inmates. Then, as now, the private visits became a tool of behaviour management, although more recent family visitation programmes in the US have tended to stress the preservation of family ties as their key aim. These visits tend to focus on sexual activity and operate as a form of incentive for prisoners to behave well and conform to prison rules. Some countries are moving towards family visits, which focus on maintaining family ties. Family visits vary in length and location: for example, in France the Unités Expérimentales de Visite Familiale (UEVF) have been operating at the Centre Pénitentiaire de Rennes since September 2003. Since then the scheme has been expanded to three prisons. The UEVF's scheme allows prisoners and their families weekend-long private visits with several family members. Sentenced prisoners can see their family members from six to forty-eight hours, being allowed a seventy-two hour visit once a year. It is interesting to note that the scope of potential visitors is wider than simply close family members or members of the extended family; rather, individuals for whom several factors provide evidence of a legitimate emotional bond to the offender can also be included. The scheme offers a means of family contact for those who are ineligible for other family contact schemes such as leave (EUROCHIPS 2006). In Ireland children are able to stay overnight with their mothers and this is useful in the absence of other programmes. These programmes of extended visits strengthen family relations and improve the probability of successful reintegration after release (EUROCHIPS 2006).

The advent of prisoner email

A promising development in the summer of 2006 was the development of pilot projects allowing prisoners' access to email. A new system, PRIS-M (Prisoners' Mail) has been piloted at HMP Downview, HMYOI Aylesbury and HMP High Down. Under the pilot scheme, mail from families is downloaded by mail room staff in each prison from a secure site on the internet, then sent directly to a printer which automatically seals each mail after printing before the message is delivered to the prisoner on the wing. The system is based on that which has been used successfully by the Armed Forces to enable British soldiers to maintain contact with their families. The initial pilots have been based on 'scanmail' which has allowed prisoners to have their handwritten letters scanned onto the computer then sent out to the family by email. The cost of mail by this method was slightly cheaper than postal rates.

In January 2007 it was announced that pilot schemes would commence in a number of London prisons which would allow prisoners internet and email access, subject to systems which could control access due to security concerns and other worries about abuse. The scheme would not allow prisoners freely to surf the net but would allow access to approved sites for educational and learning reasons, and they would be allowed to send text-only email to approved addresses (Department for Education and Skills 2006; Ford 2007). In the long term, this could open the way for other technological initiatives, such as webcams, which might assist in family contact. This, however, needs to be carefully thought through as offenders' family members may not have access to email facilities at home and it could be difficult to arrange on public computer terminals. That said, if, for example, families could access email at local support group centres, libraries or community centres then there could be many benefits. A particular benefit could be that for overseas prisoners, if the logistical problems of access to electronic resources in impoverished communities could be overcome.

Working with mothers and babies – an example

One of the dilemmas of allowing mothers to keep their children with them in prison is the question of the impact on their development. One of the groups most active in supporting family relationships is the Mothers' Union, which is currently active in ninety of the 158 prisons in the UK and which includes an emphasis on the family relationships of women prisoners (Thomas 2007). The Mothers' Union offers a worldwide perspective on prisoners' family relationships, as it works with women prisoners around the world, such as in its work in the women's prison in Kampala, Uganda.

At Holloway the Mothers' Union helped to create a roof garden with play equipment, plants and seating, and the crèche, which employs two qualified nursery nurses, offers care for babies in the Mother and Baby Unit so their mothers can work within the prison or undertake educational activities. Volunteers also take babies out of the prison for walks, so that they experience the stimuli of the outside world. The Mothers' Union also recognises the challenges that women will face on leaving prison. In other prisons the Mothers' Union run crèches at visit times, and prisoners' family members may benefit from holidays provided under the Mothers' Union Family Holiday scheme.

The role of schools: what can teachers do?

In comparison with other challenging family circumstances such as divorce, bereavement and illness, there is still relatively little guidance available for teachers. Despite the growing number of children who cope with parental imprisonment, only one local education authority, Gloucestershire, currently has an imprisoned parent policy, and one of the policy's key recommendations is that each school should identify a key contact person who is responsible for these issues (Frankel 2006). It is important however to recognise the potentially valuable contribution which can be made by schools. One teacher quoted in Frankel's (2006) article stressed that teachers are not social workers and that school children should be encouraged to leave their home problems at the door whereas others recognise the diverse consequences of imprisonment on children's emotions and behaviour. To stress that children should leave their problems at the door, for example, ignores the fact that imprisonment may involve children being taken out of school, either briefly for visits or for longer periods to care for younger siblings. Anecdotal evidence suggests that some school special needs co-ordinators are aware of the issues, whereas others are not. Schools can create an atmosphere in which children are not afraid to talk about prisons, and one way of developing this is for school libraries to stock some of the books recently published by the charity Action for Prisoners' Families, such as *Finding Dad* which is aimed at 8–11 year olds, or, for children who are more likely to read comic books, *It's a Tough Time for Everyone* which is published by Barnardo's in Northern Ireland. Questions of crime, justice, policing and prisons can be included in citizenship teaching. Action for Prisoners' Families produce a resource pack on 'Supporting Young People Affected by Imprisonment' which contains useful information and they also have a useful website.

If the school already offers or displays contact information for organisations which help families in difficulties then imprisonment can be included as well. If a child is being bullied or called names then the class teacher could directly address prison issues, for example as part of PSHE (personal, social and health education), and emphasise that just because someone's parent is in prison it does not make that child a bad child. This, of course, can be difficult where children are being encouraged by their parents to avoid contact with a prisoners' child, but the important thing is that the parent's situation is not the responsibility of the child, and it is not appropriate to treat children as if they are the same as their parents. That said, since prisoners' children are more likely to end up in prison themselves than the children of non-prisoners, it is important for teachers to recognise this and intervene as appropriate when children display potentially criminal or anti-social behaviour. This entails recognition that the cycle of imprisonment goes on through generations and for children to break this cycle they need self-esteem, goals, positive role models and appropriate support to cope with their feelings and experiences. Where a child is displaying changed behaviour or attitudes, and the school already knows about challenging family circumstances such as domestic violence, drug abuse or anti-social behaviour, it is important for teachers to be aware of imprisonment as a possible factor within the family.

One of the biggest challenges in considering the response of schools and teachers to prisoners' children is that there is little published research into the experiences of prisoners' children in school and little identification of good practice in teaching and pastoral care. Many teachers, even special needs co-ordinators who are accustomed to working with children experiencing a range of challenges, may feel ill-equipped to respond to prisoners' children. In the future, it would be beneficial for children if links could be developed between teachers and academic researchers with a view to developing relevant, focused and responsive policies, practices and training to help teachers work with children who have a prisoner in the family.

Conclusions

It was tempting to entitle this chapter 'Good news for prisoners' families' or, as inspired by Gwyneth Lewis, to subtitle it 'a cheerful chapter about prisoners' families' (Lewis 2002). Supporting prisoners' families is more multidimensional than it might at first appear, because responses to the experiences of prisoners' families can involve practical programmes of support, and also more strategic or policy-based campaigns. It is clear that there are many prison-based initiatives which are worthy of note, and also some useful and effective community projects which can be commended as examples of good practice. As tempting as this is, however, the topic of supporting prisoners' families needs to be approached with caution and a critical spirit, as discussed in the next, and final, chapter.

Notes

1 Note, however, concerns that some Christian churches could do more to either support families, support prisoners or indeed to challenge the increasing use of imprisonment (Williams 2006). For further suggestions as to how Christian churches could work with families, see Upton (2003).

2 A good example of this kind of organisation is the Criminal Information Agency, based in Liverpool. See http://www.criminal-information-agency. com.

3 The Sure Start programme consists of locally managed projects aimed at reducing social exclusion among children up to five years old in deprived areas. It has recently been announced that Sure Start is to be rolled out across the country into other areas. Connexions is a service that offers advice, guidance and support to young people aged thirteen to nineteen across England.

4 Formerly known as the Federation of Prisoners' Families Support Groups.

5 There are many examples from outside England and Wales of innovative projects to support families. For example, Renny Golden (2005) gives extensive contact details of programmes for incarcerated mothers and their families in the US context. Some of the most well-known American projects have included 'Girl Scouts Behind Bars'.

6 For brief descriptions of this and other schemes run in the US, see http://www.cjtinc.org/Aunt/Mary.htm and Golden (2005). For more information on 'Storybook Dad' see http://www.storybookdads.co.uk.

7 For further details of the charity and its work see http://www.timeforfamilies.org.uk.

8 Consider, for example, the committed friendships developed by mail in relation to death row prisoners in the US. Organisations such as Human Writes co-ordinate letter-writing with death row inmates in the US, and one only has to read their magazine to gain a sense of the profound importance to the prisoners of the letters and cards they receive, and the emotional support expressed therein.

9 The ISB is a joint Treasury/Cabinet Office initiative which aims to create sustainable improvements in the capacity to deliver public services in a more joined up manner. A key principle of the ISB programme is that investment is provided in return for reform.

Chapter 7

Conclusions

Over 40 years ago, the work of Pauline Morris (1965) gave a vivid insight into prisoners' families' lives in the context of a much lower UK prison population (Light and Campbell 2006). There have been some significant developments since 1965, especially in terms of visiting entitlements and conditions, visitors' centres, the Prisoners' Families Helpline and support groups such as POPS and Action for Prisoners' Families. At the time of writing the question of responses to prisoners' families is achieving new recognition in a number of ways, although the children of prisoners, for example, receive nowhere near as much awareness and social concern as the children of divorced parents. That said, initiatives such as the provision of debt and money advice in prisons, housing advice work in prisons, and the simple recognition of prisoners' children in the education field (Frankel 2006) offer some encouragement that, for some families and prisoners at least, the worst aspects of their experience may be beginning to be ameliorated. In many ways, however, the experiences of prisoners' family members continue to bear striking resemblances to those of family members in the early 1960s, except now these experiences have to be understood against a backdrop of a rising rate of imprisonment and shifts towards penal punitiveness. The rate of imprisonment in many jurisdictions is increasing year on year and more and more people are being processed by carceral agencies. Thus more and more families are experiencing the negative consequences of imprisonment which have been discussed in earlier chapters.

From the perspective of someone writing in the UK the most significant development in our understanding of prisoners' families in recent years has come from the ongoing stream of US-based research into the impacts of imprisonment on families and also on communities. Bearing in mind that the UK tends to follow the US in penal policy rather than the rest of Europe, if this is the case then we may begin seeing some of these things here, although played out in a different way especially in relation to rights. The situation in the UK does not currently have the same racialised focus as in the US, but the American work is significant because it links the experiences and needs of prisoners families into the broader political context of mass imprisonment or the imprisonment epidemic and does not simply view the problem as one of social service needs for particular families, but in terms of broader penal movements. The American research on mass imprisonment has likened the mass imprisonment epidemic to a new form of slavery, as a new development in the armoury of the tools of racial discrimination used by the powerful. Imprisonment in the UK is nowhere near as racialised. However, in our own country imprisonment is sweeping in more and more people, and harming their families too. It is important to note, however, questions of race and migration. Angel-Ajani (2005) quotes Wacquant (1999) who says that the over-representation of 'people of colour' in US prisons may not be 'American exceptionalism'. As Angel-Ajani writes, 'anywhere there is migration, there is an accompanying discourse of criminalisation, suspicion and mistrust' (2005: 14).

Wacquant shows that the way in which the US prison system has 'manifested itself as a force that regulates and contains the poor disenfranchised' has become a similar component of the European penal system. In some ways, I am uneasy, however, with the concept of a 'European penal system', although Wacquant's discussion of increases in the prison population in European countries is indisputable. His words are worth quoting, as they indicate that we might follow the US down the same route:

> There is every chance that the societies of Western Europe will generate analogous, albeit less pronounced, situations to the extent that they, too, embark on the path of the penal management of poverty and inequality, and ask their prison system not only to curb crime, but also to regulate the lower segments of the labor market and to hold at bay populations judged to be disreputable, derelict and unwanted. From this point of view, foreigners and quasi-foreigners would be "the blacks" of Europe (1999: 216).

Megan Comfort's work in the US is also significant in the light of UK welfare policies. Imprisonment seems to have almost entirely negative consequences for families, but her work offers some of the most innovative and insightful writing in this field. In the light of the demise of social welfare policies and the expansion of criminal justice policy in the US, it seems unsurprising that, for many women in relationships with imprisoned men, prison is the one state agency on which they can rely. Families live more and more in the shadow of the prison because other welfare-based agencies may not be there to support them. There is, of course, the possibility that the situation the US offers us is not a vision of the future but a cautionary tale, rather like that of Scrooge's funeral in Dickens' *A Christmas Carol*. We can, as a society and as influencers of policy, look at what has happened and is happening in the US, and choose to follow a different path. With the exception of the death penalty, however, in penal terms we do not have a good record of ignoring US developments. Everything from electronic tagging to mandatory minimums and sex offender registration, along with new forms of prison security, have come from the US. Whether the US situation offers us a cautionary tale or a vision of the future is difficult to answer, and of course, these two descriptors are not mutually exclusive. Since the 1990s penal policies in the UK have been more significantly influenced by America than by Europe, and the consequences of this, combined with new punitive trends in penal policy, have been the subject of discussion and debate in a number of recent publications (Tonry 2004; Jones and Newburn 2002; Pratt *et al.* 2005).

However, there are key differences between the situation in prisons in the UK and the US. For example, the *majority* of prisoners in the US are African American or of Latin American origin (Wacquant 2001), and imprisonment is emerging as a new stage in the life course of young, low-skilled black men who, as one recent study suggests, are more than five times as likely as white men to have served time in prison by the time they reach their early 30s (Pettit and Western 2004). There is no research of which I am aware which identifies such a profoundly racialised focus to mass imprisonment here, in contrast with the situation in the US where the collateral consequences of imprisonment have had their most significant and damaging effects on members of minority ethnic groups (Braman 2004; Travis and Waul 2003a). It is, of course, possible to be optimistic and consider an alternative path. In terms of prisoners' legal rights, the implementation of the Human Rights Act 1998 means that Articles 3, 8 and 12 of the

ECHR in particular are providing fruitful grounds for attempts to challenge prison regimes and conditions, albeit with mixed results (Codd 2004a; Foster 2005), and Andrew Coyle has recently reiterated the importance of recognising prisoners as citizens (Coyle 2005). While in the UK serving prisoners still cannot vote, although moves are afoot to amend this before the next election, the UK does not have the equivalent of felony disenfranchisement.

From the point of view of prisoners' families, there is a growing awareness in the UK of the relevance of the ECHR to children's rights (Munby 2004a, 2004b), and recent cases have considered contact, visits, artificial insemination and mother and baby units (see Munro 2002; Brooks-Gordon and Bainham 2004; Codd 2004b, 2005b). Yet we know from experience that penal policies and practices are more likely to cross the Atlantic in one direction more than the other. Of course, the racialised element may play out differently here, and it is interesting to note the development of the prison population of young Asian men; there has not been corresponding research into the experiences of their family members. It may well be that where young Asian men are suspected of terror-related offences their families receive support and they do not feel stigmatised. This was the experience of families of imprisoned members of paramilitary groups in Northern Ireland; the men were viewed as 'prisoners of war' and as distinct from 'criminal offenders'. The problem is, however, that we do not know anything about their experiences in research terms, although organisations such as POPS are trying to reach these marginalised populations.

Moving beyond the US and the UK, the impact of imprisonment on families is a global issue. The essays in Julia Sudbury's (2005) thought-provoking book link race, class, gender, female imprisonment and the global capitalist prison-industrial context, which serves to remind those of us working within a Western criminological academic paradigm that many of these issues are not simply matters for the US, Europe and the UK, for example, but that the punishment of prisoners' families, either explicitly or subtly by a range of means, is a worldwide phenomenon. The precise nature of the questions may vary, as in the UK we are arguing about allowing babies to stay with their imprisoned mothers whereas in India efforts are being made to remove children. What is important here, however, is to recognise the invisible punishment of prisoners' families as a global phenomenon. Concern with prisoners raises concerns about families. Similarly, many children who are already living in difficult situations, with poverty, sometimes racism and other forms of exclusion, live in communities where they are more likely to come under the scrutiny of criminal justice agencies.

Reiterating a critical perspective

Where imprisonment is concerned there is an important question of balancing social benefits with financial and social costs. In the UK, imprisonment is still the paradigmatic penalty, with a tendency for non-custodial community-based penalties to be viewed as 'soft' non-punitive sanctions. A very practical question is whether imprisonment is 'worth' its costs. Prison, after all, has long been described as 'an expensive way of making bad people worse' (Soering 2004). It is not just the prisoners, however, who are being made worse but potentially their children. Prison, after all, is very successful at perpetuating itself, both in terms of ex-prisoner reoffending and also the likelihood of prisoners' children going on to offend in the future. The work of Smith *et al.* (2007) goes some way towards offering an assessment of the real costs of imprisonment. Public protection and public safety is harder to quantify, and it is indisputable that dangerous offenders should not be at large to put the public in danger, but the costs and benefits of imprisoning property and drug offenders become more debatable. Whilst for some offenders imprisonment may offer an opportunity to come off drugs, away from usual suppliers and co-users, drugs are not hard to come by in many prisons and in addition returning a prisoner to their home environment after their sentence risks a repetition of the previous substance-abusing and offending behaviour. If resources are limited, as they clearly are, then we need to challenge the conflation of social work policy into criminal justice policy. Whilst incapacitation may in itself offer a justification for imprisonment, the consequences for family members need to be thought through. For some commentators it might be tempting to argue that parenthood should offer mitigation, but this discriminates against those without children.

In my view the kinds of programmes and innovations discussed in the preceding chapter should be welcomed if they are of benefit to prisoners' families. The question of assessing if and how these initiatives benefit families has received attention from Murray and Farrington (2007) but it is important to note that the shift towards evidence-based policy-making in criminal justice has meant that many projects have had some element of evaluation designed in. The problem for the critically minded reader is that of whether or not these reforms, whilst serving in the short term to help families, in the long term simply act as a buttress for imprisonment:

> Reforms, like democracy, can be theatre in which governing actors address publicly identified violations. The reforms function to lower scrutiny by convincing the public that human rights violations in prison are exceptional and fixable. Reforms (welfare, child welfare and sentencing reform) are often the scaffold that symbolically masks state violence or social abandonment. Instead of offering remedy, the reforms reinforce the power of governing bodies to control and coerce stigmatized populations (Golden 2005: 104).

This is a similar argument to that raised by the enormous contribution made by prisoners' female relatives to the amelioration of prison conditions: from a feminist perspective, by supporting prisoners' families we may be simply reinforcing gendered oppression, rendering women responsible for dealing with the failings of not only prison regimes but the institution of imprisonment itself. In the light of feminist research with women coping with the imprisonment of a family member, it is important to exercise caution in advocating programmes of support which reinforce the role of women as carers without recognising their own needs at a time which is often very challenging. Whilst it is obvious that support groups are mostly populated by women simply because men are more likely than women to be imprisoned, thus leaving female partners to cope outside, it is important to remember Girshick's (1996) comment that regardless of the gender of the inmate it is women who bear the burdens of caring. One of the negative implications of an increased focus on third sector sources of support is the danger of placing more burdens on prisoners' partners, mothers, daughters and sisters at a time of extreme stress and disruption. In assessing how families are and should be supported there is a key distinction to be made between assisting families from a humanitarian or 'damage limitation' based approach, and working with families as tools of offender management or as what Light and Campbell (2006) refer to as 'part of the apparatus of crime-control'. Interestingly, in an era of 'risky people' (Hudson 2003) on one hand prisoners' families are deemed 'risky' in terms of prison security (Brooks-Gordon and Bainham 2004) and in providing a crime-supportive or crime-generating environment whereas, sometimes simultaneously in policy terms, they are identified as playing a potentially valuable role in promoting offender re-entry and future non-criminal behaviour. This is a key paradox; that they are viewed at the same time both a dangerous negative influence and also potential key players in sentence planning and resettlement planning.

The broader question as to imprisonment encompasses not only an exploration of its use as a sentence but also a questioning of the dominant approach to the needs of prisoners' families which sees the effects on families as a side-effect or by-product of the sentence. Some writers argue that separation from family and damage to family relationships is inherent in imprisonment itself, that the nature of the prison is designed to break up families (No More Prison 2006). This reflects the populist tendency in the UK to view prisons still as places 'for punishment' and to resist attempts to reinforce the view that the sentence of imprisonment is punishment itself. The question of whether damage to relationships is so inherent in imprisonment itself so as to make family initiatives mere window-dressing is complex. The operation of family-focused schemes by prisons can serve to obscure the realities of the damage done to relationships; it allows prisons, and government for that matter, to say 'look what we are doing for families' whilst rendering less visible the immense damage done to relationships by imprisonment. It could be argued that it is in the very nature of the prison itself to define families as 'other', to label and to exclude, so it could be argued that a family-friendly prison undermines the very nature and meaning of the prison, which is individualist, excluding and isolating:

> Prisons cannot possibly be family friendly. They are designed to break up families, to separate people from those they love and to observe and threaten them constantly when they are together, with no respite. We know that family ties are the single biggest factor in preventing re offending but there is no consideration given to the maintenance of those ties, with some rare exceptions. The prisons run courses like 'Family man' to encourage better parenting without any questioning of the manner in which prisons themselves undermine and, in many cases, destroy family life. Organisations like Action For Prisoners' Families collude in these myths about the necessity of separation by saying that prisoners should be locked up nearer home or officers need training about the problems families face or we need better visitors' centres. What we need is to rethink the whole basis upon which we do this to people, most of them

on low incomes and deprived of support and real justice (No More Prison 2006: 4).

The answer, surely, is to challenge the very basic values on which we justify and impose prison sentences. What is needed is a concerted, courageous and fearless confrontation of the institutional power and dominance of imprisonment itself. Pursuing this challenge, of course, can be difficult for those who are dependent on government funding for their jobs. The danger is that charitable organisations which work in partnership with prisons and government agencies may fear being silenced or feel that they have to be cautious in their criticism of policies and practices in case essential funding, collaboration or co-operation is withdrawn. There needs to be the maintenance of a critical voice which independently questions these issues. It is essential, however, that those who are in a position to speak, or write, or argue, or campaign, do so alongside family members in order to bring prisoners' families issues out of the darkness and semi-visibility in which government casts them. This is not to romanticise prisoners' families; the point is to recognise that regardless of somebody's behaviour, they are still human. Thus, although arguments for family contact based on the prevention of future crime may collapse if the family is crime-supportive, human freedom involves the freedom to maintain family relationships. For the suffering of prisoners' families to be ameliorated, the programmes are a first step, but no more.

Whilst in the UK there are many books offering critical perspectives on prisons, many such books barely mention families. Yet family relationships and their erosion or destruction is a fundamental preoccupation of many prisoners. It is easy in our current risk-obsessed culture to denigrate prisoners' families for being poor, or behaving in ways which are socially unacceptable, for forming part of an undesirable underclass, thus contributing to the ongoing risk of criminality. The challenge for academics and practitioners who are concerned about the impacts of imprisonment on families is not simply to be contented with the introduction of longer visits, or email, or even home leave; the challenge is to be angry about how people are suffering *who are not themselves imprisoned*. This involves a major shift in perspective which, bluntly, is often not adopted by people until they have come into contact with imprisonment in their own family. It is too easy to distance ourselves from prisoners' families, to say that they are 'not like us'. But surely the point in our ever-imprisoning society is that it is increasingly likely to be us, or someone we know, although of course this depends on social class and structure. And surely, human rights do not depend on only applying to people we know and like; rather, for human rights to be truly meaningful they have to apply even to those people whom we may wish were not part of our species due to their conduct.

A transformative vision?

Thus, a transformative vision is needed, not simply of prisons which offer better crèches and visits schemes, but of an actual challenging of imprisonment. Rather than simply accepting the status quo and seeking to ameliorate the most harmful negative effects of imprisonment, there needs to be a questioning of the use – and abuse – of imprisonment itself, as argued by Light and Campbell (2006). After all, if, for example, a government wanted to cut the number of deaths from lung cancer, in the long term it would be better to prevent people engaging with the causes of such cancer, such as tobacco smoking, rather than simply putting money and resources into new diagnostic techniques and treatments for those who are suffering. So it is with imprisonment. Dee Cook (2006) refers to the story quoted by Adrian Sinfield (2004) of the doctor's dilemma. The doctor is standing at the shore of a fast-flowing river and hears the cry of a drowning man. He jumps in, rescues him, gives him artificial respiration and the man begins to breathe. At this point another cry is heard and again the doctor jumps into the water, rescues a man and resuscitates him. This happens again and again, by which time the doctor is so busy rescuing people that he has no time to run upstream to see who is pushing these people off the bridge into the water in the first place. In response to this, and in the context of social inequalities, Cook advocates 'upstream policies' which seek to address root causes, rather than downstream policies which seek to understand and ameliorate them. To me, however, the problem is unsatisfactory if dealt with in a binary fashion, that is, either one pulls the people out of the river or one goes to stop the person throwing them in. After all, in the time it takes to go upstream to see who is throwing the people in, others may die. What the doctor really needs, assuming that he is the best person to carry out the rescue as he is able to perform artificial resuscitation, is to try to ask someone else to go upstream, or to engage other agencies to help him. It is almost impossible to solve this dilemma if only one person is involved, without risk of people continuing to drown in the short term.

It is also important to recognise the value of professional experience and being qualified and appropriate to take on the correct role. For example, if the doctor had no relevant experience or skills, or perhaps, could not swim himself, then it would be foolhardy for him to jump in. There is also an interesting dilemma if, for example, the victims are dangerous paedophiles; from a rights perspective the humanitarian thing to do would be to pull them out, but then the doctor risks ostracism and hostility, as do those who campaign for and support prisoners' family members. The other thing about the bridge is we do not know how far away the bridge is, whether, indeed it is accessible. It might, after all, be surrounded by gun emplacements, police and the military preventing anyone from challenging the throwing of the people into the river. In some jurisdictions, the doctor could be interfering with a lawful execution process. What would the result be if all that happened was that the doctor found himself being thrown into the river too? The story does not sufficiently stress the unbalanced power differential. If the individual or group throwing people into the river is dangerously powerful and unaccountable then the best thing to be done may be for the doctor to rescue people as soon as practicable, possibly by trying to rescue them at an earlier stage after being thrown in. There are associated questions too; if people have been thrown in once, are they more likely to be thrown in again? Where do they go when they and their clothes are wet? It's all very well pulling them out of the river, but what aftercare is available? There is a question of individuals and organisations being involved in activities in which they have particular and effective strengths. For example, Action for Prisoners' Families provides a critical voice on behalf of prisoners' families. If, however, organisations such as this become too embroiled in creating initiatives and providing help and support then they may lose sight of their bigger purpose, which is to challenge the structures which continue to place prisoners' families in such difficult circumstances. The doctor's most important role may be to summon help and provide medical support as needed.

It is the same with the consequences of imprisonment. To support prisoners' families without questioning the use of imprisonment and penal policies which send more and more people to prison for longer is to potentially fall foul of the 'cerebral inertia' which Reece Walters lambasted in relation to crime science and situational crime prevention in his chapter in Barton *et al.* (2006). Although Walters' chapter is controversial, it makes some important points about the poverty of deeper theory in such contexts. Linked to this is the problem of legitimation of the use of imprisonment. By seeking to improve the immediate situation of prisoners' families without asking any of the broader questions is to administer a small pill for a chronic illness. To unquestioningly support initiatives for prisoners' families, without challenging imprisonment itself, legitimates current policies and, ultimately, serves to render less visible the devastating effects of a national imprisonment epidemic. However, if we choose to focus on 'the big picture', that is, the neo-abolitionist goal of minimising the use of imprisonment, then we are faced with the immediate prospect of families continuing to suffer. The problem for the conscientious neo-abolitionist is that of what to do, which is where the twin-track approach adopted by Golden comes into its own. The answer, I suggest, is one of a dual-pronged approach. One element involves demonstrating a commitment to challenging the nature, use and dominance of imprisonment as a punishment, which is the kind of approach which Golden (2005) called 'eyes on the prize'. Like Golden, however, I recognise the immediate needs of families, and suggest we need a 'feet on the ground' approach where more immediate measures are supported if they offer benefits to families now. To adopt one approach without the other risks either ignoring the needs of suffering families now, or blithely endorsing the ongoing use of a damaging penalty without asking more fundamental questions as to the nature and use of the penalty itself. After all, there is nothing inevitable about a state having a high rate of imprisonment.

Most readers of this book will be familiar with the costs of imprisonment in terms of the 'bed and breakfast' cost of keeping a prisoner in jail for a year. We need to also consider the social costs, and assess whether, bluntly, it is worth it. Since the development of the prison system as we know it, families have been ever-present and ever-marginalised. It is essential to recognise that the circumstances of prisoners' families are not simply a matter of concern for those who are interested in criminal justice. They are relevant to anyone interested in challenging poverty, or striving for social justice, or promoting human rights. To be committed to building a society which loves and cares for its children involves loving and caring for all children. We hear a great deal about children of divorce; disabled children; children who live with domestic violence. It dismays me that at a time when prisoners' children are visiting their parents in difficult surroundings, or ending up in care, or moving repeatedly or being bullied, the media is more interested in questioning whether it is right that children live with gay couples.

But what about prisoners' children? There is an urgent need to raise the profile of these children, to speak out, to challenge the silence.

The motivation for challenging the dominance of imprisonment is unimportant: some individuals challenge prisons on human rights grounds; others on grounds of crime prevention, prevention of reoffending by prisoners and the prevention of offending by prisoners' children in the future. For others the challenge may be spiritual, or personal. The motivation does not matter. What matters is that to truly support prisoners' families it is not enough to implement schemes, however well thought-out, well-planned and successfully implemented they might be. The challenge is to 'ask the family question' at every opportunity and in as many contexts as possible. If we as a society accord family life any respect or value then to speak – and persevere in speaking – about imprisonment in a critical voice is an imperative, not an option. The challenge is, in some ways, a small one, that is, to tell the truth to those in power. This means to tell the truth about the poverty experienced by families, to tell the truth about the shocking public transport provision to some establishments (or the lack of it), to tell the truth about the loneliness and sorrow of children when their mothers are jailed. This should be a topic of major public concern, yet sadly it is not yet.

One of the consequences of the dominance of imprisonment, and the ubiquitousness of its negative effects, is to feel that nothing can be done and to accept the situation. But, those of us who are committed to supporting prisoners' families need to campaign vociferously and bravely around the vision of a different approach to the use of incarceration. For those of my generation growing up in the 1970s, the Berlin Wall was standing and looked like it would be there for our lifetimes; the Cold War was in full flow; South Africa was in the grip of apartheid; Nelson Mandela was in jail and the IRA was bombing British cities. At that time the possibility of any of these situations changing seemed remote, but within less than thirty years all these things have undergone radical transformations. The fight to improve the situation for prisoners' families, and to challenge damaging policies of incarceration, is one which incorporates struggles involving citizenship, human rights, family life and social justice. In the long term, only by challenging imprisonment itself can we truly make a difference to those women, men and children who live their lives in the shadow of prison.

Bibliography

Action for Prisoners' Families (2002) *Supporting Young People with a Prisoner in the Family: Guidance Notes for Adults Working with Young People*. London: Action for Prisoners' Families.

Action for Prisoners' Families (2004) 'Home Office Plan Undermines Blair's New Crime Strategy', Press Release, 19 July 2004.

Adams, K. (1992) 'Adjusting to Prison Life' in M. Tonry (ed.) *Crime and Justice: A Review of Research*, 16, 275–359. Chicago: Chicago University Press.

Agozino, B. (2005) 'Nigerian Women in Prison: Hostages in Law' in J. Sudbury (ed.) *Global Lockdown: Race, Gender and the Prison–Industrial Complex*. New York: Routledge.

Allard, P. (2002) *Life Sentences: Denying Welfare Benefits to Women Convicted of Drug Offenses*. Washington, DC: The Sentencing Project.

American Bar Association (2002) *Task Force on Collateral Sanctions, Introduction, Proposed Standards on Collateral Sanctions and Administrative Disqualification of Convicted Persons*. Unpublished report.

Angel-Ajani, A. (2005) 'Domestic Enemies and Carceral Circles' in J. Sudbury (ed.) *Global Lockdown: Race, Gender and the Prison-Industrial Complex*. New York: Routledge.

Arditti, J. A. (2002) 'Ecological Nightmares of the Worst Kind: Families and Incarceration', *Discussion Paper for the 32nd Theory Construction and Research Methodology Workshop*, Houston, TX, November 2002.

Arditti, J. A. (2003) 'Locked Doors and Glass Walls: Family Visiting at a Local Jail', *Journal of Loss and Trauma*, 8(2): 115–138.

Aungles, A. (1993) 'Prisons – Penal Policies: The Hidden Contracts', in P. Easteal and S. McKillop (eds) *Women and the Law: Proceedings of a Conference held 24–26 September 1991*. Canberra: Australian Institute of Criminology.

Aungles, A. (1994) *The Prison and the Home.* Sydney: The Institute of Criminology.

Aungles, A. and Cook, D. (1994) 'Information Technology and the Family: Electronic Surveillance and Home Imprisonment', *Information Technology and People,* 7(1): 69–80.

Bandele, A. (1999) *The Prisoner's Wife: A Memoir.* New York: Washington Square Press.

Barton, A., Corteen, K., Scott, D. and Whyte, D. (2006) *Expanding the Criminological Imagination: Critical Readings in Criminology.* Cullompton: Willan Publishing.

Bates, R., Lawrence-Wills, S. and Hairston, C. F. (2003) 'Children and Families of Incarcerated Parents: A View from the Ground', *Research Brief on Children, Families and the Criminal Justice System,* Summer 2003. Chicago: University of Illinois.

Baunach, P. (1985) *Mothers in Prison.* New Brunswick, NJ: Transaction Publishing.

Beckerman, A. (1989) 'Incarcerated Mothers and Their Children in Foster Care: The Dilemma of Visitation', *Children and Youth Services Review,* 11(2): 175–183.

Beckerman, A. (1994) 'Mothers in Prison: Meeting the Prerequisite Conditions for Permanency Planning', *Social Work,* 39(1): 9–13.

Benedict XVI (2007) *Post-Synodal Apostolic Exhortation Sacramentum Caritatis of the Holy Father Benedict XVI to the Bishops, Clergy, Consecrated Persons and the Lay Faithful on the Eucharist and Summit of the Church's Life and Mission.* Vatican, 22 February 2007.

Bernstein, N. (2005) *All Alone in the World: Children of the Incarcerated.* New York: The New Press.

Berry, P. and Eigenberg, H. (2003) 'Role Strain and Incarcerated Mothers: Understanding the Process of Mothering', *Women and Criminal Justice,* 15(1): 101–119.

Bloom, B. (1992) 'Incarcerated Mothers and Their Children: Maintaining Family Ties' in American Correctional Association (ed.) *Female Offenders: Meeting the Needs of a Neglected Population.* Laurel, MD: American Correctional Association.

Bloom, B., Owen, B. and Covington, S. (2004) 'Women Offenders and the Gendered Effects of Public Policy', *Review of Policy Research,* 21(1): 31–48.

Boswell, G. (1996) *Young and Dangerous: The Backgrounds and Careers of Section S3 Offenders.* Aldershot: Avebury.

Boswell, G. (2002) 'Imprisoned Fathers: The Children's View', *Howard Journal of Criminal Justice,* 41(1): 14–26.

Boswell, G. and Wedge, P. (2001) *Imprisoned Fathers and their Children.* London: Jessica Kingsley.

Bosworth, M. (1999) *Engendering Resistance: Agency and Power in Women's Prisons.* Aldershot: Ashgate.

Boudin, K. (1998) 'Lessons from a Mother's Program in Prison: A Psychosocial Approach Supports Women and their Children' in J. Harden and M. Hill (eds) *Breaking the Rules: Women in Prison and Feminist Therapy*. New York: Haworth Press.

Boudouris, J. (1996) *Parents in Prison: Addressing the Needs of Families*. Lanham, MD: American Correctional Association.

Bowlby, J. (1946) *Forty-four Juvenile Thieves: Their Characters and Home-life*. London: Bailliere, Tindall and Cox.

Bowlby, J. (1973) *Attachment and Loss: Separation, Volume 2*. New York: Basic Books.

Bozzuti, J. (2003) 'Judicial Birth Control? The Ninth Circuit's Examination of the Fundamental Right to Procreate in *Gerber v. Hickman*', *St. John's Law Review*, 77: 625.

Braman, D. (2002) 'Families and Incarceration' in M. Chesney-Lind and M. Mauer (eds) *Invisible Punishment: The Collateral Consequences of Mass Imprisonment*. New York: The New Press.

Braman, D. (2004) *Doing Time on the Outside: Incarceration and Family Life in Urban America*. Ann Arbor, MI: University of Michigan Press.

Braman, D. and Wood, J. (2003) 'From One Generation to the Next: How Criminal Sanctions are Reshaping Family Life in Urban America' in J. Travis and M. Waul (eds) *Prisoners Once Removed: The Impact of Incarceration and Re-entry on Children, Families and Communities*. Washington, DC: The Urban Institute Press.

Broadhead, J. (2002) 'Visitors Welcome – Or Are They?', *New Law Journal*, 152(5): 7014–7015.

Brodsky, S. (1975) *Families and Friends of Men in Prison: The Uncertain Relationship*. Lexington, KY: Lexington Books.

Brookes, M. (2005) 'Investing in Family Ties: Reoffending and Family Visits to Prisons', *NPC Research Insight October 2005*. London: New Philanthropy Capital.

Brooks-Gordon, B. and Bainham, A. (2004) 'Prisoners' Families and the Regulation of Contact', *Journal of Social Welfare and Family Law*, 26(3): 263–280.

Brown, K. (2001) *No-one's Ever Asked Me: Young People with a Prisoner in the Family*. London: Action for Prisoners' Families.

Brown, K., Dibb, L., Shenton, F. and Elson, N. (2002) *No-one's Ever Asked Me: Young People with a Prisoner in the Family*. London: Action for Prisoners' Families.

Bunyan, N. (2006) 'Prison Bans Kissing to Cut Drug Deals', *Daily Telegraph*, 17 January 2006.

Caddle, D. and Crisp, D. (1997) 'Mothers in Prison', *Home Office Research Findings No. 38*. London: Home Office.

Cameron, M. (2001) *Women Prisoners and Correctional Programs*. Canberra: Australian Institute of Criminology.

Carlen, P. (1983) *Women's Imprisonment*. London: Routledge & Kegan Paul.

Carlen, P. (1990) *Alternatives to Women's Imprisonment*. Milton Keynes: Open University Press.

Carlen, P. (ed.) (2002) *Women and Punishment: The Struggle for Justice*. Cullompton: Willan Publishing.

Carlen, P. and Worrall, A. (eds) (1987) *Gender, Crime and Justice*. Milton Keynes: Open University Press.

Carlen, P. and Worrall, A. (2004) *Analysing Women's Imprisonment*. Cullompton: Willan Publishing.

Carlen, P., Hicks, J., O'Dwyer, J., Christina, D. and Tchaikovsky, C. (1985) *Criminal Women*. Cambridge: Polity Press.

Carter, P. (2004) *Managing Offenders, Reducing Crime*. London: Home Office.

CASC (1999) *Women in Prison*. London: Catholic Agency for Social Concern.

Casey-Acevedo, K. and Bakken, T. (2002) 'Visiting Women in Prison: Who Visits and Who Cares?', *Journal of Offender Rehabilitation*, 34(3): 67–83.

Casey-Acevedo, K., Bakken, T. and Karle, A. (2004) 'Children Visiting Mothers in Prison: The Effects on Mothers' Behaviour and Disciplinary Adjustment', *The Australian and New Zealand Journal of Criminology*, 37(1): 418–430.

Cheney, D., Dickson, L., Uglow, S. and Fitzpatrick, J. (2001) *Criminal Justice and the Human Rights Act 1998, Second Edition*. Bristol: Jordans Ltd.

Christian, J. (2005) 'Riding the Bus: Barriers to Prison Visitation and Family Management Strategies', *Journal of Contemporary Criminal Justice*, 21(1): 31–48.

Clarke, C. (2005) 'Where Next for Penal Policy?' *Speech to the Prison Reform Trust*, London, 19 September 2005.

Cobean, S. C. and Power, P. W. (1978) 'The Role of the Family in the Rehabilitation of the Offender', *International Journal of Offender Therapy and Comparative Criminology*, 22(1): 29–39.

Codd, H. (1998) 'Prisoners' Families: the "Forgotten Victims"', *Probation Journal*, 45(3): 148–154.

Codd, H. (2000) 'Age, Role Changes and Gender Power in Family Relationships: The Experiences of Older Female Partners of Male Prisoners', *Women and Criminal Justice*, 12(2/3): 63–93.

Codd, H. (2002) '"The ties that bind": Feminist Perspectives on Self-Help Groups for Prisoners' Partners', *Howard Journal of Criminal Justice*, 41(4): 334–347.

Codd, H. (2003) 'Women Inside and Out: Prisoners' Partners, Women in Prison and the Struggle for Identity', *Internet Journal of Criminology*. http://www.flashmousepublishing.com.

Codd, H. (2004a) 'Prisoners' Families: Issues in Law and Policy', University of London, Institute of Advanced Legal Studies public lecture, June 2004.

Codd, H. (2004b) 'Prisoners' Families: Issues in Law and Policy', *Amicus Curiae*, 55: 2–7.

Codd, H. (2005a) 'The Collateral Consequences of Mass Imprisonment: A Cautionary Tale or a Vision of the Future?', *Paper presented at the British Criminology Conference*, Leeds University, July 2005.

Codd, H. (2005b) 'Integrating Empirical Research: Prisoners' Rights, the Law and the Family', *Paper presented at the WG Hart Legal Workshop*, University of London, Institute of Advanced Legal Studies, June 2005.

Codd, H. (2006) 'Prisoners and their Families: Human Rights and Human Dignity', *Paper presented at the 1st Anglo–German Legal Workshop*, Keele University, November 2006.

Codd, H. (2007a) 'Prisoners' Families and Resettlement: A Critical Analysis', *Howard Journal of Criminal Justice*, 46(3): 255–263.

Codd, H. (2007b) 'The Slippery Slope to Sperm Smuggling: Prisoners, Artificial Insemination and Human Rights', *Medical Law Review*, 15: 220–235.

Combessie, P. (2002) 'Marking the Carceral Boundary: Penal Stigma in the Long Shadow of the Prison', *Ethnography*, 3(4): 535–555.

Comfort, M. (2002) 'Papa's House: The Prison as Domestic and Social Satellite', *Ethnography*, 3(4): 467–499.

Comfort, M. (2003) 'In the Tube at San Quentin: The "Secondary Prisonization" of Women Visiting Inmates', *Journal of Contemporary Ethnography*, 32(1): 77–107.

Comfort, M. (2007) *Doing Time Together: Love and Family in the Shadow of the Prison*. Chicago, IL: University of Chicago Press.

Commission on Women and the Criminal Justice System (2004) *Women and the Criminal Justice System*. London: Fawcett Society.

Commission on Women and the Criminal Justice System (2006) *Justice and Equality: Second Annual Review of The Commission on Women and the Criminal Justice System*. London: Fawcett Society.

Condry, R. (2004) *After the Offence: The Construction of Crime and its Consequences by Families of Serious Offenders*. Unpublished Ph.D. Thesis, University of London.

Condry, R. (2007) *Families Shamed: The Consequences of Crime for Relatives of Serious Offenders*. Cullompton: Willan Publishing.

Cook, D. (2006) *Criminal and Social Justice*. London: Sage.

Corcoran, M. (2006) *Out of Order: The Political Imprisonment of Women in Northern Ireland 1972–1998*. Cullompton: Willan Publishing.

Corston, J. (2007) *The Corston Report: A Report by Baroness Jean Corston of a Review of Women with Particular Vulnerabilities in the Criminal Justice System*. London: Home Office.

Covington, S. (2003) *Beyond Trauma: A Healing Journey for Women*. Center City, MN: Hazelden.

Cox, C. (1999) *To Grandmother's House We Go and Stay: Perspectives on Custodial Grandparents*. New York: Springer.

Coyle, A. (2001) 'Prisons and the Democratic Process', *Presentation at the 'New Initiatives in Penal Reform and Access to Justice' Conference*, Hyderabad, India, October 2001.

Coyle, A (2005) 'On Being a Prisoner in the United Kingdom in the 21st Century: Does the Wilberforce Judgement Still Apply?', *Inaugural Lecture*, International Centre for Prison Studies, King's College London, 22 March 2005.

Cregan, J. and Aungles, A. (1997) 'The Criminal Justice System and Prisoners' Families: Socio-psychological Issues', *Paper presented at The Hidden Victims of Crime: Families of Prisoners CRC Justice Support*, Hunter Region, Forum, Newcastle, May 1997.

Creighton, S., King, V. and Arnott, H. (2005) *Prisoners and the Law*. Haywards Heath: Tottel Publishing.

Crawley, E. and Sparks, R. (2005) 'Older Men in Prison: Survival, Coping and Identity', in A. Liebling and S. Maruna (eds) *The Effects of Imprisonment*. Cullompton: Willan Publishing.

Cummings, E., Davies, P. and Campbell, S. (2000) *Developmental Psychopathology and Family Process*. New York: Guilford Press.

Cunningham, A. (2001) 'Forgotten Families: The Impacts of Imprisonment', *Family Matters*, 59: 35–38.

Currie, E. (2002) 'Preface' in K. Carrington and R. Hogg (eds) *Critical Criminology: Issues, Debates, Challenges*. Cullompton: Willan Publishing.

Davies, R. P. (1980) 'Stigmatization of Prisoners' Families', *Prison Service Journal*, 40: 12–14.

Davis, A. (1992) 'Men's Imprisonment: The Financial Cost to Women and Children' in R. Shaw (ed.) *Prisoners' Children: What Are the Issues?* London: Routledge.

Dennison, C. and Lyon, J. (2001) *Young Offenders, Fatherhood and the Impact of Parenting Training*. Brighton: Trust for the Study of Adolescence.

Department for Education and Skills (2006) *Reducing Reoffending through Skills and Employment: Next Steps*. London: HMSO.

Devlin, A. (2002) *Cell Mates/Soul Mates: Stories of Prison Relationships*. Winchester: Waterside Press.

Diduck, A. and Kaganas, F. (2006) *Family Law, Gender and the State: Text, Cases and Materials, Second Edition*. Oxford: Hart Publishing.

Ditchfield, J. (1994) 'Family Ties and Recidivism', *Home Office Research Bulletin No. 36*. London: Home Office.

Dixon, B. (2005) 'Mass Incarceration is an Abomination', *The Black Commentator*, 147: 1.

Dodge, M. and Pogrebin, M. (2001) 'Collateral Costs of Imprisonment for Women: Complications of Reintegration', *The Prison Journal*, 81(1): 42–54.

Doka, K. (1995) 'Disenfranchised Grief' in L. DeSpelder and A. Strickland (eds) *The Path Ahead*. Mountain View, CA: Mayfield.

Douglas, M. C. (1993) 'The Mutter-Kind-Heim at Frankfurt-am-Main: "Come Together- Go Together": An Observation', *International Journal of Comparative and Applied Criminal Justice*, Spring.

Dressel, P. and Barnhill, S. K. (1994) 'Reframing Gerontological Thought and Practice: The Case of Grandmothers with Daughters in Prison', *The Gerontologist*, 34(5): 685–691.

Dunlap, E., Golub, A., Johnson, B. and Wesley, D. (2002) 'Intergenerational Transmission of Conduct Norms for Drugs, Sexual Exploitation and Violence: A Case Study', *British Journal of Criminology*, 42(1): 1–20.

Dunn, S. (2002) 'The "Art" of Procreation: Why Assisted Reproduction Technology Allows for the Preservation of Female Prisoners' Right to Procreate', *Fordham Law Review*, 70: 2561–2602.

Eaton, M. (1993) *Women After Prison*. Milton Keynes: Open University Press.

Eddy, J. M. and Reid, J. (2003) 'The Adolescent Children of Incarcerated Parents' in J. Travis and M. Waul (eds) *Prisoners Once Removed: The Impact of Incarceration and Re-entry on Children, Families and Communities*. Washington, DC: The Urban Institute Press.

Enos, S. (2001) *Mothering from the Inside*. Albany, NY: SUNY Press.

EUROCHIPS (2006) *Children of Imprisoned Parents: European Perspectives on Good Practice*. Paris: EUROCHIPS.

Evans, P. (2002) 'Inside Story', *The Guardian*, 17 April 2002.

Fallon, P., Blueglass, R., Edwards, B. and Daniels, G. (1999) *Report of the Committee of Inquiry into the Personality Disorder Unit, Ashworth Special Hospital* (Cm. 4194–ii). London: HMSO.

Farrall, S. and Maruna, S. (2004) 'Desistance-Focused Criminal Justice Policy Research: Introduction to a Special Issue on Desistance from Crime and Public Policy', *Howard Journal of Criminal Justice*, 43(4): 358–367.

Farrington, D. P. (1995) 'The Development of Offending and Anti-social Behaviour from Childhood: Key Findings from the Cambridge Study in Delinquent Development', *Journal of Child Psychology and Psychiatry*, 36(6): 929–964.

Farrington, D. P., Barnes, G. C. and Lambert, S. (1996) 'The Concentration of Offending in Families', *Legal and Criminal Psychology*, 1: 35–60.

Farrington, D. P., Jolliffe, D., Loeber, R., Stouthamer-Loeber, M. and Kalb, L. M. (2001) 'The Concentration of Offenders in Families, and Family Criminality in the Prediction of Boys' Delinquency', *Journal of Adolescence*, 24(5): 579–596.

Ferraro, K. J. and Moe, A. M. (2003) 'Mothering, Crime and Incarceration', *Journal of Contemporary Ethnography*, 32(1): 9–40.

Fishman, S. H. (1983) 'The Impact of Incarceration on Children of Offenders' in M. Frank (ed.) *Children of Exceptional Parents*. New York: Haworth Press.

Fishman, L. T. (1988a) 'Stigmatization and Prisoners' Wives: Feelings of Shame', *Deviant Behavior*, 9: 169–192.

Fishman, L. T. (1988b) 'Visiting at the Prison: Renewed Courtship and the Prisoner's Wife', *Free Inquiry in Creative Sociology*, 16(1): 115–121.

Fishman, L. T. (1990) *Women at the Wall: A Study of Prisoners' Wives Doing Time on the Outside*. Albany, NY: University of New York Press.

Flanagan, T. J. (1980) 'The Pains of Long-term Imprisonment: A Comparison of British and American Perspectives', *British Journal of Criminology*, 20(2): 148–156.

Ford, R. (2007) 'Security Fear as Prisoners are Told: You Have E-mail', *The Times*, 2 January 2007.

Fortin, J. (2003) *Children's Rights and the Developing Law, Second Edition*. London: Butterworths.

Foster, S. (2005) 'Prison Conditions, Human Rights and Article 3 ECHR', *Public Law*, Spring: 35–44.

Frankel, H. (2006) 'Unlock Their Future', *Times Education Supplement*, 24 November 2006.

Fraser, B. (2001) 'The Mediator as Power Broker' in E. Weigand and M. Dascal (eds) *Negotiation and Power in Dialogic Interaction*. Philadelphia, PA: John Benjamins.

Friends World Committee for Consultation (Quakers) (2005a) *Submission by Friends World Committee for Consultation (Quakers) on the Rights of the Child Day of Discussion 2005*. Geneva: Quaker United Nations Office.

Friends World Committee for Consultation (Quakers) (2005b) *Submission by Friends World Committee for Consultation (Quakers) on the Rights of the Child Day of Discussion 2005: Children of Imprisoned Mothers*. Geneva: Quaker United Nations Office.

Gabel, K. and Johnston, D. (1995) *Children of Incarcerated Parents*. New York: Lexington Books.

Gallie, P. L. (2002) *Prisoners Responsible for Family Anguish – Not Prison System*, Press Release, 8 July 2002.

Gampell, L. (1999) *Response to the Government Consultation Document 'Supporting Families'*. London: Federation of Prisoners' Families Support Groups.

Gampell, L. (2004) *Minutes of Joint Meeting of the Associate Parliamentary Group for Parents and Families and the All-Party Parliamentary Penal Affairs Group, on the theme of Prisoners' Families and Resettlement*, 14 September 2004.

Garland, D. (2001) 'Introduction: The Meaning of Mass Imprisonment', *Punishment and Society*, 3(1): 5–7.

Gentry, P. (1998) 'Permanency Planning in the Context of Parental Incarceration: Legal Issues and Recommendations', *Child Welfare*, 77(5): 543–559.

Girshick, L. (1996) *Soledad Women*. Westport, CT: Praeger.

Glaser, D. (1964) *The Effectiveness of a Prison and Parole System*. New York: Bobb-Merrill.

Glasser, I. (1993) 'Mothers in Prison in World Perspective', *Proceedings of the Fourth North American Conference on Family and Corrections*, Quebec City, Canada, 10–12 October 1993.

Goffman, E. (1963) *Stigma: Notes on the Management of Spoiled Identity*. New York: Penguin.

Golden, R. (2005) *War on the Family: Mothers in Prison and the Families they Leave Behind*. New York: Routledge.

Gordon, J. (1999) 'Are Conjugal and Familial Visitations Effective Rehabilitative Concepts?', *The Prison Journal*, 79(1): 119–135.

Grassroots (2006) *Grassroots Family Days and Support Project Update*, November 2006. Blackburn: Diocesan Board of Social Responsibility.

Green, D. (2004) *Crime Reduction: Are Government Policies Likely to Achieve its Declared Aims?* http://www.civitas.org.uk.

Greene, J. (2002) 'Entrepreneurial Corrections: Incarceration as a Business Opportunity' in M. Mauer and M. Chesney-Lind (eds) *Invisible Punishment: The Collateral Consequences of Mass Imprisonment*. New York: The New Press.

Grinstead, O., Faigeles, B., Bancroft, C. and Zack, B. (2001) 'The Financial Cost of Prison Visiting: A Survey of Women Visitors to a State Prison', *Journal of African-American Men*, 6(1): 59–70.

Grounds, A. and Jamieson, R. (2003) 'No Sense of an Ending: Researching the Experience of Imprisonment and Release Among Republican Ex-prisoners', *Theoretical Criminology*, 7(3): 347–362.

Hairston, C. F. (1991) 'Family Ties During Imprisonment: Important to Whom and for What?', *Journal of Sociology and Social Welfare*, 18(1): 87–104.

Hairston, C. F. (1998) 'The Forgotten Parent: Understanding the Forces that Influence Incarcerated Fathers' Relationships with their Children', *Child Welfare*, 77(5): 617–638.

Hairston, C. F. (2003) 'Prisoners and Their Families: Parenting Issues During Incarceration' in J. Travis and M. Waul (eds) *Prisoners Once Removed: The Impact of Incarceration and Re-entry on Children, Families and Communities*. Washington, DC: The Urban Institute Press.

Hale, B. (2005) 'The Sinners and the Sinned Against: Women in the Criminal Justice System', *Longford Lecture*, 5 December 2005. London: The Longford Trust.

Halsey, K., Ashworth, M. and Harland J. (2002) *Made for Prisoners by Prisoners: A Summary of NFER's Evaluation of the Safe Ground Family Relationships and Parenting Programme*. Slough: NFER.

Hames, C. and Pedreira, D. (2003) 'Children with Parents in Prison: Disenfranchised Grievers Who Benefit from Bibliotherapy', *Illness, Crisis and Loss*, 11(4): 377–386.

Hannah-Moffat, K. (2001) *Punishment in Disguise: Penal Governance and Canadian Women's Imprisonment*. Toronto: University of Toronto Press.

Hannah-Moffat, K. (2007) 'Gendering Dynamic Risk: Assessing and Managing the Maternal Identities of Women Prisoners' in K. Hannah-Moffat and P. O'Malley (eds) *Gendered Risks*. London: Glasshouse Press.

Harris, J. (1998) 'Rights and Reproductive Choice' in J. Harris and S. Holm (eds) *The Future of Human Reproduction*. Oxford: Clarendon Press.

Hastings, J. and Typpo, M. (1994) *An Elephant in the Living Room*. Minneapolis, MN: Hazelden Publishing & Educational Services.

Heidensohn, F. (1985) *Women and Crime*. London: Macmillan.

Henry-Lee, A. (2005) *Women in Prison: The Impact of the Incarceration of Jamaican Women on Themselves and their Families*. Kingston, Jamaica: The Planning Institute of Jamaica, Social Development and Gender Unit.

Herman, N. J. (1993) 'Return to Sender: Reintegrative Stigma-management Strategies of Ex-psychiatric Patients', *Journal of Contemporary Ethnography*, 22(3): 295–330.

Hessisches Ministerium der Justiz (2005) '30 *Jähriges Bestehen des Mutter-Kind-Heims der Justizvollzugsanstalt Frankfurt am Main*', Press Release, 10 November 2005.

Hewson, B. (2003) 'Privacy Claims Hit the Rocks', *New Law Journal*, 14 November 2003.

HMIP (2001) *Follow-up to Women in Prison: A Thematic Review by HM Chief Inspector of Prisons*. London: HMIP.

HMIP (2006) *Foreign National Prisoners: A Thematic Review*. London. HMIP.

HM Prison Service (2007) 'Hibiscus Helps Cater for Foreign National Needs', *Prison Service News*, April/May 2007.

Holt, N. and Miller, B. (1972) *Explorations in Inmate–Family Relationships*. Sacramento, CA: California Department of Corrections.

Home Affairs Committee (2005) *Report on the Rehabilitation of Prisoners*. London: HMSO.

Home Office (2001) 'The Prison Population in 2000: A Statistical Review', *Home Office Research Findings No. 154*. London: Home Office Research, Development and Statistics Directorate.

Home Office (2004) *Reducing Re-offending: National Action Plan*. London: Home Office Communication Directorate.

Home Office (2005) 'Resettlement Outcomes on Release from Prison in 2003', *Home Office Research Findings No. 248*. London: HMSO.

Home Office (2006) A *Five Year Strategy for Protecting the Public and Reducing Re-offending*. London: HMSO.

Hopper, C. (1969) *Sex in Prison: The Mississippi Experiment with Conjugal Visiting*. Baton Rouge, LA: Louisiana State University Press.

Howarth, G. and Rock, P. (2000) 'Aftermath and the Construction of Victimisation: "The Other Victims of Crime"', *Howard Journal of Criminal Justice*, 39(1): 58–78.

Hull Daily Mail (2003) 'Let Me Have Killer's Baby', *Hull Daily Mail*, 6 September 2003.

Hudson, B. (2003) *Justice in the Risk Society*. London: Sage.

Hudson, B. (2006) 'Punishing Monsters, Judging Aliens: Justice at the Borders of Community', *Australian and New Zealand Journal of Criminology*, 39(2): 232–247.

Jackson, E. (2001) *Regulating Reproduction: Law, Technology and Autonomy*. Oxford: Hart Publishing.

Jackson, E. (2002) 'Conception and the Irrelevance of the Welfare Principle', *Modern Law Review*, 65(2): 176–203.

Jackson, E. (2006) 'Prisoners, Their Wives and the Right to Reproduce', *Bionews*, 30 April 2006.

Jarvis, J., Graham, S., Hamilton, P. and Tyler, D. (2004) 'The Role of Parenting Classes for Young Fathers in Prison: A Case Study', *Probation Journal*, 51(1): 21–33.

Jewkes, Y. (2005) 'Prisoners and the Press', *Criminal Justice Matters*, Spring 2005: 27–29.

Johnston, D. (1993) *Children of the Therapeutic Intervention Project*. Pasadena, CA: Pacific Oaks Center for Children of Incarcerated Parents.

Johnston, D. (1995) 'Effects of Parental Incarceration' in K. Gabel and M. D. Johnston (eds) *Children of Incarcerated Parents*. New York: Lexington Books.

Johnston, D. (2001) 'Incarceration of Women and Effects on Parenting', *Paper prepared for conference 'Effects of Incarceration on Children and Families'*, Northwestern University, Evanston, IL, 5 May 2001.

Jones, J. (2004) 'Common Constitutional Traditions: Can the Meaning of Human Dignity Under German Law Guide the European Court of Justice', *Public Law*, Spring 2004: 167–187.

Jones, T. and Newburn, T. (2002) 'Learning from Uncle Sam? Exploring US Influences on British Crime Control Policy', *Governance*, 15(1): 97–119.

Jose-Kampfner, C. (1995) 'Post-Traumatic Stress Reactions in Children of Imprisoned Mothers' in K. Gabel and M. D. Johnston (eds) *Children of Incarcerated Parents*. New York: Lexington Books.

Juby, H. and Farrington, D. P. (2001) 'Disentangling the Link Between Disrupted Families and Delinquency', *British Journal of Criminology*, 41(1): 22–40.

Kadison, D. and Weiss, M. (2002) 'Mob Sperm Bust', *New York Post*, 3 December 2002.

Kirsch, M. (2005) 'Sleep Tight, Dear, From Mum in Jail', *The Times*, 19 January 2005.

Kitzinger, S. (1997) 'Sheila Kitzinger's Letter from Europe: How Can We Help Pregnant Women and Mothers in Prison?', *Birth*, 24(3): 197.

Klein, S., Bartholomew, G. and Hibbert, J. (2002) 'Inmate Family Functioning', *International Journal of Offender Therapy and Comparative Criminology*, 46(1): 95–111.

Kotarba, J. A. (1979) 'The Accomplishment of Intimacy in the Jail Visiting Room', *Qualitative Sociology*, 2: 80–103.

Kroll, B. (2004) 'Living with an Elephant: Growing up with Parental Substance Misuse', *Child and Family Social Work*, 9: 129–140.

Laing, J. and Oderberg, D. (2005) 'Artificial Reproduction, the "Welfare Principle" and the Common Good', *Medical Law Review*, 13(3): 328–356.

Laing, K. (2003) *Supporting Prisoners and their Families*. London: Young Voice.

Laing, K. and McCarthy, P. (2005) *Risk, Protection and Resilience in the Family Life of Children and Young People with a Parent in Prison: A Literature Review*. Newcastle: Newcastle Centre for Family Studies.

Lancashire Evening Post (2006a) 'Parents of Text Pervert are Hounded', *Lancashire Evening Post*, 22 July 2006.

Lancashire Evening Post (2006b) 'Five Jailed for Selling Heroin', *Lancashire Evening Post*, 24 July 2006.

Larman, G. and Aungles, A. (1991) 'Children of Prisoners and their Outside Carers: The Invisible Population' in P. Easteal and S. McKillop (eds)

Women and the Law: Proceedings of a Conference held 24–26 September 1991. Canberra: Australian Institute of Criminology.

Laub, J. and Sampson, R. (2003) *Shared Beginnings, Divergent Lives: Delinquent Boys to Age 70.* Cambridge, MA: Harvard University Press.

Laub, J., Nagin, D. and Sampson, R. (1998) 'Trajectories of Change in Criminal Offending: Good Marriages and the Desistance Process', *American Sociological Review,* 63: 225–238.

Lefley, H. P. (1987) 'Family Burden and Family Stigma in Major Mental Illness', *American Psychologist,* 44(3): 556–560.

Lester, M. (2004) *'Wainwright v. Home Office,* Case Comment', *European Human Rights Law Review,* 2: 193–199.

Leverentz, A. (2006) 'The Love of a Good Man? Romantic Relationships as a Source of Support or Hindrance for Female Ex-Offenders', *Journal of Research in Crime and Delinquency,* 43(4): 459–488.

Levi, R. and Appel, J. (2003) *Collateral Consequences: Denial of Basic Social Services Based Upon Drug Use.* New York: New York City Drug Policy Alliance.

Lewis, G. (2002) *Sunbathing in the Rain: A Cheerful Book about Depression.* London: Harper Collins.

Liebling, A. (1992) *Suicides in Prison.* London: Routledge.

Liebling, A. (1999) 'Prison Suicide and Prisoner Coping' in M. Tonry and J. Petersilia (eds) *Prisons, Crime and Justice: A Review of Research,* 26, 283–360. Chicago, IL: University of Chicago Press.

Liebling, A. and Krarup, H. (1993) *Suicide Attempts and Self-injury in Male Prisons.* London: Home Office.

Light, R. (ed.) (1989) *Prisoners' Families: What Are the Issues?* Bristol: Bristol Centre for Criminal Justice.

Light, R. (1992) *Prisoners Families: Keeping in Touch.* Bristol: Bristol Centre for Criminal Justice.

Light, R. (1993) 'Why Support Prisoners' Family-Tie Groups?', *Howard Journal of Criminal Justice,* 32(4): 322–329.

Light, R. (1995) 'Black and Asian Prisoners' Families', *Howard Journal of Criminal Justice,* 34(3): 209–217.

Light, R. and Campbell, B. (2006) 'Prisoners' Families: Still Forgotten Victims?', *Journal of Social Welfare and Family Law,* 28(3/4): 297–308.

Literacy Trust (2006) *Reading Initiatives – Prisons,* see http://www.literacytrust. org.uk.

Londono, P. (2007) 'Applying Convention Jurisprudence to the Needs of Women Prisoners', *Public Law,* Summer 2007: 198–208

Lopoo, L. and Western, B. (2005) 'Incarceration and the Formation and Stability of Marital Unions', *Journal of Marriage and the Family,* 67(3): 721–734.

Loucks, N. (2002) *Just Visiting? A Review of the Role of Prison Visitors' Centres.* London: Prison Reform Trust/Action for Prisoners' Families.

Loucks, N. (2004) *Prison Without Bars: Needs, Support and Good Practice for Work with Prisoners' Families.* Edinburgh: Tayside Criminal Justice Partnership/ Families Outside.

Lowenstein, A. (1984) 'Coping with Stress: The Case of Prisoners' Wives', *Journal of Marriage and the Family,* 46(3): 699–708.

Macaskill, C. (2002) *Safe Contact? Children in Permanent Placement and Contact with Birth Relatives.* Lyme Regis: Russell House Publishing.

McCarthy, C. (2004) 'Prison Suicides: The Death Toll Rises', *HLM,* 22(1): 5.

McDermott, K. and King, R. (1992) 'Prison Rule 102: "Stand by Your Man": The Impact of Penal Policy on the Families of Prisoners' in R. Shaw (ed.) *Prisoners' Children: What are the Issues?* London: Routledge.

McEvoy, K., O'Mahony, D., Horner, C. and Lyner, O. (1999) 'The Home Front: The Families of Politically Motivated Prisoners in Northern Ireland', *British Journal of Criminology,* 39(2): 175–197.

McIntire, R. (1973) 'Parenthood Training or Mandatory Birth Control: Take Your Choice', *Psychology Today,* October: 34.

Maidment, M. (2006) *Doing Time on the Outside: Deconstructing the Benevolent Community.* Toronto: University of Toronto Press.

Manning, R. D. (2000) *Credit Card Nation: The Consequences of America's Addiction to Credit.* New York: Basic Books.

Manza, J. and Uggen, C. (2004) 'Punishment and Democracy: Disenfranchisement of Non-incarcerated Felons in the United States', *Perspectives on Politics,* 2(3): 491–505.

Maruna, S. (2001) *Making Good: How Ex-Convicts Reform and Rebuild Their Lives.* Washington, DC: American Psychological Association.

Maruna, S. and Immarigeon, R. (2004) *After Crime and Punishment: Pathways to Offender Reintegration.* Cullompton: Willan Publishing.

Mauer, M. and Chesney-Lind, M. (eds) (2002) *Invisible Punishment: The Collateral Consequences of Mass Imprisonment.* New York: The New Press.

May, H. (2000) 'Murderers' Relatives: Managing Stigma, Negotiating Identity', *Journal of Contemporary Ethnography,* 29(2): 198–221.

Mazza, K. (2002) 'And Then the World Fell Apart: The Children of Incarcerated Fathers', *Families in Society,* 83(5/6): 521–529.

Medlicott, D. (2007) 'Women in Prison' in Y. Jewkes (ed.) *Handbook on Prisons.* Cullompton: Willan Publishing.

Mills, A. (2005) '"Great Expectations?": A Review of the Role of Prisoners' Families', *Selected papers from the British Society of Criminology Conference,* Portsmouth University 2004, http://www.britsoccrim.org/v7.htm.

Mills, A. and Codd, H. (2007) 'Prisoners' Families' in Y. Jewkes (ed.) *Handbook on Prisons.* Cullompton: Willan Publishing.

Mills, A. and Codd, H. (2008) 'Prisoners' Families and Offender Management: Mobilising Social Capital', *Probation Journal,* 55(1): 7–22.

Minkler, M. and Roe, K. (1993) *Grandmothers as Caregivers: Raising Children of the Crack Cocaine Epidemic.* Newbury Park, CA: Sage.

Monture-Angus, P. (2002) *The Lived Experience of Discrimination: Aboriginal Women Who Are Federally Sentenced*. Ottawa: Canadian Association of Elizabeth Fry Societies.

Morgan, J. (2004) 'Privacy Torts: Out with the Old, Out with the New', *Law Quarterly Review*, 120: 393–398.

Morgan, R. and Newburn, T. (2007) 'Youth Justice' in M. Maguire, R. Morgan and T. Newburn, *The Oxford Handbook of Criminology, Fourth Edition*. Oxford: Oxford University Press.

Morris, P. (1965) *Prisoners and Their Families*. London: George Allen & Unwin.

Mumola, C. J. (2000) 'Incarcerated Parents and Their Children', *Bureau of Justice Statistics Special Report*. Washington, DC: US Department of Justice.

Munby, J. (2004a) 'Making Sure The Child Is Heard: Part 1 – Human Rights', *Family Law Journal*, 34: 338–347.

Munby, J. (2004b) 'Making Sure The Child Is Heard: Part 2 – Representation', *Family Law Journal*, 34: 427–435.

Munro, V. (2002) 'The Emerging Rights of Imprisoned Mothers and their Children', *Child and Family Law Quarterly*, 14(3): 303–314.

Murray, J. (2005) 'The Effects of Imprisonment on Families and Children of Prisoners' in A. Liebling and S. Maruna (eds) *The Effects of Imprisonment*. Cullompton: Willan Publishing.

Murray, J. and Farrington, D. P. (2005) 'Parental Imprisonment: Effects on Boys' Anti-social Behaviour and Delinquency Through the Life Course', *Journal of Child Psychology and Psychiatry*, 46(12): 1269–1278.

Murray, J. and Farrington, D. P. (2006) 'Evidence-based Programs for Children of Prisoners', *Criminology and Public Policy*, 5(4): 721–736.

Murray, J. and Farrington, D. P. (2007) 'Parental Imprisonment: Long-lasting Effects on Boys' Internalizing Problems through the Life-course', *Development and Psychopathology*, 20(1): 273–290.

Murray, J., Janson, C. G. and Farrington, D. P. (2007) 'Crime in Adult Offspring of Prisoners: A Cross-national Comparison of Two Longitudinal Samples', *Criminal Justice and Behavior*, 34(1): 133–149.

Myers, B. J., Smarch, T. M., Amlund-Hagen, K. and Kennon, S. (1999) 'Children of Incarcerated Mothers', *Journal of Child and Family Studies*, 8(1): 11–25.

Nelson, M., Deess, P. and Allen, C. (1999) *The First Month Out: Post-incarceration Experiences in New York City*. New York: Vera Institute of Justice.

Newnham, D. (2002) 'Inside Story', *Times Educational Supplement*, 10 January 2002.

Niven, S. and Stewart, D. (2005a) 'Resettlement Outcomes on Release from Prison in 2003', *Home Office Research Findings No. 248*. London: Home Office.

Niven, S. and Stewart, D. (2005b) 'The Role of Family and Friends in Successful Resettlement', *Prison Service Journal*, 159: 21–24.

Noble, C. (1995) *Prisoners' Families: The Everday Reality*. Ipswich: Ormiston Trust.

No More Prison (2006) *Members' Newsletter*, October 2006.

O'Brien, P. (2001) *Making it in the 'Free World'*. Albany, NY: SUNY Press.

Ohlin, L. (1954) *The Stability and Validity of Parole Experience Tables*. Unpublished Ph.D. Thesis, University of Chicago.

Owen, B. (1998) *In the Mix: Struggle and Survival in a Women's Prison*. Albany, NY: SUNY Press.

Owen, T., Livingstone, S. and Macdonald, A. (2003) *Prison Law, Third Edition*. Oxford: Oxford University Press.

Page, J. (2004) 'Eliminating the Enemy: The Import of Denying Prisoners Access to Higher Education in Clinton's America', *Punishment and Society*, 6(4): 357–378.

Pandey, S. P. and Singh, A. K. (2006) *Women Prisoners and their Dependent Children (The Report of the Project Funded by Planning Commission, Government of India, New Delhi)*. New Delhi: Serials Publication.

Parke, R. D. and Clarke-Stewart, K. A. (2003) 'The Effects of Parental Incarceration on Children: Perspectives, Promises, and Policies' in J. Travis and M. Waul (eds) *Prisoners Once Removed: The Impact of Incarceration and Re-entry on Children, Families and Communities*. Washington, DC: The Urban Institute Press.

Paylor, I. and Smith, D. (1994) 'Who are Prisoners' Families?', *Journal of Social Welfare and Family Law*, 16(2): 131–144.

Peckham, A. (1985) *A Women in Custody*. London: Fontana.

Peelo, M., Stewart, J., Stewart, G. and Prior, A. (1991) 'Women Partners of Prisoners', *Howard Journal of Criminal Justice*, 30(4): 311–327.

Petersilia, J. (2003) *When Prisoners Come Home: Parole and Prisoner Re-entry*. New York: Oxford University Press.

Pettit, B. and Western, B. (2004) 'Mass Imprisonment and the Life Course: Race and Class Inequality in US Incarceration', *American Sociological Review*, 69(2): 151–169.

Piper, C. (2007) 'Should Impact Constitute Mitigation? Structured Discretion Versus Mercy', *Criminal Law Review*, February 2007: 141–155.

Pollock, J. (2002) 'Parenting Programs in Women's Prisons', *Women and Criminal Justice*, 14(1): 131–154.

POPS (2003) *Through the Crystal Maze: Celebrating 15 Years: Annual Review, 2002–3*. Manchester: POPS.

Pratt, J., Brown, D., Hallsworth, S., Brown, M. and Morrison, W. (2005) *The New Punitiveness: Trends, Theories, Perspectives*. Cullompton: Willan Publishing.

Prince's Trust (2001) *It's Like That: The Views and Hopes of Disadvantaged Young People*. London: The Prince's Trust.

Prison Reform Trust (2004) *Forgotten Prisoners: The Plight of Foreign National Prisoners in England and Wales*. London: Prison Reform Trust.

Prison Reform Trust (2007) *Bromley Briefings: Prison Factfile,* May 2007. London: Prison Reform Trust.

Proctor, P. (2003) 'Procreating from Prison: Evaluating British Prisoners' Right to Artificially Inseminate their Wives under the United Kingdom's New Human Rights Act and the 2001 Mellor Case', *Georgia Journal of International and Comparative Law,* 31(2): 459

Ramsden, S. (1998) *Working with Children of Prisoners: A Resource for Teachers.* London: Save the Children.

The Reading Agency (2006) *Inside Outside: The Big Book Share Phase 3.* St. Albans: The Reading Agency. http://www.readingagency.org.uk/projects/children/documents/BBS3update06.doc.

Richards, B. (1978) 'The Experience of Long-term Imprisonment', *British Journal of Criminology,* 18(2): 162–169.

Richards, M. and McWilliams, B. (1996) 'Imprisonment and Family Ties', *Home Office Research and Statistics Bulletin No. 38.* London: HMSO.

Richards, M., McWilliams, B., Allcock, L., Enterkin, J., Owen, P. and Woodrow, J. (1994) *The Family Ties of English Prisoners: The Results of the Cambridge Project on Imprisonment and Family Ties,* Occasional Paper No. 2, Cambridge: Centre for Family Research.

Roberts, J. V. and Gabor, T. (2004) 'Living in the Shadow of Prison: Lessons from the Canadian Experience in Decarceration', *British Journal of Criminology,* 39(1): 92–112.

Robertson, J. (2004) 'Procreative Liberty and Harm to Offspring in Assisted Reproduction', *American Journal of Law and Medicine,* 30: 7–40.

Robertson, O. (2007) *The Impact of Parental Imprisonment on Children.* Geneva: Quaker United Nations Office.

Roth, R. (2004) '"No New Babies": Gender Inequality and Reproductive Control in the Criminal Justice and Prison Systems', *American University Journal of Gender, Social Policy and Law,* 12: 391–424.

Rubinstein, G. and Mukamal, D. (2002) 'Welfare and Housing: Denial of Benefits to Drug Offenders' in M. Mauer and M. Chesney-Lind (eds) *Invisible Punishment: The Collateral Consequences of Mass Imprisonment.* New York: The New Press.

Salmon, S. (2007) *Memorandum submitted by Action for Prisoners' Families,* Home Affairs Select Committee Written Evidence, March 2007.

Sampson, R. J. and Laub, J. H. (1993) *Crime in the Making: Pathways and Turning Points through Life.* Cambridge, MA: Harvard University Press.

Sampson, R. J. and Laub, J. H. (2003) 'Life-course Desisters? Trajectories of Crime Among Delinquent Boys Followed to Age 70', *Criminology,* 41(3): 555–592.

Sampson, R. J. and Laub, J. H. (2005) 'A Life-Course View of the Development of Crime', *The ANNALS of the American Academy of Political and Social Science,* 602(1): 12–45.

San Francisco Children of Incarcerated Parents Partnership (2005) *Children of Incarcerated Parents: A Bill of Rights (Revised)*. San Francisco, CA: San Francisco Children of Incarcerated Parents Partnership.

Schneller, D. P. (1978) *The Prisoner's Family: A Study of the Effects of Imprisonment on the Families of Prisoners*. San Francisco, CA: R & E Research Associates.

Schoenbauer, L. J. (1986) 'Incarcerated Parents and their Children – Forgotten Families', *Law and Inequality*, 4: 579–601.

Seymour, C. (1998) 'Children with Parents in Prison: Child Welfare Policy, Program and Practice Issues', *Child Welfare*, 77(5): 469–493.

Shafer, N. (1994) 'Exploring the Link between Visits and Parole Success', *International Journal of Offender Therapy and Comparative Criminology*, 38: 17–32.

Shaw, R. (1987) *Children of Imprisoned Fathers*. London: Hodder & Stoughton.

Shaw, R. (ed.) (1992) *Prisoners' Children: What are the Issues?* London: Routledge.

Sinfield, A. (2004) 'Preventing Poverty in Market Societies', *Paper presented to ESPAnet Annual Conference*, University of Oxford, September 2004.

Smith, B. V. (2006) 'Analyzing Prison Sex: Reconciling Self-expression with Safety', *Columbia Journal of Gender and Law*, 15: 185–234.

Smith, M. (1992) 'Stigma', *Advances in Psychiatric Treatment*, 8: 317–323.

Smith, R., Grimshaw, R., Romeo, R. and Knapp, M. (2007) *Poverty and Disadvantage Among Prisoners' Families*. London: Joseph Rowntree Foundation.

Social Exclusion Unit (2002) *Reducing Re-offending by Ex-prisoners*. London: Social Exclusion Unit.

Soering, J. (2004) *An Expensive Way to Make Bad People Worse: An Essay on Prison Reform from an Insider's Perspective*. New York: Lantern Books.

Solokoff, N. (2005) 'Women Prisoners at the Dawn of the 21st Century', *Women and Criminal Justice*, 16(1/2): 127–137.

Stringer, A. (2000) 'Women Inside in Debt: The Prison and Debt Project', *Paper presented at the Women in Corrections: Staff and Clients Conference*, convened by the Australian Institute of Criminology in conjunction with the Department of Correctional Services SA, Adelaide, 31 October–1 November 2000.

Struckhoff, D. R. (1977) *Adjustments of Prisoners' Wives to Separation*. Unpublished Ph.D. Dissertation, Southern Illinois University.

Sudbury, J. (ed.) (2005) *Global Lockdown: Race, Gender, and the Prison-Industrial Complex*. New York: Routledge.

Sunday Times (2002) 'Prisoners Take up their Right to Father Children from Prison', *Sunday Times*, 15 December 2002.

Sunday Times (2006) 'Divorcee Fights to Have Child by Rabin's Jailed Assassin', *Sunday Times*, 23 April 2006.

Sutherland, E. (2003) 'Procreative Freedom and Convicted Criminals in the United States and the United Kingdom: Is Child Welfare Becoming the New Eugenics?', *Oregon Law Review*, 82: 1033–1065.

Swan, A. (1981) *Families of Black Prisoners: Survival and Progress*. Boston, MA: GK Hall & Co.

Sykes, G. (1958) *The Society of Captives: A Study of a Maximum Security Prison*. Washington, DC: American Psychological Association.

Tabib, M. and Mole, N. (2006) 'Imprisoned Parents and the Right to Family Life', *International Family Law Journal*, 97: 97–103.

Taylor, M. L. (2001) *The Executed God*. Minneapolis, MN: Augsburg Fortress.

Thomas, F. (2007) 'Life Beyond Bars', *Home and Family*, Spring 2007: 34–36.

Tonry, M. (2004) *Punishment and Politics: Evidence and Emulation in the Making of English Crime Control Policy*. Cullompton: Willan Publishing.

Travis, J. and Waul, M. (2003a) *Prisoners Once Removed: The Impact of Incarceration and Re-entry on Children, Families and Communities*. Washington, DC: The Urban Institute Press.

Travis, J. and Waul, M. (2003b) 'The Children and Families of Prisoners' in J. Travis and M. Waul (eds) *Prisoners Once Removed: The Impact of Incarceration and Re-entry on Children, Families and Communities*. Washington: The Urban Institute Press.

Uggen, C. and Wakefield, S. (2005) 'Young Adults Re-entering the Community from the Criminal Justice System: The Challenge of Becoming an Adult', in W. Osgood, E. M. Foster, C. Flanagan and G. R. Ruth (eds) *On Your Own Without a Safety Net: The Transition to Adulthood for Vulnerable Populations*. Chicago, IL: University of Chicago Press.

Uggen, C., Manza, J. and Behrens, A. (2003a) 'Less than the Average Citizen: Stigma, Role Transition and the Civic Reintegration of Convicted Felons' in S. Maruna and R. Immarigeon (eds) *After Crime and Punishment: Pathways to Offender Reintegration*. Cullompton: Willan Publishing

Uggen, C., Manza, J. and Behrens, A. (2003b) 'Felony Voting Rights and the Disenfranchisement of African Americans', *Souls*, 5(3): 48–57.

Upton, R. (2003) *Reaching Those Affected by Prison*. Cambridge: Grove Books.

US Department of Justice (2000) *Report on Minor Children Who Have a Mother or Father in Prison*. Washington, DC: US Department of Justice, Bureau of Justice Statistics.

Van Nijnatten, C. (1998) *Detention and Development: Perspectives of Children of Prisoners*. Mönchengladbach: Forum Verlag Godesberg.

Visher C. A. and Travis, J. (2003) 'Transitions from Prison to Community: Understanding Individual Pathways', *Annual Review of Sociology*, 29: 89–113.

Wacquant, L. (1999) 'Suitable Enemies: Foreigners and Immigrants in the Prisons of Europe', *Punishment and Society*, 1(2): 215–222.

Wacquant, L. (2001) 'Deadly Symbiosis: When Ghetto and Prison Meet and Mesh', *Punishment and Society*, 3(1): 95–134.

Wahidin, A. (2004) *Older Women and the Criminal Justice System: Running Out of Time*. London: Jessica Kingsley.

Walker, J. (2006a) 'Risk, Protection and Resilience in the Family Life of Children and Young People with a Parent in Prison', *Paper presented at the International Symposium on 'Pathways into and out of Crime: Taking Stock and Moving Forward'*, De Montfort University, Leicester, April 2006.

Walker, J. (2006b) 'Silent, Forgotten and Vulnerable: Examining the Risks and Resilience of Children with a Parent in Prison', *Paper presented at the Institute of Advanced Legal Studies Discussion Evening on 'Prisoners' Children and the Law'*, May 2006.

Walker, J. and McCarthy, P. (2005) 'Parents in Prison: The Impact on Children' in G. Preston (ed.) *At Greatest Risk: The Children Most Likely to be Poor*. London: Child Poverty Action Group.

Warr, M. (1998) 'Life Course Transitions and Desistance from Crime', *Criminology*, 36: 183–216.

Welch, M. (2005) *Ironies of Imprisonment*. Thousand Oaks, CA: Sage.

Wells, G. (1986) *The Meaning Makers: Children Learning Language and Using Language to Learn*. London: Hodder & Stoughton.

Western, B., Pettit, B. and Guetzkow, J. (2002) 'Black Economic Progress in the Era of Mass Imprisonment' in M. Chesney-Lind and M. Mauer (eds) *Invisible Punishment: The Collateral Consequences of Mass Imprisonment*. New York: The New Press.

Wheelock, D. (2005) 'Collateral Consequences and Racial Inequality', *Journal of Contemporary Criminal Justice*, 21(1): 82–90.

Williams, J. (2002) 'Have the Courts Got it Right? The Queen on the Application of *Mellor v. Secretary of State for the Home Department'*, *Child and Family Law Quarterly*, 14(2): 218–228.

Williams, R. (2006) *Speech on Penal Policy given at Worcester Cathedral*, 17 July 2006.

Wilson, A. N. (2007) 'The Peversion of Human Rights as Jail Thug is Allowed to Become a Dad', *Daily Mail*, 6 December 2007.

Wilson, D. (1996) *Sentenced to Paternal Deprivation: Contact Between Children and their Imprisoned Fathers*. Unpublished MA Dissertation, University of East Anglia.

Wilson, W. J. and Neckerman, K. M. (1986) 'Poverty and Family Structure' in S. Danziger and D. Weinberg (eds) *Fighting Poverty*. Cambridge, MA: Harvard University Press.

Wolff, N. and Draine, J. (2004) 'Dynamics of Social Capital of Prisoners and Community Re-entry: Ties That Bind?', *Journal of Correctional Health Care*, 10(3): 457–490.

Woolf, L. J. (1991) *Prison Disturbances April 1990: Report of an Inquiry* (Part II of Report with S. Tumin). London: HMSO.

Woolf, M. (2004) 'Hazel Blears: Blair's "Little Ray of Sunshine" Keen to Shed New Light on the Old Cops and Robbers Story', *The Independent*, 16 August 2004.

Wright, L. and Seymour, C. (2000) *Working with Children and Families Separated by Incarceration.* Washington, DC: Child Welfare League of America Press.

Wyner, R. (2003) *From the Inside: Dispatches from a Women's Prison.* London: Aurum Press.

Young, D. S. and Smith, C. J. (2000) 'When Moms are Incarcerated: The Needs of Children, Mothers and Caregivers', *Families in Society*, 81(2): 130–141.

Young, J. (1999) *The Exclusive Society: Social Exclusion, Crime and Difference in Late Modernity.* London: Sage.

Ziebert, R. (2006) *No Easy Answers: The Effects of Parental Incarceration on Children.* Milwaukee, WI: Alliance for Children and Families.

Index